MIMIERNEUURDENSIS
MIMIERNEVORDIS
MIMIGADEFURENSIS
MIMIGARDA
MIMIGARDE
MIMIGARDEFORD
MIMIGARDEFORDIENSIS
MIMIGARDVORDENSIS
MIMIGARNEFORDIENSIS
MIMIGERNAFARDENSIS
MIMIGERNAFORD
MIMIGERNAFORDE
MIMIGERNAUORDENSIS
MIMIGERNAVORDE
MIMIGERNEFORD
MIMIGERNEFORDENSIS
MIMIGERNOFORD
MIMMEGARDEUURDENSIS
MINIGARDEVURDA
MINMIGARDAVURDENSIS
MINNINGARDEVORD
MONASTERIENSIS
MONASTERIUM
MONESTERE
MONSTER
MÖNSTER
MUNESTERE
MUNESTRE
MUNSTER

MÜNSTER

MUNSTERE
MUNSTRE
MYMINGROD

QUO VADIS? - STADT- UND REISEFÜHRER

Edited by Wolfgang Neumann

1. Bennewitz, Holger:
   BONN. Ein Stadtführer.
   Münster: NW-Verlag 1990
   ISBN 3-9802540-0-3

2. Neumann, Wolfgang / Schaepe, Ralf:
   MÜNSTER. Ein Stadtführer.
   Münster: NW-Verlag, 4th rev. edition 1998
   ISBN 3-9802540-8-9

3. Neumann, Wolfgang / Schaepe, Ralf
   (translated by *Rund um Buch & Skript*):
   MÜNSTER. A City Guide.
   Münster: NW-Verlag, 1st edition 1998
   ISBN 3-932927-10-9

NW-Verlag Münster

Wolfgang Neumann / Ralf Schaepe
translated by *Rund um Buch & Skript*

MÜNSTER

A CITY GUIDE

NW-VERLAG MÜNSTER

Front cover: Gable of the historic City Hall

Pages 2-3: Münster seen from the south-west (aerial photograph)

Impressum

NW-Verlag, Wolfgang Neumann
Frauenstr. 25

D - 48143 Münster
Tel. & fax: 02 51 / 51 14 01

Cover design, lay-out, advertisements:
Wolfgang Neumann

Lithog. & exposure: *TSG Röder*, Münster

Printed by:
Druckerei Fritz Hartmann

D - 48683 Ahaus

Printed on chlorine-free bleached paper.

© NW-VERLAG MÜNSTER 1998
ISBN 3-932927-10-9

1st
edition

Misprints
by

Welcome to 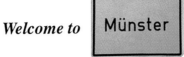 Münster

Whether you want to visit Münster for just a short time, or whether you are planning to live here, you will certainly want to know more about this city. We invite your curiosity. This city guide invites you to have a stroll through Münster; it will take you to the most interesting and most beautiful places and will provide you with a lot of valuable background information about the Westphalian Metropolis.

*A stroll through Münster might take quite a bit of time, and you will probably look forward to a short spell of rest. Whether you just want to browse or whether you are looking for more detailed information, you will be able to find both in the following chapters. If necessary, the **index** will help you to locate the exact passage in the guide.*

You will find out about Münster's history when you read about the terror of the Anabaptists' reign. Next, there is a chapter about the divers aspects of contemporary culture. And then we will introduce you to some of the popular meeting places in Münster like "Pinkus Müller" or "Cavete" ... But before finishing the day in one of the local pubs or restaurants, you will certainly want to go and see some of the many sights in and around Münster. A few tips for an interesting day trip (maybe by bike) might certainly prove helpful. Then you will meet some of the illustrious sons and daughters of Münster; and you will even have a taste of Westphalian cooking.

*Finally, "Münster at a Glance" provides **maps of the city and the surrounding area** as a means of quick orientation. Even those in a hurry will be satisfied by informative descriptions of the **sights**, museums and exhibitions or sculptures.*

*But where can you get a ride in a hot-air balloon? Rent a bicycle? And where will you find a pub or restaurant that serves your favourite food? Well, you can find all the answers in a large and detailed section providing **useful information for tourists**.*

After reading the first chapter about Münster today, you will probably be keen on exploring the city on your own. This city guide is very simple to use and very similar to a human tourist guide. Just as you would meet him or her, you will "meet" the "City Guide" to Münster. Where? Right in the city centre, in Münster's "front parlour", the Prinzipalmarkt ... (i.e. on p. 21)

☞ One more hint: The circled numbers following each sight refer to the folded city map between pp. 144 and 145.

M Ü N S T E R   T O D A Y

"It either rains or the church bells ring - and, when these two things coincide, it is bound to be Sunday". This popular saying does not necessarily have to come from someone living outside Münster. It could also be an ironic statement from one of Münster's own citizens. Nevertheless, the average citizen of this city is either a well-to-do civil servant or an industrious business man - and he regards himself as a citizen of a town that is said to be "one of the most beautiful among the beautiful cities in Germany". Keeping this in mind, it is easy to laugh - even at yourself.

Maybe one of Münster's many students was the first to use this description. Münster University is the third largest in Germany, and many of its students, who like to make fun of the city when they arrive here, decide to stay in Münster after finishing their exams.

However, nobody will ever know for sure who used this apt description of Münster for the first time. It is a fact that it has been handed down from generation to generation in the Münsterland 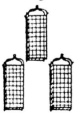 and that it is also well known in relatively far-off regions. There might be a fairly simple reason: it is the attempt to capture Münster's essentials in a few words.

Indeed, rumour has it that troughs of low pressure developing over the Atlantic Ocean tend to spend themselves around Münster. This is partly true, as Münster is in fact mainly influenced by the Atlantic cauldron with an average of 195 days of rain each year. Yet surprisingly, it is also one of the sunniest regions in Northern Germany with approximately 1,600 hrs of sunshine each year. In general, the  Münsterland is characterized by its mild winters (in 1990, the accumulation of snow totalled only 1(!)cm) and its relatively cool summer months. The recorded temperatures in the last 135 years reached an average of 9.2°C per year and 16.1°C in the summer.

There is no doubt that the allusion to the constant ringing of church bells is true. After all, Münster has been a bishopric since 805 A.D. and houses numerous churches of rich architectural variety that are greatly valued in art history. ... And they certainly account for a fairly large amount of church bells.

Münster itself is situated right in the centre of the Münsterland, which borders on the Teutoburg Forest in the north and the Emsland in the east and reaches the River Lippe in the south and the Netherlands in the west. The Münsterland forms a part of the so-called Westphalian Lowlands, a geological formation that dates back 70 to 100 million years, a time when the whole area was still covered by water. With only a few exceptions - for example the Baumberge in the west of Münster - it is a rather flat region. Münster's altitude is just 61.3 metres. Owing to its geological history, the Münsterland is characterized by its heavy, clayey but nevertheless fertile

Round the "Aaseekugeln"

soil as well as marshy soils and heath-land areas. There are even large regions with sandy loess, where the tasty asparagus thrives. Hedges, small wooded areas, small lakes and brooks divide the fields and meadows, all of which creates the typical parkland, for which the Münsterland is so famous. It is a wonderful region for cycle tours or for horseriding. The more than 281,000 inhabitants of Münster (1996) are indeed fortunate that their home town is situated right in the middle of this natural park that offers so many leisure-time activities. However, they also enjoy all the advantages of a principal economic and cultural centre with about 1.5 million people living in the immediate area. Münster has been expanding outwards for several centuries and today covers an area of 302.37 km². From north to south Münster covers 24.4 km, from east to west 20.6 km.

In comparison, the old part of the town, which is approximately 1200 metres in diameter, appears relatively modest. The first settlements - at Münster's present location - were already, for purposes of trade, conveniently situated near a small ford through the River Aa. There, several important trade routes intersected, which, by and by, gained more importance. Today's traffic connections are quite impressive, too. Münster gained its structural importance from its central location and its role as a connecting link between the Rheno-Westphalian industrial areas and the North Sea ports. From Münster you can directly reach two motorways: the A1 from Cologne to Bremen connecting the Ruhr area to the north of the country, and the A43 - another feeder road from the Ruhr and cities on the Rhine. The inter-city trains connecting Bremen and Hamburg to

11

Cologne, Düsseldorf and Frankfurt stop in Münster. By the way, far-seeing local politicians have been trying for some time to introduce a very different kind of train to the Münsterland: the magnetic levitation railway that has been successfully tested in the Emsland. This  type of railway could connect Münster and the International Airport Münster / Osnabrück (FMO) 25 km away from the city. This airport has recorded a steady growth in the numbers of passengers and freight over the last years and is an ideal starting point for trips to destinations all over the world. If you are an amateur pilot, you can also use the small airport in Telgte (near Münster), which is used by glider pilots, too. Furthermore, the Dortmund-Ems Canal, which traverses the city, is an important waterway for this region. Münster's port accounts for a rather impressive volume of traffic - all sorts of goods needed for the supply of the city are handled here. On a different note, the inner-city traffic - with all its negative and positive aspects - is something to be reckoned with, too. Never before have there been so many (1996: 126,873) cars crowding through the centre of the town (round about 50% of Münster's citizens own a car). But still, there have never been so many bicycles either, and the number is still growing. The bike - or "Leeze" as it is called here in Münster - is used for almost 40% of all trips, which probably makes more than one tourist wonder whether he has ended up in the Netherlands. Rumour has it that you will probably find more bicycles than people in

the city ... If that is true, one can only wonder why a large number of bicycles is stolen every year (1996: 5451 thefts), when - at least statistically - every citizen is the proud owner of 1.1 bikes ... Münster is definitely a city of and for cyclists. As a result, it was awarded the "Goldene Speiche" (Golden Spoke) for the "most bicycle-friendly city in Germany". (Incidentally, the counterpart called "Rusty Spoke" was presented to Essen.) You might now presume that only Münster's penniless students are compelled to go everywhere by bike ... But no, the mayoress, the nun in her habit or the university professor can all be seen riding their bikes in Münster. As do the many civil servants or employees ... And these form a large part of Münster's citizens as the city is the administrative capital of Westphalia. Münster is the seat of the Regional Association of Westphalia-Lippe, the head of administration of Münster, the vicar-general of the bishopric, the Oberfinanzdirektion Münster (regional finance office responsible for Westphalia-Lippe), the Constitutional Court of Law and the Administrative Court of Appeal of the Land North Rhine-Westphalia, several professional associations, numerous national banks as well as trade associations. Around 78% of the working population of this city are employees and blue collar workers, followed by civil servants (16%) and independent business men and their relatives (6%). Otherwise, Münster's economy is mainly characterized by small or medium-sized busi-  nesses, which account for a varied and well-balanced economic structure. In 1996, the strength of the economy amoun-

Cathedral, Cathedral Square and the Church of Our Lady

ted to roughly 3.8 thousand million DM industrial turnover with an export quota of round about 24%. As in the old days, when Münster was a member of the Hanseatic League, the city manages relatively well economically. The rate of unemployment amounts to 8.9% (1996); one has to bear in mind, though, that this includes a very large number of young academics recently graduated from Münster University.

Münster's Westfälische Wilhelms-Universität is an important economic factor that should not be neglected. Obviously, the achievements of the university in research and teaching and their long-term and indirect effects are not easy to measure. But the importance for industry, however, can easily be deduced from the amount of emphasis that is put on the field of modern technology and information transfer. The technology centre (Technologiehof) was established in order to establish and integrate innovative firms near the university. There are plans for a very large technology park, which will further link university and business. In the winter term of 1997/98, there are 45,500 registered students, which makes Münster the third largest university in Germany preceded by Cologne and Munich. Add to that the students from the College of Applied Sciences and you will reach the impressive number of about 55,000 students. This corresponds to roughly 20% of Münster's population. However, this does not mean that the born and bred "Münsteraner" is threatened with extinction. However, these days you seldom find one of the rare "natives". And, if you do happen to meet one of these specimens, then it will most certainly be extremely stubborn, provincial, business-

13

minded and Roman Catholic ... At least, this is what you expect if you believe in the common stereotypes. However, one characteristic of stereotypes is that most of them are only partly true. There are, at least, reliable details as far as the denomination of Münster's citizens is concerned: Roman Catholic: 60.1%, Protestant: 21.6%, others: 18.3% (1996). The supposed provincialism is the butt of many jokes and anecdotes which unfortunately do not translate well at all, so that we have to do without any examples at this point. To make up for that, we would like to cite a few of the ten commandments from the *Catechism for the True Citizens of Münster*, which are no less revealing than the above-mentioned anecdotes. This catechism - the author of which very wisely chose to remain anonymous - was published in 1835, and here are a few excerpts:

> *"Thou shalt not suffer a stranger near thee; and thou shalt never get a favourable impression of some-one who is not born and bred in the Münsterland."*
>
> (1st Commandment)

> *"Thou shalt not strive for innova-tion."*
>
> (2nd Commandment)

> *"Thou shalt never suffer thirst."*
>
> (5th Commandment)

There were special commandments intended for the fair sex, for example the 6th Commandment:

> *"Thou shalt never show a friendly face to thy husband except when thou asketh him for money or a new dress."*
>
> (6th Commandment)

However, you do not do justice to the people of the Münsterland at all if you accuse them of provincialism. They show a sound love of their region as well as a great sense of tradition. They stick to the Münsterland cuisine with its traditional trinity consisting of "Pumpernickel" (a special type of wholemeal rye bread with a slightly sweet taste), smoked ham and "Korn" (a distilled spirit made from grain), and they keep up traditions. If you are lucky, you might even get to meet a genuine "Kiepenkerl" ... You wonder what that might be? Have a closer look at the chapter entitled "The Kiepenkerl Quarter". In spite of their great love of tradition, the citizens of Münster have an advantage over people living in other regions. They manage to cultivate traditions and love of their region and - at the same time - refrain from closing their eyes to the outside world and current progress. Besides the integration of Münster University, which has already been mentioned above, and which symbolizes the pro-European atmosphere of this city, Münster is twinned with cities all over the world: York (Great Britain, 1958), Orléans (France, 1960), Kristiansand (Norway, 1967), Monastir (Tunisia, 1969), Rishon le Zion (Israel, 1981), Fresno (United States, 1986), Ryasan (Russia, 1989), Lublin (Poland, 1991).

The Anabaptists' cages attached to St Lambert's Church

In addition, there is a town twinning between Münster-Hiltrup and Beaugency as well as a partnership between Münster and Mühlhausen in the former East Germany (Thuringia, 1990). Münster is a very popular city for hosting congresses and other big events. There is the "Send" - a huge fair on the Hindenburgplatz - the "Turnier der Sieger" - an equestrian event in which national champions take part - or the World Skateboarding Championship, and even an economic summit.

Münster also hosts open-air sculpture exhibitions at irregular intervals. However, a few people in Münster will most certainly shake their heads in wonder at some of the sculptures. There will be no open complaints, though, as such events are taken notice of outside the region, too, which adds to the renown of the city

The "Kiepenkerl"

and attracts quite a few wealthy tourists to the city. And people in Münster are definitely business-minded ... Rumour has it that - after the light earthquake in April 1992 - one of Münster's business men had the brilliant idea of selling T-shirts with the catchy slogan "I was there! - Earthquake in Münster!" printed on them. Today, Münster's merchant tradition is best reflected in the busy pedestrian precincts and shopping streets. The Prinzipalmarkt, in particular, which is often described as the "front parlour" of the city, is best known for its large number of exclusive shops under its arcades.

It is on the Prinzipalmarkt that the visitor to Münster can get a first impression of the special atmosphere of this city. This is why we chose the Prinzipalmarkt as a starting point for several walks through the city which are described in the following chapters. Here on the Prinzipalmarkt, you can easily see evidence of the two main forces that have formed more than 1200 years of Münster's local history. On the one hand, there is the church, represented by the dominant St Lambert's Church and the Cathedral of St Paul not far away, on the other hand the group of proud burghers and merchants, represented by the stately gabled houses and the historic City Hall. Over the centuries, the two sides have formed a fruitful symbiosis. All the same, there were also times characterized by conflicts and attempts at emancipation on both sides. Nevertheless, or rather because of that, these two forces have played an important part in the very special culture and atmosphere that has developed over the centuries in the Metropolis Westphaliae. In this context, one should not forget to mention two

Arcaded houses on the Prinzipalmarkt

very important persons who played a vital role for this region. Firstly, Münster was one of the main spheres of activity of the famous baroque architect Johann Conrad Schlaun. More than eighty buildings in the Münsterland bear witness to his work, amongst which you will find such well-known buildings as the Erbdrostenhof - a beautiful noble residence right in the city centre -, the Schloss (Castle) and sacred buildings such as the Church of St Clemens (Clemenskirche). Secondly, we would like to mention Clemens August Graf von Galen, the former bishop of Münster, nicknamed the "Lion of Münster", a priest who dared to speak openly and - maybe even more importantly - publicly from the pulpit against the regime during the Nazi period. Two more historic events which made everyone turn to Münster have to be mentioned here: the short period of the reign of the

Anabaptists, a group of radical reformers, and the Treaty of Westphalia in 1648. In the Hall of Peace in the City Hall, diplomats entered into negotiations which finally led to the signing of the Treaty of Westphalia, which in turn brought about the end of the Thirty Years' War. Catastrophes like the numerous wars, sieges and fires as well as the recurrent outbreaks of the plague have not managed to wear Münster's citizens out. Whatever happened, the inhabitants of this city have always managed to pick themselves up again. They did so after the Second World War, too, which had terrible consequences for Münster. 63% of the town was destroyed by allied air raids, and more than 90% of the old part of the town was left in ruins. In view of such a degree of destruction, one really has to be grateful that Münster has decided to rebuild the historical

All in all, people in Münster are entitled to feel a little proud of their bustling city. This was also reflected in the lavish celebrations to mark the 1200 years' jubilee of Münster in 1993. In order to secure Münster's position as a centre of culture, there were many attractions in the course of the festivities, which attracted many visitors from outside the town. Münster's citizens are very fond of their city, and - according to a recent big survey - they strongly identify with their region.

There is also a very small but nevertheless unerring indication of this strong identification: in quite a few of the students' papers you will find small ads from students trying to swap their current university place with someone in Münster. The opposite is not so easy to find, which may be seen as another sign of Münster's attractiveness.

We would like to close this chapter with a quotation from the writer Ricarda Huch and hope to arouse your curiosity so that you will discover Münster with the help of the next chapters.

Prinzipalmarkt in a new form instead of giving in to the temptation of designing a completely new and modern city centre. This was was done in Kassel, which had also suffered a great deal of destruction during World War II. Today, there are many doubts about this decision.

Perhaps one of the most impressive examples of Münster's post-war reconstruction is the Gothic City Hall, which - as the site of the Treaty of Westphalia - was meant to become a special symbol after the Second World War. Nevertheless, some strikingly modern buildings were also erected in post-war Münster, for example the new Municipal Theatre. Today, Münster still follows this tradition of innovative building projects, which you can see if you have a look at the City Museum and the new Municipal Library.

"Of all the cities in Westphalia Münster is the most distinguished. Indeed, in the whole of Germany there is no other city to equal it."

(Ricarda Huch, 1927)

The Schloss / Castle: Ornamented gable of the middle projection

The Prinzipalmarkt with St Lambert's Church
Oil painting by Jacques François Carabain (1868)

STROLLING THROUGH MÜNSTER

Münster's "Front Parlour": The Prinzipalmarkt

You are now right in the middle of Münster's "front parlour", the city's best address, a place full of tales and history. From the 12th century onwards, the **Prinzipalmarkt** has been the centre of business life as well as of shopping and of trade.

In the early Middle Ages, the fairs on the Cathedral Square, the Prinzipalmarkt and its vicinity became more and more popular. From far away traders came to these fairs, which usually took place after the Church synods - this is where the German expression "**Send**" is derived from. To this day, owners of shooting galleries, merry-go-rounds and also traders selling flowers and specialities meet on the Hindenburgplatz three times a year.

In 1574, the "Send" sword was displayed for the first time on the wall of the City Hall as a reminder for every troublemaker that special and very strict laws were in force during the time of "Send". "Send" was meant to be a time of trade, not of trouble. Any bloodshed during the "Send" was punished by the death sentence. By the way, the original "Send" sword - like so many other historical relics in Münster - still exists today and is displayed at the City Hall during the period of the "Send".

In the 13th century, there were only simple wooden shops and premises along the walls and the moat of the Cathedral precinct; later, patrician houses in the Gothic style followed until - in the middle of the 16th century - Renaissance made its appearance in Münster. Then wealthy and influential merchants started to build the typical gabled houses, which are to this day still used for their original purpose.

If you stroll along the Prinzipalmarkt, you'll soon find yourself in front of the **City Hall (Rathaus) (33)**. This was one of the many buildings in this area destroyed by bombing in October 1944. Like most of the neighbouring buildings, it was faithfully reconstructed in the original style on the basis of old building plans. As a result, you can now admire one of the most beautiful 14th-century secular Gothic buildings. Its impressive front with its pointed arches and the elegant gable was built without model.

On the ground floor of the City Hall you'll find the **"Hall of Peace" (Friedenssaal)**, the former Council Chamber. One of its attractions is the richly ornamented wooden panelling. This 16th-century masterpiece of craftsmanship was - along with many other valuable items - removed from the City Hall during World War II and evacuated to the Weser Uplands and therefore escaped the bombing. You should also have a look at the wrought-iron chandelier, the massive fireplace, and the various portraits of the envoys involved in the negotiations leading to the Treaty of Westphalia.

Today, the "Hall of Peace" is visited mainly by tourists, but on May 15th, 1648, it was the place that witnessed the final negotiations that then brought about the end of the Thirty Years' War. These

The "Send" sword

The Municipal Wine House

Wooden panelling in the "Hall of Peace"

22

negotiations have gone down in the annals of history as part of the "**Treaty of Westphalia**" ("**Westfälischer Frieden**"). The scene of the solemn oath was immortalized in the famous painting by Gerard Ter Borch. Likewise, the inscription in the great fireplace with the timeless words "Pax Optima Rerum" ("Peace is the Greatest Good") is a constant reminder of this historic event.

Take in the special atmosphere of this historic building and stay a little while. Soon, a friendly voice on tape will provide you with all sorts of information about the "Golden Cockerel" ("Goldener Hahn") or the strangely withered hand that has been preserved for several centuries, and further details of the Peace negotiations.

Guided tours of the City Hall: Sun: 11.30 am - 12.30 pm (except during official meetings or functions), cf. p. 180.

To the left of the City Hall you will find the "**Municipal Wine House**" ("**Stadtweinhaus**") **(33)**, which dates back to the years 1615/16 and which forms an interesting contrast, as far as art-history is concerned, to the neighbouring City Hall. The latter is a fine example of Gothic architecture - the former is regarded as one of Münster's most important buildings of the late Renaissance period. Its gable is richly ornamented with spiral-shaped decorations, and at the front of the building there is another projecting portico, called the "Laube" which reaches up to the first floor, the upper part of which forms a balcony. In years gone by, the Municipal Wine House was the traditional place for measuring and weighing goods. The very best cloth of the region was brought to Münster by the merchants. The City Council stored its wine in the cellars of the Wine House - hence the name. Under or right in front of the "Laube" judicial sentences were pronounced. Thus, the two arches of the "Laube" were referred to as "Sentenzbogen". In order to deter others from crime, the culprits received their punishment directly after the verdict was announced - right at the place where you are standing now. A nice assortment of instruments of torture was available including the ever-popular pillory. However, death sentences were usually carried out on the "Galgheide" ("Galgen" = gallows) outside the city gates. There, just one gibbet was not enough. People in those days were highly imaginative, so the poor wretches were beheaded, broken upon the wheel, burnt alive, or quartered, according to circumstances.

Today, the Municipal Wine House is all about politics. In 1998, the Social Democrats and the Green Party are the ruling parties in the Münster City Council, while the Christian Democrats form the opposition. Not only those who have recently moved to Münster but also visitors should take the opportunity to attend one of the public Council meetings - definitely quite an experience for those who like that sort of thing.

If you are not in the mood to listen to our council members, then you can always walk a bit further and admire **St Lambert's Church** (**Lambertikirche**) **(31)**. You are standing in front of a wonderful example of late Gothic architecture - certainly one of Münster's finest churches, with a tower surmounted by a spire reaching some 300 feet into the air. If you look closely at the base of this spire, you can see three cages attached to it. In the year 1536, the corpses of the executed

Christmas-time on the Prinzipalmarkt

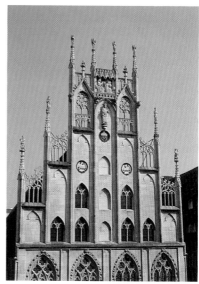

The "Krameramtshaus"   *Gable of the City Hall*

24

Anabaptists' leaders, Bernt Knipperdolling, Jan van Leiden, and Bernd Krechting were put on public display in these cages as a grim warning to deter others.

High up in the tower, the watchman still goes about his business. From 9-12 pm (except Tuesdays) he watches over the city. As in the old days, he has to look out for fire in the city or approaching enemies and - with his copper horn - he also has to proclaim the time half-hourly. You have to climb almost 300 steps of a narrow spiral staircase if you want to have a look at his work-place and admire the breathtaking view - when you have recovered your breath after the strenuous climb - from the top of the tower. We have saved you the climb ...

St Lambert's Church was built between 1375 and 1460, but it was not until 1898 that it took on its present appearance. As the old Romanesque west tower was in danger of collapse, it was - after eleven years' work - completely rebuilt in the neo-Gothic style on the model of Freiburg Minster. There has been a church on this very same site ever since 1000 A.D. The almost square elevation with its nave and two side aisles of equal height make it clear that this church was built for all burghers and merchants, and, even more important, all of them had the same rights. St Lambert's Church is certainly one of Westphalia's most beautiful Gothic

"Hallenkirchen". Situated right in the middle of three markets - the Alter Fischmarkt (Fishmarket), Roggenmarkt (Ryemarket) and Prinzipalmarkt - St Lambert's Church was always in-volved in the busy market life in front of its portals. Market wives and traders simply carried their goods through the church from one side portal to the other without worrying about any devotions taking place. Even today quite a few people decide to take a short cut through St Lambert's Church. You should not simply walk through this church though, take your time and have a look at its many art treasures. The figures of the Apostles in the choir and those of the Church Fathers in the side choir as well as the modern stained glass items are certainly worth seeing. By the way, in the Nazi period, it was in St Lambert's Church that Bishop Clemens August Graf von Galen preached against the Nazis. After visiting St Lambert's, we suggest you take a stroll through the pedestrian precinct starting directly in front of the church. But do not miss having a look beforehand at the **Krameramtshaus (32)** to the right of St Lambert's; this is the fine hall of the mercers' guild and dates back to the Renaissance.

Copper horn of the watchman of St Lambert's Church

To the Schloss, past the Dom

Our next sight is quite easy to reach. The narrow Domgasse leads from the Prinzipalmarkt straight to the Domplatz (Cathedral Square). If it happens to be Wednesday or Saturday, the big semiweekly market will probably keep you from visiting the Dom at once. A vast variety of mouthwatering fresh food, all sorts of paraphernalia, kitsch and examples of craftsmanship entice you into a leisurely stroll over the market. Well, do not hesitate to give in to the temptation; after all, the Dom has been there in its present form for 700 years and will probably still be there after the market closes at 1.30 pm. If Wednesday or Saturday happen to be public holidays, the market takes place a day earlier; as you can't have trading on the Cathedral Square on a holiday.

From the outside the **Cathedral of St Paul (Paulus-Dom) (29)** is not nearly as magnificent as St Lambert's Church. Big and immense, the cathedral dominates the Cathedral Square, the last of three cathedrals built on this site and an example of structural transition. The forty years (1225 - 1265) needed to complete the building saw the transition from the Romanesque to the Gothic period; as a result, characteristics of both periods can be traced in the building. The first cathedral was erected under the supervision of Münster's "founder", the monk and later bishop Liudger, at the beginning of the 9th century. Almost on the same site Bishop Erpho had the second cathedral built and consecrated in the year 1090. Today, you'll find a nave with two aisles, a west and east transept. The western façade and the towers of the cathedral were erected in the period between the end of

the 12th and the middle of the 13th century. Part of the radial chapels around the choir are from the middle of the 17th century. You will find many a treasure in the ambulatory, for example the **astronomical clock**. This beautiful piece from the late Middle Ages shows the course of the stars and also features a perpetual calendar (up to the year 2071) - a vast technical achievement for the constructors.

Also very impressive is the almost five metre high **statue of St Christopher** dating from 1627, which has left the authors quite puzzled. St Christopher holds a genuine tree in his left hand. The top of the tree and the lower part of the tree-trunk with its root are thicker than the middle part held by the saint. How did the tree get into the hand of the saint? There is no apparent damage to the tree - so it was not cut in two halves and then fitted into the opening of the hand. Or was it?

Also worth having a visit is the magnificent baptistery with its 14th-century bronze baptismal font.

The old western façade destroyed in World War II was not reconstructed after the war. After years of rebuilding, the Dom was reconsecrated in 1956. Since then, there has no longer been any west portal through which the bishops used to enter the nave for mass in the past, and you enter the Dom through the so-called **Paradies** (Vorhalle) on the south side of the Dom facing the big Cathedral Square. In the "Paradies", a portico where formerly the episcopal court sat in judgement, you will find some excellent examples of sculpture, for example the life-size 13th-century statues of the Apostles. You should also take some time and look at the wartime photographs of the cathe-

Former west front of the Dom (oil painting from 1780)

Market on the Cathedral Square   *Madonna in the west transept (Dom)*

27

The astronomical clock in the Dom

dral in ruins on display there. Like most of the buildings in the city centre, the Dom was badly damaged by bombing during World War II but meticulously reconstructed in the post-war period.

Today, the western façade is dominated by a rosette of twelve round windows arranged in a circle, which symbolizes the twelve Apostles surrounding the Evangelists in the middle, who are represented by four more windows. (Mockers, however, like to compare the new western façade to a telephone dial. But judge for yourself.) The windows were designed by Ewald Mataré, an artist who was the mentor of Joseph Beuys. The latest acquisition in the cathedral are the windows in the choir chapels designed by another of Mataré's pupils, Georg Meistermann. When you have finished looking at all the treasures in the cathedral, you should not neglect to visit the **cathedral chamber**

(**Domkammer**) in a new wing of the Dom next to the cathedral cloister. The 1200-year history of the cathedral is illustrated by valuable exhibits depicting the holy relics, liturgy and art history of the cathedral. The exhibits include the precious golden head-shaped reliquary of St Paul dating from the 12th century, which is the oldest occidental reliquary of this kind.

Back on the Cathedral Square - the entrance to the "Paradies" right behind you - turn right and walk down the alley between the Bishop's palace (Bischöfliches Palais) and Ketteler'sche Doppelkurie (an aristocratic mansion). In former days the whole Cathedral Square was surrounded by similar noble residences. You now cross the bridge over the River Aa and leave the former cathedral precinct and are now "beyond the water", so to speak, which corresponds to the literal translation of "Überwasserviertel", which is the quarter of Münster you have just entered. Right in front of you towers the mighty Church of Our Lady (Liebfrauenkirche), also, with reference to its location, called **Überwasserkirche (14)**. It is best to walk straight up to the portal to admire this Gothic church with nave and aisles of equal height built in the 14th century. The interior was almost completely destroyed in World War II, but you'll be compensated by the richly ornamented portal and the massive tower. However, you'll soon realise that the portal has not remained intact, either - some of the sculptures originally framing the portal are missing. This is due to events dating back much further than the last war: during the siege of Münster in 1534/35, the Anabaptists had to strengthen their ramparts and, for lack of other material, irreverently used the portal sculptures. Only about 350 years later did the sculptures, an exquisite cycle of the Madonna and the Apostles, reappear. Today, they are put on display in the Westphalian Museum of Art and Cultural History on the Cathedral Square. But this was by no means the only heinous deed committed by the Anabaptists. As you can see, there is no characteristically Gothic spire. The Anabaptists dragged it down to form a platform for their cannons. Please, do not ask how they managed to heave the weapons onto the top of the tower ... A new spire was erected in later years, but a storm at the beginning of the 18th century swept it off again.

Now, for the time being this has certainly been more than enough as far as architecture and church buildings are concerned. Let's continue on our way and walk along the Frauenstrasse. Keep walking straight on, and it will be only a few minutes before you can see the magnificent **Schloss (Castle) (15)**. It is mainly the work of the famous architect Johann Conrad Schlaun, who died, however, before the building was completed. Those who take an interest in architecture are bound to come across his name again in Münster. Schlaun designed the plans for the late baroque building intended as the residence of Prince Bishop Maximilian Friedrich von Königsegg-Rothenstein. Construction work started in 1767, but Schlaun died in 1773 before the building was completed. His successor, Wilhelm Ferdinand Lipper, included new architectural styles when he completed the interior design. With reference to Schlaun's plans, Lipper simply noted that there was too much "inconsistent foliage and flourish". However, construction work on the castle was completed in 1787 without Lipper exercising much influence on the exterior design, Thus, the castle has

Statue of St Christopher

gone down in art history as the last baroque residence. It has also been noted for the stark contrast between the light-coloured sandstone taken from the Baumberge near Münster and the red brickwork. The middle section of the wide three-winged residence dominates the rest of the building, which is typical of baroque architecture. Ornamental and figured decoration complete the picture of a prestigious residence. The castle served for only a short time as the residence of the prince bishops of Münster. Later, people like General Blücher or Freiherr vom Stein lived here. Today, the Castle houses lecture halls and is the seat of the administration of Münster University. It is quite obvious that the Schloss is located at quite some distance from the historic city centre. This is due to a certain shift of power from the city to the prince during the period of absolutism. The prince, then,

The canons' cemetery

Medieval sculptures in the "Paradies" of the Dom

The Schloss

The Botanical Gardens

wished for prestigious buildings and grounds for himself and his court, thereby expressing his self-assessment also through the distance created between himself and the city. In Münster, it was less problematic to realize such plans as the medieval and modern fortifications had been razed to the ground. Thus, there was enough space between the former citadel and the fortifications to build the castle that we see today. The contours of the citadel (Ital. "little city"), a typical small bastion that was part of the fortifications to protect the sovereign even against his own city may still be seen today, as remains of the former rampart and moat surround the park behind the castle. The extensive grounds of the Schloss (**Schlossgarten**) are to be found to the rear of the building. This is a very popular meeting place, especially during the summer months. Jugglers use the lawns for practising, there are concerts in the garden pavilion, and those who prefer a more leisurely time out can go and visit the **Botanical Gardens (Botanische Garten)** of the university right next to the Schloss. You should really go and have a look at it - it's certainly worth seeing! They are open from 8 am till 7 pm (during the winter months till 4 pm only). The gardens were laid out in 1803 and contain a vast assortment of nearly all species of plants in an area of 11.12 acres. Whatever grows on this planet - poisonous plants and medicinal herbs, plants from mountainous regions, useful plants, cacti, exotic trees and shrubs - the chances are that you'll be able to find it here. As they do not expect all visitors to be experts, you will find lots of signs with the names of the plants. Plants that do not thrive in our climate are kept in greenhouses - like the "Schwiegermuttersessel" (Mother-in-

law's armchair). Never heard of it before? Well, this is the affectionate term Germans use when they refer to Echinocactus Grusonii, which is - a nasty cactus!

If you have enough staying power left, go on to read the next four chapters, which guide you along the Aasee to the trinity loved by tourists: the All-weather Zoo, the Museum of Natural History and the open-air museum Mühlenhof. If you prefer to discover more of the city centre, you will have to go back to St Lambert's Church on the Prinzipalmarkt and continue reading on p. 43, where you'll find more details about the Salzstrasse and the so-called "baroque triangle".

To the Aasee (Lake Aa)

Now we suggest you go back to the entrance of the Botanical Gardens. When you are standing on the Schlossplatz again, turn right and walk straight ahead and then follow the Promenade. After a ten minutes' walk, you will reach the **Aasee**. Next to the water's edge you will see a large lawn dominated by three large concrete balls, the "**Giant Pool Balls**", created by the artist Claes Oldenburg in 1977. When the weather is fine, this lawn is usually crowded with people. They are the lucky ones that have managed to leave the dreary daily round behind for a short while and enjoy the wonderful sunshine instead. Around the Aasee there are lots of recreational and leisure-time facilities. You can choose whether to go and relax with the sun-worshippers or to rent a rowing boat, a canoe or maybe a pedal boat. Of course, you can also go for a walk around the Aasee. If you walk along the shore, you will soon reach the All-weather Zoo. But I'm afraid you will have

"Münster on Ice" - the Aasee in the winter

The Aasee at sunset

to walk alone. The lazy author much prefers to take the "Wasserbus" - a boat that sets off every hour on the hour from spring to late autumn. This is definitely a much less strenuous way of getting to the zoo, and you can build up your strength before you explore the grounds of the zoo.

The All-weather Zoo:
Come and See Other Faces

When you reach the landing-stage of the "Wasserbus", you can already see the entrance of the zoo. If the water should not only be below you in the Aasee but also pour down on you from clouds above, there is still no need to worry. Münster's zoo is a so-called **All-weather Zoo (59)**. Therefore you can go and see some of the most interesting animals (almost) without getting wet. If the weather is fine - so much the better! - because then you can explore the grounds of the zoo at your leisure. It covers an area of 61.78 acres. Discover the dolphinarium, try to find the "Streichelzoo", a special part of the zoo where you can actually stroke the animals, let your children check out the playgrounds, or go and have a nice meal in the zoo's own restaurant. But this will have to wait a little longer. First, you will certainly want to see some more.

The "all-weather tour" is not only an ideal solution when it rains; it is also an ideal starting point for a tour through the zoo when the weather is fine. The tour is split up into two different routes. You need less than two minutes to get from one building complex to the next.

On the tour you will find, for example, the "Tropenhaus" with animals from the tropics. Here, the caymans, in particular, are of special interest. Take your time

watching them - you will not find greedy monsters but pleasantly lethargic creatures with a distinct pattern of social behaviour. Of course, this positive impression is helped a lot by the thick pane of bullet-proof glass between the visitors and the animals. Equally helpful are the strong bars in the house for beasts of prey. It is fairly gruesome to watch these big cats tear up one half of an ox. After you have seen this, it is even more surprising to see how tenderly the lions behave towards their partners. A prime example of up-to-date animal keeping is the spacious "tropical house" (Tropenhalle) designed for the Indian elephants, complete with rocky background, waterfall and a lot of space for the elephants to move around. For the visitors there are pagodas, lush vegetation as well as multimedia effects to remind them of the tropical home of the elephants. Not only the young visitors are allowed to feed the elephants fruit and vegetables provided by the zoo. Anyway, this is all part of the new concept of the zoo management, whose main aim is to create the closest possible contact between the visitors and the animals. So this is why you may suddenly come across a couple of cheetahs being taken for a walk by their keepers. There are also plans for direct contact between primates and visitors. Other inhabitants of the zoo, such as the very popular jackass or cape penguins, are already quite often to be found outside their compound. They regularly march around the polarium with their keeper as part of their "fitness training". It is also fun to watch the grey seals at their daily training. At the end of the session you will see a seal move on dry ground, as "Egbert", one of the young seals, loves to leave his enclosure and crawl towards the audi-

ence. There are unusual encounters in the dolphinarium, too, when the dolphins play with the sea-lions and children are allowed to stroke the big sea mammals.

Altogether, the stock of animals in the zoo amounts to approx. 2800, far too many to describe them in detail here. Just stroll through the zoo and discover the variety for yourself. But - whatever happens - do not forget to visit the Aquarium and the Terrarium. Round about 1000 fish, from the well-known guppy to the fairly bizarre porcupine fish, invite you to spend some time there.

Münster owes the impressive zoological gardens to one of the city's most enigmatic characters, the "crazy Professor" Landois (see pp. 131-133). He had his small zoo built between the Schloss and the Aasee. When the city was looking for a suitable new location for the Westdeutsche Landesbank, the whole zoo was moved in 1974 without hesitation to the new and much larger site you are now

exploring. It is fairly obvious that the move was by no means easy to accomplish. Especially if you, like Noah, want to take everything from the tiny worm to the elephants with you. So it happened that - for some months at least - Münster had in fact two zoological gardens. The move was a stroke of luck. It would never have been possible to house such a large number of animals in the old zoo.

To get back to the city, you can use either the "Wasserbus" or the better-known asphalt variety (take no. 14). But perhaps you would like to know something about the Westphalian Museum of Natural History situated right next to the zoo? Then you should go on reading.

Allwetter Zoo Münster (59). Sentruper Str. 315, tel.: 02 51/89 04-0. Open daily from 9 am. Ticket offices close at 6 pm (Apr. - Sept.); 5 pm (Oct. + Mar.); 4 pm (Nov. - Febr.). Animal houses close 30 mins later. The zoo must be left 1 hour after the closing of the ticket offices.

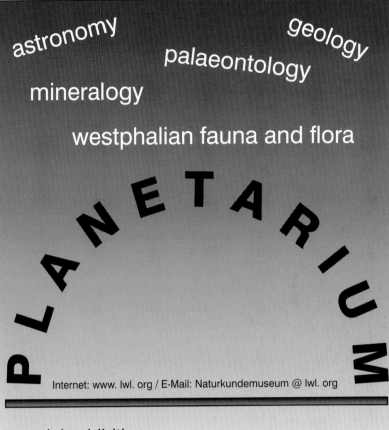

The Westphalian Museum of Natural History

This museum certainly presents some of the most varied exhibitions in and around Münster. But, above all, the staff of the **Westphalian Museum of Natural History (Westfälisches Museum für Naturkunde)** (**58**) always take extra care to present their exhibitions in a way that is both gripping and easy to understand. The museum is situated opposite the main entrance to the zoo. You can easily spot it because of the huge sculptures of prehistoric dinosaurs in front of the building.

The first eye-catching exhibition already arouses a lot of interest. It has become one of the permanent exhibitions and almost an institution: the weather - everyone is prepared to spare some time for this topic. Here, you can have a look behind the scenes and get to know more about the work of the weathermen. On two monitors you can watch what is going on above us, for the weather satellite "Meteosat" regularly transmits pictures of the earth to the tracking station in the museum.

But there are also topics that are - literally - more down to earth. In the mineralogical section you will find information about crystals, geology and the continental drift. In addition, earthquakes are registered and constantly monitored. Experts in Münster probably had the greatest moment in their lives at the time of the local earthquake in 1992, which measured as much as 5.5 on the Richter scale. Very impressive indeed are the world's biggest ammonites, on display in the museum. The exhibition "Evolution of Man" tells you about man's place in the process of evolution and the gradual development of the human species. And those who are tired of the very often grey skies in the Münsterland can go and look at the starry sky shown in its entirety in the **Planetarium (58)** right in the centre of the museum. There are regular presentations such as "From the Big Bang to Infinity" or "A Space Journey Through the Planetary System". From time to time, there is also a special treat: classical music or synthesizer sounds under the stars in the Planetarium.

As the single exhibitions are grouped around the Planetarium, you will automatically come across the two "crowd-pullers": "Prairie and Plains Indians" and "World of the Dinosaurs". Currently, in particular, the huge prehistoric reptiles fascinate both young and old. Remains of these rulers of the Mesozoic such as single bones or skeletons, teeth, eggs or imprints of their skin structure can tell us more about their size, build or food. To this day, no one has fully explained the circulatory system of the huge herbivores or the pattern of their social behaviour. Unique in Europe are the lifelike reconstructions of the Deinonychus or the big predatory Allosaurus.

The second highlight is to be found right around the corner: now you can immerse yourself in the world of the American Indians. On about 500 m² the exhibition presents the life of the Prairie and Plains Indians today and in former times. The Indians' outlook, their world view, their system of values and especially their attitude towards nature become clear.

Thus, a visit to the Westphalian Museum of Natural History is definitely an unforgettable experience.

Patient guard of the museum

The world's largest ammonites in the Museum of Natural History

THE "MÜHLENHOF" OPEN-AIR MUSEUM
- open all year round -

Mar. 16th - Oct. 15th: open daily from 10 am - 6 pm (ticket offices close at 5 pm) • Oct. 16th - Mar. 15th: Sun: 11am - 4.30pm, Tue - Sat: 1 - 4.30pm (ticket offices close at 5pm)

Theo-Breider-Weg 1 • tel.: 02 51 / 9 81 20-0 • fax: 02 51 / 9 81 20-40

The "Mühlenhof" Open-Air Museum

Authenticity is probably the biggest attraction of an open-air museum: a whole village has been turned into a museum, and nothing technical disturbs the special atmosphere. You almost expect to find 18th century village children to come charging around the corner any minute now. Though all working tools are carefully stacked away, you can still imagine the farmer coming along to harness his horse to the plough and going to work on the field.

Of course, the tools of the blacksmith are normally carefully put away, and the visitor can find explanations on a board. The same applies to the baker's utensils and to those of all the other craftsmen to be found here. But on some days, these old crafts actually come back to life again: shoemaker, blacksmith, baker, carpenter, spinner or beekeeper use their historical tools. And when the delicious aroma of freshly baked bread wafts across from the baking-house, the visitor can feel for himself that no film, no history book or historical novel can present history in quite the same way as an open-air museum like this one.

You get there by simply walking or cycling up the Sentruper Strasse from the Westphalian Museum of Natural History. After a few minutes, a sign indicates that you have to turn right. Soon you'll arrive at the entrance to the village. If you should start from the Prinzipalmarkt, take a number 14 bus and simply ask the driver to tell you when the bus reaches the stop "Bockwindmühle".

The **"Mühlenhof" open-air museum (Mühlenhof Freilichtmuseum) (57)** was founded in 1960 by a group of Münster citizens and businessmen headed by Theo Breider. The museum was opened in 1961. About twenty different historical buildings from both Westphalia and the Emsland region were carefully dismantled and transported from their original sites to the museum. There, the buildings were meticulously rebuilt. The **Bockwindmühle**, a windmill built in 1748 using a method of construction known for more than 1000 years, is certainly one of the biggest attractions of the museum. The rotating part of the windmill weighs round about 700 centners (35,000 kilograms), and its sails span approximately 33 metres. On your tour through the grounds of the museum you'll gain a fascinating insight into everyday life in the old days. Although the houses of the craftsmen often do not look quite as impressive as the Mühlenhaus (miller's house) (1619) or the "Gräftenhof" (farmhouse of a moated farmstead) (1720) from the outside, you'll nevertheless find lots of interesting things inside. The blacksmith, for example, had to know and work with a fairly confusing number of different tools. And the baker, too, had to stock a variety of tools and utensils in his hut to be able to earn his living. Or would you have expected a to find a waffle-iron in an 18th-century baking-hut? Most of the items in the houses are explained with the help of tags and boards, and you can always ask the friendly museum guides if you need further information. By the way, the male guides

The "Bockwindmühle"

are dressed in the traditional costume of the "Kiepenkerl".

When you continue your tour, you'll soon reach the small **bee-hut** housing a number of beehives. As beekeepers always assure you that bees are relatively harmless insects, you can risk a careful look inside. If, however, you are not totally convinced, you can always walk on and put a safe distance between yourself and the buzzing creatures. But do not walk too far - you should by no means miss the next house, which is the **Mühlenhaus (miller's house)** built in 1619. Inside the big building with its thatched roof you will find lots of interesting items. You are even allowed to peep into the small cosy-looking bedrooms. In those days you could shut out the world outside by simply closing the sliding doors in front of the small bunks and then go to sleep. When you have seen all the rooms, go and have a closer look at the fire-place; take a look up the chimney, to be more precise ... There you will find heaven - that is the "Westphalian heaven" full of sausages and ham. When they are well-hung and thoroughly smoked and dried by the fire beneath, these specialities are taken down and sold to the visitors. You can eat them at once, accompanied by a drop of Korn, or you can take home a little supply of traditional Münsterland food and savour them later.

Next, you should go and look at the small **country school** built in 1823: a single classroom, a few wooden benches, a desk, a blackboard and a cast-iron stove right in the middle of the room. One can easily imagine the poor village youths reciting verse and doing mental arithmetic while under the constant threat of the cane. And almost involuntarily you search the desks for carved scribblings of the pupils.

Soon you will come to a semi-detached house dating from the 18th century. In the left-hand side of the building you will find a cosy restaurant; the right-hand side houses the "Kramladen" (small shop). Passing the coach house and the "Zichorienmühle" (chicory mill), you will then see the impressive **Gräftenhof**. This building is from Schonebeck near Nienberge and about 270 years old. Everything inside was preserved in its original form.

Groups can also visit the Mühlenhof open-air museum in the evening (advance booking only). An evening tour through the museum is certainly a special experience with many a tale told by the "Kiepenkerle" and tasty Westphalian food being offered as refreshment.

Along the Salzstrasse

The Salzstrasse begins at the small square in front of St Lambert's Church with its fountain erected in 1956 and leads towards the central station. It is one of the most attractive pedestrian precincts in Münster, and the local residents and businessmen are right when they state that the Salzstrasse owes its special flair to the so-called **"baroque triangle"**. The three corners are marked by the Church of St Clemens (Clemenskirche) **(35)**, the Erbdrostenhof **(36)** and the Dominican Church (Dominikanerkirche) **(34)**. Even today, you can still feel the difference between the Prinzipalmarkt with its more Hanseatic atmosphere and the rather "noble" air of the "baroque triangle" with its aristocratic past.

However, before we go and follow the traces of the baroque period, we just have to take a short detour first. Not more than a stone's throw away on the left-hand side, walking past St Lambert's Church and the remarkable Renaissance **Krameramtshaus (guild hall) (32)**, you can spot the new **Municipal Library (Stadtbücherei) (5)** (cf. p.44f). Seen from the point of view of architecture, you are standing on rather international terrain, as the rather individual postmodern building (opened in 1993) designed by the architects Bolles-Wilson was discussed worldwide. The new library is characterized by its postmodern and self-assured yet also very careful embedding in the inner-city surroundings with its historical buildings. However, it is also worth taking a look at the interior of the new library as the visitor can not only see one of the most modern and functional libraries, but also see for himself that this does not necessarily exclude the more playful elements of architecture.

But let's go back to the Salzstrasse - preferably taking the same route. Walking up the Salzstrasse from St Lambert's Church you will soon see the Dominican Church (**Dominikanerkirche**) **(34)** to your left. This church was designed by the architect Lambert Friedrich von Corfey, one of the mentors of the baroque architect Johann Conrad Schlaun; it was built between 1705 and 1725. The most striking feature of the church, which today is used as the Catholic university church, is its sandstone façade. The baroque building is decorated with Roman elements. To the left of the church you can see a detached façade, which is all that is left of the former monastery. Inside the Dominican Church you will be impressed by the richly decorated 17th-century altar.

Not very far from the Dominican Church, you can admire one of the masterpieces of the late baroque period, the **Erbdrostenhof (36)** built between 1753 and 1757. This noble residence - like so many buildings in Münster - was designed by the famous architect Johann Conrad Schlaun. The most striking feature of this residence is certainly its almost concave façade. In this case, necessity was the mother of invention. Adolph Heidenreich von Droste-Vischering chose this rather confined site for a new and representative noble residence in the city cen-

The Municipal Library   Die Stadtbücherei

tre. As the site was not big enough for such a project, Schlaun opted for a three-winged building with a concave ground-plan, which he placed diagonally on the almost rectangular site. Because of this brilliant trick by the architect the Erbdrostenhof still possesses an air of spaciousness and architectural lightness. It is certainly worth comparing the Erbdrostenhof and the Schloss. Both buildings are characterized by the contrast between sandstone elements and red brick. However, the curvature of the building which is mirrored in the cast-iron railing enclosing the court is definitely unique and creates the special kind of dynamic that is typical of the baroque period. In 18th-century Münster there were around forty noble residences. They were usually occupied during a few months in winter. The owners usually preferred to spend the warm summer months - when roads to the city were dry and nearly always passable - on their moated castles in Münster's surrounding area.

The Erbdrostenhof, like many other buildings, was destroyed in a fire in World War II; if you look at the residence today though, you simply have to admire the work of the restorers. Today, the Erbdrostenhof is mainly used as a venue for concerts, and each September the residence is the centre of the Baroque Festival, which itself has become an institution of cultural life in Münster.

The Church of St Clemens (**Clemenskirche**) **(35)** is not so easy to find. You can best get there from the Erbdrostenhof if you turn right into the nearby Ringoldsgasse. Follow the narrow street and you'll automatically reach the Church of St Clemens, another baroque building designed by the architect Schlaun. The building of this beautiful church was commissioned by the Prince-Bishop Clemens August, who was - apparently with some justification - referred to as having been "bitten by the bug" as far as building projects were concerned. Today, the church, which was built between 1745 and 1753, is mainly used for weddings.

Strictly speaking, the church only consists of a cylindrical body with a dome-shaped roof and therefore seems to stand quite isolated from the surrounding buildings. However, originally the Church of St Clemens was part of a complex consisting of the church, the monastery of the order of the "Brethren of Charity" and the St Clemens hospital. As with the design of the Erbdrostenhof, one had to make do with a rather restricted site, thus the architect opted for erecting the church right in the centre of the acute angle formed by the wings of the hospital. You can still see some blind doors indicating that the church was connected to the other buildings, all of which were completely destroyed in World War II. It was only due to the enormous commitment of the curators of monuments that this church was able to rise again from the ruins. While it was possible to use at least part of the ruins for the restoration of the façade, the remarkable **fresco in the cupola** (Kuppelfresko) is a complete and true reproduction of the original fresco. The bright light - weather permitting - streaming in through the shaft of the cupola, the so-called "lantern", into the church falls

The Erbdrostenhof

The Church of St Clemens

on a child to be baptized or on a coffin. In both cases, the "lantern" symbolizes the nearness of God. This idea is also taken up in the motif of the fresco depicting the Ascension of St Clemens.

While the façade of the church is dominated by baroque elements, the circular interior radiates a lighter atmosphere because of its rococo elements. The unique atmosphere of this church with its special infusion of light, the azure altar columns, its sculptures and the dominant fresco in the cupola was and still is so impressive that it was once even (wrongly) considered to be the work of the famous architect Balthasar Neumann, though it is in fact the work of the Westphalian architect J.C. Schlaun alone. Certainly, he also had some models: Rome's S. Andrea al Quirinale by Bernini provided him with ideas for the interior of the church. Individual items of the furnishing were of course produced by contemporary artists under the direction of Schlaun himself. The small garden surrounding the church is an attempt to lessen the isolation of the church from the neighbouring buildings.

The garden was designed by the Münster architect Harald Deilmann. Whether the metal obelisk erected in the centre of the garden, which automatically brings up the question of its relation to the baroque church nearby, can be seen as a self-confident demonstration of modern style, a successful act of confrontation or simply an unintentional admission of stylistic mediocrity is purely a matter of opinion. You will have a good view from the inviting benches in the garden.

After a look around St Clemens you should go back to the Salzstrasse via the Ringoldsgasse, as there is something else to be seen, which is the pride not only of the city fathers. The **"Salzhof"** (**37**) is the latest addition on the Salzstrasse. It is a shopping arcade, the concept of which reflects today's trend. The big building houses a number of different chain stores. The customer can have an ice cream or a cup of coffee, then go and buy some clothes and finally have a meal in the whole-food restaurant. On the upper floors of the Salzhof, which is also highly interesting as far as its unusual architecture is concerned, you will find the **City Museum (Stadtmuseum)** (**37**), which offers an interesting and varied tour through 1200 years of Münster's history. (For further information see the chapter "The City Museum Münster".)

We would now like to draw your attention to a historical building, which has only recently turned from a ruin into a place full of life and which is not easy to find. It is the **"Lortzingsaal"** (near **37**), named after the composer and master of the German 19th-century comic opera, Albert Lortzing (1801-1851), who spent seven years in Münster and was greatly admired by the citizens of Münster. The Lortzingsaal is situated near the Erbdrostenhof on the Arztkarrengasse, a narrow street which runs behind the Salzhof. At the end of the 19th-century, the new theatre was named after Lortzing. Later, the hall, which was built in the 18th century, was given the name of the composer. As of 1921, it became *the* favourite haunt of musicians and artists in the roaring twenties.

The Lortzingsaal was severely damaged in World War II. The reconstruction of the hall had often been discussed, but it was only a few years ago that these plans were finally realized. The result is a very careful reconstruction of the neo-Gothic building, which now houses a restaurant serving Mexican food. The combination of the original fabric of the hall and modern gastronomy forms an interesting contrast, which attracts many visitors.

Outside, the Salzstrasse is full of life. In front of the many different and bustling shops you can fairly often see street musicians, jugglers and other artists. A couple of street cafés and restaurants with outside tables invite you to sit down and watch the bustling crowds in the street. On the terrace of the Café Grotemeyer you can even enjoy the view of the Erbdrostenhof at the same time.

Putto in the Church of St Clemens

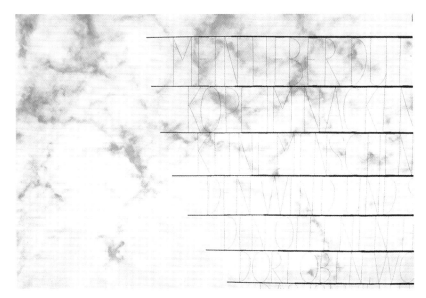

"Looking up. Reading the words ...", sculpture by Ilya Kabakov (1997)

"32 cars for the 20th century ...", sculpture by Nam June Paik (1997), now removed

Around the Promenade

Once again the Prinzipalmarkt is the starting point. This time the reader of our city guide will arrive there by bicycle. (Perhaps you are with a small group of people, then you might go on your little tour together). First turn into the Rothenburg with its variety of shops and shortly afterwards turn left, into the Königsstrasse. Having done so, you go on - with St Ludgeri to your left - towards the "Kreisel", the bustling roundabout on the Ludgeriplatz. Shortly before reaching it, turn left into the avenue of linden trees, the Promenade. Especially on hot days, it is extremely pleasant to cycle on the old city fortifications in the shade of the linden trees. But it does not necessarily have to be hot to lure the cyclist to the Promenade. Riding a bicycle or maybe going for a nice walk there is definitely a pleasant way to relax. No cars are allowed on the Promenade, which is an attractive route to get to know Münster off your own bat.

But first of all, what exactly is the **Promenade**? Well, since the dim and distant past the location of Münster has been attractive. As a result, time and again envious people tried to drive the settlers at the ford of the Aa from their settlement. So each generation used the means at their disposal to protect itself against intruders. While - after the pre-Christian settlements - it was the cathedral stronghold and a small trade settlement which were protected by ramparts and a trench, the city expanded more and more over the years. During the Middle Ages a ring of fortifications with eleven gates and six towers was erected, and additional trenches were dug. With that, the old town was fenced off at the end of the 12th century, as we still find it today, well recognizable from the course of the Promenade. With the appearance of firearms in the course of the 14th century the medieval fortifications were no longer able to serve their purpose reliably, so that the fortifications were later on enlarged in Italian-Dutch style into a modern defensive system with protruding bastions. Yet, although these strong fortifications earned Münster the reputation of an almost impregnable city, around the middle of the 18th century the installations had to be dismantled. One reason for this was certainly the now even further advanced military technology. But most of all, the city walls once built for protection, had turned into a tight corset. The prospering city with its steadily growing population could not expand. From 1764 onwards, therefore, the minister under the prince bishop, Baron Franz von Fürstenberg, had the ramparts turned into a promenade, as you now find it. So the town was able to expand and at the same time received a green belt in the middle of today's city, without which Münster simply cannot be imagined. Now this ring of linden trees not only gives the citizens of Münster the opportunity for a walk, but time and again provides an excellent point of orientation for people new to the city.

Now, thus equipped with some historical knowledge, we can start on our journey. You will not cycle for long, just a few minutes, then to your right you will see a pretty park with a pond,

"Rotating Squares"

the citizens' park **Engelenschanze** (between **50** and **65**), the remains of a former rampart. It does invite you to repose, but, as you have only just started your trip, you will leave it to one side for the time being. Perhaps you would also like to take the time to look at the sculpture **"Rotating Squares"** erected here by George Rickey in 1973 before continuing your journey. Then cycle parallel to the Von-Vincke-Strasse. On this part of the route to your left the new, old **synagogue** is located (**41**). In 1938 the synagogue was burnt down at this place during the Reichspogromnacht. Then in 1961 the simple place of worship you can see here now was erected.

Then you will come to the Salzstrasse. To your right the Servatiiplatz, with a multi-storey building quite high by Münster standards. Also to your right

you can admire a very modern sculpture, a little older, though: the memorial **"Indivisible Germany"** by Anni Buschkötter (1960), impressive in its simple, but therefore even more insistent expressiveness, which makes the problematic nature of the division of Germany perceptible to the senses.

To the left of the Promenade the pedestrian precinct, the Salzstrasse begins with the "baroque triangle" already described, consisting of the Erbdrostenhof, the Church of St Clemens and the Dominican Church. The small, but no less interesting church **St Servatii** (**40**) has not been described yet, though, so that a small detour is recommended. Cycling to the left onto the square and once more immediately turning off left, you will come to the newly restored church dating from the 13th century.

"Indivisible Germany"

The hall with its raised nave and aisles is of late Romanesque origin; yet the pointed arches in the vaults already mark the transition to the early Gothic period. The late Gothic choir was only added in the second half of the 15th century. As far as the interior is concerned, there is a winged altar dating from around 1500, which is of special interest. It can be found in the left side-aisle.

Take the same route back to the Promenade. If you happen to have a lot of time on your hands, we at this point recommend a visit to the **City Museum (Stadtmuseum) (37)** at the entrance to the pedestrian precinct. Here, for example, you can relive your small trip along the promenade with the help of clearly arranged city models. Cycling further along the Promenade, you will soon come to a larger arterial

The Buddenturm

road, at this point called the Mauritz-tor, which means it was also guarded by a city gate. Yet all that remains of it is the small classical **Wachhäuschen (guard-house)** on the right-hand side. Now, it is better to go under this road. Work up a bit of momentum to reach the rampart level again on the other side without too much struggle.

You will now cycle quite a bit until you come to the Hörstertor. The linden trees are very young here, as the old trees unfortunately had to be cut down not too long ago. Signs explain the measure which was met with a lack of understanding by some of the citizens. On the lawn to your right you can see another large sculpture. The war memorial by the Münster artist Bernhard Frydag dates from 1909 and in its shape recalls the famous monument of Theoderic the Great in Ravenna.

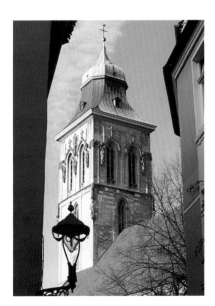

The Church of St Martin

Upon reaching the Hörstertor, you will find, to your right, at the street corner Fürstenbergstrasse / Bohlweg the **State Archives (Staatsarchiv) (6)**. A concrete extension building has been attached to the colossal Neo-Renaissance building (end of 19th century); whether these two buildings are a good match, architecturally speaking, is certainly open to doubt.

To your left, further into town, the former **Church of the Lotharingian Canonesses (Kirche der Lotharinger Chorfrauen) (7)** is situated; once again a work of J. C. Schlaun, which today houses the Municipal Archives, where the documents of town history are collected. Perhaps you would now wish to take another trip to the city centre. Then you will have to follow the Hörsterstrasse, until - to your right - you will be able to catch sight of the Gothic **Church of St Martin (St. Martinikirche) (8)** through a small alley next to a beautifully restored town house dating from 1763. The church's baroque tower roof, designed by Schlaun, was twice destroyed by fire and had to be renewed. You have now reached the Neubrückenstrasse, where, to your left, the **Municipal Theatre (9)** is located. When it was opened in 1956, the architectural design was thought to be highly progressive. Apart from the special overall design, the integration of the garden front of a historic noble residence is of interest. This remaining part of the ruin of the **Romberger Hof** located in a small inner court can be reached by a staircase right next to the theatre box office.

Back down the Neubrückenstrasse again and past the Church of St Mar-

tin, you will reach the Wasserstrasse, and to the right of the car park you will also quickly find your way back to the Promenade. Turn left, and after only a few metres you will come across one of the few remains of the historic ramparts of the city, the imposing **Zwinger (outer court) (54)**. Built in 1536, the Zwinger was originally a battery tower located on a sensitive spot of the city ramparts, the point at which the River Aa flows out of the city, which had to be specially protected. Later, a gunpowder factory is said to have been situated in the tower, which in an explosion promptly blew off the roof of the building. In 1732, the eager Johann Conrad Schlaun converted the Zwinger into a prison. During World War II, the Nazi henchmen used the building to take into custody and to assassinate Jews and opponents of the regime.

By the way, the modern prison, the **Justizvollzugsanstalt (place of detention)**, is located not far from here on the other side of the Promenade behind the Gartenstrasse. It is a building dating from the middle of the 19th century, anachronistically decorated with battlements (designed by a colleague of Schinkel). Nevertheless, with its pentagonal, star-shaped form the prison optimized the methods of supervision in a functional Prussian way. A single supervisory head office in the middle of the five-winged building is still sufficient today to control all sections with several floors each, connected by bridges. However, to have a look at this building from the inside you would need a legally confirmed prison sentence. This, of course, we cannot recommend, as you would then miss seeing the many other sights of the city.

"Attention please, the platform is leaving!"

Flea market on the Promenade

Now, back to the Promenade. Keep on cycling until you come to a street called the Neubrückentor - once again the former location of a historic city gate, of which unfortunately only the name has remained. For your information: to your left you will find a real attraction if you have small children - a playground with a genuine steam locomotive to climb on and to play with.

The Kreuztor is the next crossroads you will pass, and to your left you will find the **Buddenturm (2)**. As one of the fortified towers, it was an original part of the medieval rampart (around 1200), on the site of which you are just cycling. On the outer wall you can still see today the connecting points of the city wall. It was only later that the tower was transformed into a prison and around 1880 into a water tower and used accordingly.

Batardeau on the Promenade

Just for your information: diagonally opposite the Buddenturm, further into town, Münster's most famous pub quarter is located, the Kreuzstrasse with numerous original pubs. To your right you will find the Kreuzviertel (quarter), just as well known and often confused with the first-mentioned pub quarter. But you keep on cycling ahead, as none of the pubs there have opened yet anyway.

You will leave behind to your right the **Kreuzschanze (entrenchment)** (see **2**), in former times part of the modern fortifications, today a popular park with an Annette von Droste Hülshoff statue.

After cycling about one hundred metres, you can take a look at an interesting part of the former fortifications in the trench to your right, a so-called **Graben-** or **Wasserbär (batardeau)**. This is a pointed wall with a turret added to it, to stop intruders from climbing over it. The "Grabenbär", as part of a floodgate system, ensured that the ditches never ran dry, thereby losing their protective function, even when the Aa was running low. You can find another "Grabenbär" near the old zoo, a place you will soon be visiting.

Another few metres, and you will come to a bigger road you will have to cross: the Neutor. To your right you will be able to see two small early classical **gate houses**, just for once not designed by Schlaun, but by Wilhelm Ferdinand Lipper. Lipper was the architect who finished the construction work on the castle after Schlaun's death. The Neutor on the left-hand side turns into the Hindenburgplatz, and with that you are approaching one of the sights of Münster: **the Schloss (Castle) (15)**. As it has already been presented in the chapter "To the Schloss, past the Dom", we will skip it at this point.

By the way, you are just cycling along that part of the Promenade that is regularly lined in the summer by countless flea market stalls. If you are lucky enough to get into the hustle and bustle, you will have to wheel your bicycle. But that does not really matter. As it is widely known that you can find anything at flea markets, you will certainly find some piece or other that you have been looking for in vain for a long time.

When you come to another road - to your left the **Amtsgericht (law court) (19)** (Neo-Renaissance), a building classified as a historical monument - the Promenade will continue to your right, slightly staggered. If - after a few metres - you can see the municipal swimming baths, you are going in the right direction. Next to the swimming baths one finds the **Westerholtsche Wiese** (lawn), where important horse shows and show jumping competitions of Münster, an equestrian centre of some importance, are held. The River Aa runs along the lawn, and behind it remains of the historic city fortifications - the so-called Neuwerk - are still to be found. The Neuwerk especially protected the point of entry of the Aa into the fortified city, analogous to the point where the river flows out of it close to the Zwinger (outer court) already visited. If you are lucky, i.e. it is summer, you can here also see another small sight that is even alive: a long, artistically trimmed hedge with various, surprisingly easily recognisable animal motifs.

On the right-hand side of the Promenade in former times the **Alte Zoo (Old Zoo)** (see **17**) was located. Today you can find here a large bank building with numerous sculptures in the surrounding park. The park also contains the second remaining "Grabenbär" already mentioned. Next door, the highly fanciful residential building of the zoo founder, the so-called **Tuckesburg**, can be found. Cycling on along the promenade, you will then quickly discover the miniature artificial lake, the **Aasee**, with its numerous possibilities for spending one's leisure time. If you have some physical strength left, you might hire a rowing boat and enjoy the panorama of Münster from the lake.

Otherwise, you go on following the Promenade, now turning to the left, and you will come to the Stadtgraben. On the other side of the road, the Kanonenberg (hill) and the small Kanonengraben (trench) with a small lake invite you to repose. In the summer, it is a little quieter here than on the lawn in front of the Aasee, which is mostly occupied by the young people of Münster.

Now it is only a short way back to our starting point, the Prinzipalmarkt. Going straight on along the Promenade, you will soon reach the roundabout ("Kreisel") on the Ludgeriplatz. You have now travelled once around the whole city centre, and, in doing so, you have covered roughly 4.5 kilometres, not counting detours. At the roundabout you once again turn left into the Königsstrasse. At the end of this street you turn right into the Rothenburg, and you will find yourself back on the Prinzipalmarkt.

"Kiepenkerle"

Münster - a shopping paradise

The Kiepenkerl Quarter

After an extended stroll through town, the **Kiepenkerlviertel (Kiepenkerl Quarter) (12)** is the right place to go to on an early summer evening or even in the afternoon, in search of refreshments. The quarter is located at the Spiekerhof, the old storehouse for the city's grain supplies. Again starting from the Prinzipalmarkt, you follow the arcades in the direction of St Lambert's Church, which you now already know. This way takes you further along the Drubbel and the Roggenmarkt. You just have to follow the curved course of the street. The terraced ice-cream parlour you will notice first does not strictly speaking belong to the Kiepenkerl Quarter, but it might be regarded as its atmospheric gateway. Keep on walking under the arcades of the old buildings, now mainly expensive shops, until you come to a small square reminiscent of medieval times.

If there on a pedestal you discover the statue of the itinerant salesman, you have come to the right place. He is called the **"Kiepenkerl" (12)**. Wandering through the Münsterland, he carried on his back a large basket, the "Kiepe", and, wherever he found his customers, he sat down for a short time. But it was not only his goods which he sold, but also his news. In times when there were no newspapers, and only a few people were able to read letters, and, of course, television and radio had not been invented yet, it was the Kiepenkerl's task not only to keep up the exchange of information between the villages but also especially to report valuable informa-

tion from the city. Of course, one can imagine that some of the news had undergone considerable changes, partly because of misunderstandings, but also perhaps for reasons of entertainment, of gruesome effect or of positive self-portrayal. This might seem amusing, but we should not forget that the "pepping up" of news or the vanity of people who have seen or heard events happening are still an important part of the news business. Perhaps the Kiepenkerl today would be a radio reporter with a good salary, because telling stories is what he must have been very good at.

Regarded from this point of view, the sculpture of the typical Kiepenkerl with basket, scarf and long pipe has a symbolic value here. Like every location where people come together for the sole reason of enjoying themselves, the small monument, around which tables and chairs are grouped, naturally also inspires communication. And over a nice cup of coffee, a glass of lemonade or an "Alsterwasser" (a refreshing mixture of beer and orangeade) many a story is modified for the sake of a good punch line.

The quarter is very popular not only because it is so close to the hustle and bustle of the city centre with its shopping streets, but also because the leisurely afternoon might later end nicely with a proper meal at one of the numerous restaurants lining the little square.

If you feel like going on a "Pättkestour", a proper bicycle ride, the next day, you might now take the chance of properly fortifying yourself. After all, there are more than 250 km of cycle paths alone in the city centre.

Ludgeri and Aegidii Quarters:
Of Noble Residences and Venerable Churches

The Prinzipalmarkt is the starting point for Münster's two largest pedestrian precincts. One of them, the Salzstrasse, you already know. The other one, the **Ludgeristrasse**, begins at the southern end of the Prinzipalmarkt and reaches almost to the Promenade ring. Along this street, you will find not only larger department stores but also ordinary and high-priced retail shops. At the end of the Prinzipalmarkt, you will first pass the **Stadthausturm** (**Town Hall Tower**), built in the Neo-Renaissance style at the beginning of this century. The accompanying town hall was destroyed. You then turn left into the Ludgeristrasse. Approximately halfway down the pedestrian area it is worth making a detour into the Hötteweg to your right, because there you will find the Königspassage, an attractive shopping arcade. Keep on walking down the Ludgeristrasse until it opens into St Mary's Square, which is shaded by a number of tall, old trees.

The adjoining massive **Ludgerikirche** (**Church of St Ludgeri**) (**43**) is a building stylistically set between the Gothic and the Romanesque periods. It is supposedly the oldest "Stufenhallenkirche" with raised nave but no nave windows in the Münsterland, i.e. a church with a nave only a little higher than the aisles and with the light entering through the aisle windows. The original church is thought to have been built around the end of the 12th century, but experts' estimates vary. It does not seem possible to give details of the architectural models. The search for early evidence is especially difficult because the church was completely destroyed in the Great Fire of 1383. The choir, as well as the western spires, had to be pulled down. Around 1400, the Gothic choir was built anew and a Gothic "crown" was put on the Romanesque crossing tower. St Ludgeri has a Romanesque nave, which in a visually attractive way is connected to the Gothic choir. The two western spires were only added in 1875. The church was once again destroyed in World War II - what you see here is a reconstruction.

As far as art history is concerned, it is the choir-stall carvings dating from the 16th century and the two panels from the year 1598, created by the painter Nikolaus tom Ring the Younger, that are of importance. Especially impressive is also the font, dating from the beginning of the 16th century. Not quite as old is the crucifix at the western end of the south side aisle: when the artist Heinrich Bäumer created it in 1929, the figure still possessed both its arms. In the last war, they were then blown off by an exploding bomb - the hole in the heart (!) of the figure of Christ was also caused by a bomb fragment. As a symbol of destruction caused by the war, the wooden crucifix has been left in this state and instead of the arms the sentence *"I have no other hands than yours"* is now engraved in the side wings of the cross.

Standing outside again in the grass-covered St Mary's Square, you will be able to see the **Mariensäule (St Mary's Column)**, which was consecrated in 1899 and goes back to a model from the beginning of the 17th century. South of the column is the Ludgeriplatz with a roundabout. But we want to move forward in the other direction, along the Königsstrasse (King's Street), which, as one can tell from the name, was once a very noble street. For quite a long time the Königsstrasse was lined by noble residences from the 16th to the 18th century. But a very large number of noble residences were also located in the area of the Aegidiistrasse, the Domplatz and the Ludgeristrasse. It was due to this fact that Münster in its history was given the name "City of Nobility" and, because of the considerable influence of this class, was called an "aristocratic republic". In the age of absolutism the citi-

The Church of St Ludgeri

zens increasingly lost their independence. Where town houses were located earlier, the nobility built their impressive city residences to be able to take part directly in the social life of the provincial capital instead of sitting bored in their moated castles in the country.
Because of the destruction during the war unfortunately only a few remains of these grand mansions are still standing or could be reconstructed. On the Königsstrasse, where we now want to stroll, this applies to the **Senden'sche Hof** of Baron Droste zu Senden, which dates back to the 18th century; in an interesting way it has been integrated into the new building of the Commerzbank. Only a few steps further, again on the western side of the street, we will find the **Oer'sche Hof** (1748) designed by J. C. Schlaun with the contrast of red brickwork and Baum-

Crucifix in the Church of St Ludgeri

St Mary's Column in front of St Ludgeri   *The Heeremannsche Hof*

Renaissance arcaded gabled house   *Front of the Church of St Aegidii*

berge sandstone so characteristic of Münster. Quite befitting its rank, the Oer'sche Hof today, among other things, houses a fine restaurant. A little further away, there follows the restored **Beverfoerder Hof**, a three-wing building dating from the beginning of the 18th century, though only its right wing still retains a historic exterior today. The small car park next to this building once again gives way to a noble residence, the 16th-century **Heeremannsche Hof** - today the seat of the Administrative Court of Appeal of the Land North Rhine-Westphalia. The residence's reconstructed street façade (design by Hermann tom Ring) impresses with its shaping typical of the Renaissance. Below the oriel gable, the inscription "POST TENEBRAS SPERO LUCEM" can be found, meaning approximately "After darkness (death of night) I hope for the light (salvation)", a saying which is interpreted as expressing relief at the end of the cruel reign of the Anabaptists. A little further down the other side of the road, the Stadtsparkasse (municipal savings bank) can be found today. In the past, the classical **Druffel'sche Hof** (1784/88) was located here, of which only the façade and the flight of steps have remained. But next to the Heeremansche Hof, we turn left onto the cobbled road, the Krumme Strasse, and we reach the Aegidiikirchplatz (church square) with St Aegidii, the Constitutional Court of Law of North Rhine-Westphalia as well as the Administrative Court of Appeal of the Land North Rhine-Westphalia. In between, a fountain with the figure of the Madonna from 1965.

What you see today of **St Aegidii (44)** is a post-war restoration. The original building was a Capucin monastery and an early work of the architect Johann Conrad Schlaun. It took four years, from 1724 to 1728, to complete this building. Following the strict rules of the mendicant order, the church is remarkably simple in style. The sandstone west façade is also kept simple but attracts attention with the clear shape of the ledge and the portal with an arched gable protruding from the flat façade. If you look closely, you can still discover the bullet holes in the façade caused by small arms or grenade splinters from the last war. Inside, the carvings decorating the wooden pulpit from the 18th century are of importance. Worth seeing in choir and nave are also the paintings of the Nazarenes, an organisation of painters who supported a renewal of religious art.

If you are a real fan of museums, you are now in just the right place. Only a few metres to your right, the **Westphalian Museum of Archaeology (Westfälisches Museum für Archäologie) (27)** is awaiting its visitors. Here, the prehistory of Westphalia is documented by burial objects, stone tools, pottery, jewellery and other small finds. Whoever is interested in ages even further back in the past should visit the **University Museum of Geology and Palaeontology (Geologisch-Paläontologisches Museum) (25)** in the Pferdegasse, which can be reached by taking a few steps in the direction of the Domplatz. Here, geology is vividly presented and the history of the earth is made comprehensible through rocks and fossils. The most spectacular exhibit is certainly the huge ice-age skeleton of a **mammoth**.

63

Mammoth in the University Museum of Geology and Palaeontology

Walking a little further, you will come to the Cathedral Square, where you will find the **Westphalian Museum of Art and Cultural History (Westfälisches Landesmuseum für Kunst- und Kulturgeschichte) (27)** already mentioned, but also, a little concealed, the **University Archaeological Museum (Archäologisches Museum) (26)** in the Fürstenberghaus. The latter, though, is only open at the following times:
Tue, Thur, Fri: 1 - 3 pm; Wed: 4 - 6 pm, Sat: 11 am - 1 pm, Sun: 2 - 4 pm. The opening hours are rather difficult to remember; however, admission is free.

While some of you may want to visit the many museums the city has to offer, we are turning back to the starting point of our tour, the Prinzipalmarkt. To get there, we have to walk down the Rothenburg, starting opposite the Aegidiimarkt. Originally one of the oldest streets of Münster, the Rothenburg today contains only a few old houses, e.g. the house No. 44 at the point where the Königsstrasse, which we left only a short time ago, meets the Rothenburg. It is a **Renaissance arcaded gabled house** resembling the Krameramtshaus opposite St Lamberti because of its typical stepped gable with the semi-rosettes trimmed with spheres on the gable steps. To the right of this outstanding example of Renaissance architecture the probably structurally oldest house of the street, No. 45, with its Gothic sandstone façade, can be found. Just a few steps further on, you'll find yourself back at the Prinzipalmarkt again. Perhaps out of curiosity you have not yet found the time to stop and eat. Now, restaurants can be found under the arcades.

The Town Hall Tower

Fresco in the Erbdrostenhof

Deckengemälde im Erbdrostenhof

H I S T O R I C A L   F A C T S

The History of the City of Münster

The Münsterland is known to have been inhabited by Neolithic settlers as of 3000 B.C. Finds from this age can be seen today in the Westphalian Museum of Archaeology; and a huge mammoth skeleton from an even earlier age can be found in the Museum of Geology and Palaeontology.

From the 6th century B.C. onwards, the favourable geographical location, the traversable ford on the Aa and the fertile soil all around led, as has been proved, to the settlement of the Horsteberg, which later became the Cathedral Hill and the centre of the city. Around the turn of the millennium, the Romans with their army camps invaded the Münsterland, but after their famous defeat in the battle in the Teutoburg Forest they withdrew again behind the Rhine. There is proof of the existence of a Frankish settlement on the Horsteberg in the 2nd century A.D. But in the 5th - 7th centuries A.D., the Saxons invaded the Münsterland from the east and settled there; the Saxon settlement "Mimigernaford" arose. The name "Mimigernaford" - later "Mimigardeford" - according to a theory stems from an ancient sacri- ficial altar near a ford, dedica- ted to Mimir, the pagan god of wisdom. But the Saxons did not reckon with the persistence of the expelled Franks. It was, however, not until some

centuries later, in the time of Charlemagne (747 - 814), that the Franks succeeded in reconquering the Westphalian territories from the heathen Saxons. Not content with doing that, they forced Christianity on them, and this shaped Westphalia from this time onward. In the year 792 A.D., and here the actual history of the city of Münster begins, Charlemagne sent the Frisian monk Liudger (742 - 809) to convert the West Saxons. On a hill close to the settlement "Mimigernaford" on the banks of the River Aa, Liudger established a protected diocese which he called "Monasterium", i.e. "monastery". From the beginning, the monastery housed not only clergymen, but also artisans, and so Monasterium enjoyed a certain independence. In 805, Monasterium became a bishopric, and Liudger was consecrated its bishop. Liudger also founded the first of altogether three cathedral buildings.

In the course of the 10th century, the protected cathedral stronghold attracted more and more traders so that a merchant settlement arose around the cathedral building, followed later on by another settlement on the left bank of the Aa around the diocese of St Mary in the Überwasser quarter. The shopkeepers - for business reasons - were interested in maintaining a lively contact with the artisans. Later, the settlement was called "Monestere". The first reference to this term dates back to the year 1106. In the year

1090, the Bishop Erpho consecrated the second cathedral building, where the third cathedral, the Cathedral of St Paul, stands today.

Monestere experienced its first great endurance test in 1121, when the later Emperor Lothar of Supplinburg conquered Münster and reduced the town to rubble: the cathedral stronghold and the merchant settlement were destroyed and had to be arduously rebuilt. Consequently, in 1150, the fortification of the bishop's castle was abandoned in favour of ramparts surrounding the whole settlement.

With the fall of Henry the Lion in 1180, the structure of rule changed in Münster: Henry's duchy was split up, and, in Münster, the bishop also became the secular sovereign, the prince-bishop. Over the next 20 years, the first city wall was built in the area of the ramparts: Münster kept these marked borders until far into the 19th century. They are still clearly visible in today's urban landscape in the form of the Promenade. So the external requirements facilitating the gradual development of a city with its own rights (Town Charter sealed around 1200) and also with a growing independence from the bishop were fulfilled.

In the meantime, Münster had developed into an important trading city with far-reaching trade relations. The town traded with (among others) Riga, Nowgorod, Bergen and London and consolidated this position even further: the "Treaty of Ladbergen" (1246) for the mutual protection of the travelling merchants against robbery was signed by Münster, Osnabrück, Minden, Coesfeld and Herford. Seven years later, Münster entered into an alliance

Great Seal of the City from 1536

of cities with Dortmund, Lippstadt and Soest to secure and extend their mutual trade. The development of Münster as a trading city was heading for a peak when, in 1305, the city first took part in a meeting of the Hanseatic League in Lübeck.

At the end of the 13th century, the bishopric developed into a corporate state, i.e. the bishop and the body of representatives of the various medieval classes, that is the nobility, the city representatives and the members of the cathedral chapter, ruled together. The increasing autonomy of the citizens from the clergy is, for example, reflected in the following oath which the bishop had to swear to his fellow rulers from 1309 onwards: "Nobody's lord, nobody's servant, that is the right of the citizens." It was only because of the military independence achieved in 1278 in the course of these emancipation efforts that the city was able to apply for full admission to the Hanseatic League. There is proof of Münster's participation in the Hanseatic League as early as 1368.

Jan van Leiden - King of the Anabaptists

guilds taking control of the council in 1457 and with the city once again strengthening its rights in relation to its sovereign, the prince-bishop. From this time onwards, the guilds clearley dominated the citizen's politics, which was expressed in the representative Early-Gothic City Hall, intentionally placed opposite the main gate of the cathedral precinct.

But the everlasting conflict did not stop. From 1500 onwards, there were mutterings of displeasure at the church property's exemption from taxes and, finally, the Reformation also reached Münster. But in Münster these attempts were to culminate in the Anabaptists' reign. First, the approval of the population was enormous. Since 1531, the Catholic clergyman Bernd Rothmann had been preaching Luther's doctrines and with that gained the support not

The first great outbreak of the plague struck Münster in 1350 and caused a break in the development of the city. Altogether, the Black Death was to afflict Münster eight times. After the first outbreak of the plague, the supposedly guilty Jews were persecuted, and the destruction of the first Jewish community in Münster soon followed.

The city recovered from the plague and soon started trading again. The artisans' guilds, first mentioned in a document from 1354, were in control of production and competition and kept an especially watchful eye on outside competitors.

From 1450 onwards, the bishop and the guilds quarrelled about political power in the city in the so-called diocese feud. The feud ended with the

The Church of Our Lady

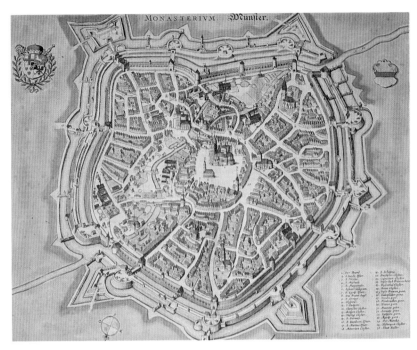

Bird's-eye view (around 1655)

only of numerous citizens, but also of an important leader of the opposition, the cloth merchant Bernd Knipperdollinck. The population's positive response was so great that the bishop at that time, Franz von Waldeck, in 1533 in the Settlement of Dülmen was compelled to accept the fact that Münster had become Lutheran. On January 6, 1534, Bernd Rothmann was secretly baptized by a follower of the Dutchman and self-appointed prophet Jan Matthys. He thereby publicly professed his faith in the forbidden community of the Anabaptists. The Anabaptists modelled themselves on the apostolic community and rejected the customs and traditions of the official church. They wished to live in a pious community of property. Their name was derived from the rejection of child christening: they were, instead, baptized as adults. The Anabaptists also believed in the return of Christ at Easter 1534. For them, Münster was to become the "New Jerusalem". For Franz von Waldeck, the declaration of belief in the Anabaptists' teachings meant a violation of the Settlement of Dülmen. This is why he no longer felt tied to the agreements reached there. In 1534, the Anabaptists came to power in the city hall. Many citizens were persuaded by their ideas and adopted them of their own free will. At the end of February of that year, the charismatic Jan Matthys came to Münster and preached his ideas about the Christian

Torture and execution of the Anabaptists

community of property, the abolition of money, in short, a form of Christian communism. Several thousand inhabitants of Münster could not acquire a taste for these new ideas and left the city. On the other hand, supporters of the movement moved in from the outside. Münster became one of the strongholds of the Anabaptists, and Jan Matthys took over as their leader. In the meantime, the bishop had gathered an army outside the walls to besiege Münster. In a heroic but pointless attack, Matthys was killed by the bishop's troops. After Matthys' death, the only twenty-five-year-old tailor Jan van Leiden, whose real name was Johann Bockelson, took command. First of all, he crowned himself king of a world to be established anew with all the insignia of power: royal coat of arms, sceptre and crown. Van Leiden intro-

duced a number of reforms, all of which - like his kingship - he justified as revelations of the Heavenly Father. Among other things, he introduced polygyny, the right of men to marry several women - mind you, not the other way round! Not only that, but polygyny even became a duty; and those who did not obey, be it man or woman, were beheaded or imprisoned. When one of van Leiden's sixteen concubines dared to criticize him and accused her husband of living the high life while the population was starving, van Leiden made short work of her. He personally beheaded her in public and then, on top of that, danced around her corpse in a frenzy, singing.

In many people's opinion, that went too far. A rebellion broke out that was bloodily suppressed. Morale was low among the besieged: food was getting so scarce that dogs, cats and rats had to serve as iron rations.

But it is amazing how the Anabaptists nevertheless succeeded in defying the siege for 16 months, at the same time keeping internal unrest under control and perfecting the fortifications of the city. In some way, the Anabaptists time and again must have been able to fill the citizens with enthusiasm; otherwise, it is almost impossible to explain the extensive work of the citizens on the ramparts. Militarily speaking, the Anabaptists proceeded cleverly anyway. To raise the height of the ramparts and entrenchments, stones from churches and even sacred sculptures were used, as filling material was scarce. Today, in the portal of the Church of Our Lady (Überwasserkirche) several statues are still missing, which, however, were found again during excavations at the end of the 19th century and can be seen today in the Westphalian Museum of Art and Cultural History next to the Cathedral Square. The Anabaptists' tactics of taking down six church spires also considerably confused the episcopal besiegers. But soon von Waldeck's troops learned for themselves what was happening there. The besieged were using the levelled spires as ideal gun emplacements for well-aimed shots. For this deed, which actually amounted to a desecration of the places of worship, biblical authorization was of course at hand, based on the motto *"What is high shall be abased and what is low shall be exalted"*.

By now, it seemed only a matter of time until von Waldeck would capture the city. The situation of the besieged was hopeless. But they had to remain in the city because von Waldeck had

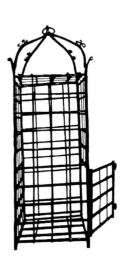

Anabaptists' cages

MVLIER PLEBEIA MONAST
gienfis in VVeftphalia.

Burgher's wife from Münster, 1577

hundreds of those citizens killed who tried to go over to the episcopal troops. On June 24, 1535, the bishop stormed the city, thanks to the betrayal by a citizen, who gave away a weak point in the fortifications to the besiegers. The leaders of the Anabaptists, Bernd Krechting, Bernd Knipperdollinck and the self-appointed "king" Jan van Leiden were captured, tortured with glowing tongs in public and then stabbed to death. Their corpses were exposed in three cages attached to the base of the spire of St Lambert as a deterrent. Power was back in the hands of the

bishop, who immediately withdrew many of the city's rights. By the way, the empty cages are still attached to St Lambert's Church, but surely you have already discovered that.

From 1541 onwards, the restoration of the city's rights and liberties was carried out. Again, Münster recovered economically and in 1580 led the principal cities in the Westphalian section of the Hanseatic League.

With Ferdinand of Bavaria, Münster then had a bishop (1612 - 1650) who was a convinced supporter of the Counter-Reformation and with that a special patron of Catholic life. The diocese of Münster in the course of the 16th century also blossomed into Germany's largest episcopal principality. At the beginning of the 17th century - as everywhere else in Europe - the city was given another modern ring of fortifications, consisting of ramparts and entrenchments allowing the raking of the trenches by guns without a dead angle remaining. This was still the case with the medieval fortifications of towers and later with rondels. For Münster, the year 1618, the beginning of the Thirty Years' War, was not a date of importance at first - the city was not really affected by the war.

In 1643, when the Emperor and the Empire were in a state of war, Münster obtained a status of neutrality: Emperor Ferdinand released the city from the "allegiance to His Imperial Majesty and to the Empire". The reason for this: the European peace congress was sitting in Münster.

In 1648, all the world at that time turned their eyes towards the Westphalian metropolis. On May 15, about 230 ambassadors from almost all over

"Arrival of the ambassador Adriaen Pauw"

"Ratification of the peace treaty", Oil painting by Gerard Ter Borch

Auß Münster vom 25. deß Weinmonats im Jahr
1648. abgefertigter Freud- vnd Friedenbringender Postreuter.

A pamphlet tells everyone the good news (1648)

"Ich komm von Münster her gleich Sporn-streich geritten/ und habe nun das meist deß Weges überschritten/ Ich bringe gute Post und neue Friedenszeit/ der Frieden ist ge-macht/ gewendet alles Leid. (...)

Mercur fleugt in der Lufft/ und auch der Friede Je/ Gantz Münster/Oßnabrugg und alle Welt ist froh/ die Glocken thönen starck/ die Orgeln lieblich klingen/ Herr Gott wir loben dich/ die frohen Leute singen. Die Stücke donneren und sausen in der Lufft/ die Fah-nen fliegen schön/ und alles jauchzend rufft: der Höchste sey gelobt/ der Friede ist getrof-fen/ fortan hat manniglich ein besser Jahr zu hoffen/ (...)

Es tauren mich allein die armen Degenfe-ger/ Die haben nichts zu thun: Last Degen/ Degen seyn/ macht einen Pflug darfür/und eine Pflugschar drein. (...)"   (1648)

"I have come riding post-haste from Mün-ster/ and have by now covered most of my road./ I bring good news of a time of peace/ peace has been made/ all sorrow is turned away. (...)

Mercury flies the skies/ and in addition Peace/ All Münster/ Osnabrück and all the world rejoices/ the bells ring out and organs sweetly play/ Lord God we praise Thee/ the joyful people sing. Salutes thunder and roar in the air/ flags fly bravely/ and everyone joins in to cheer:
Praise to God in the Highest/ Peace is made, henceforth shall each and every one look forward to better times. (...)

I am only sorry for the poor sword-smiths/ For they have nothing to do: Let swords alone/ make out of them a plough instead/ and a ploughshare too. (...)"   (1648)

Europe met in the council chamber of the City Hall - today's Hall of Peace - on the Prinzipalmarkt, to seal the peace treaty between Spain and the Netherlands. In October, the Emperor's peace treaties with France and Sweden followed. This was the end of the Thirty Years' War.

The good tidings of the peace agreement was sent all over the world in a pamphlet bearing the motif of the "Postrider bringing Joy and Peace" and the message opposite, written in verse (excerpts).

For five long years, during which the City Hall time and again served as a meeting point, the negotiations went on, finally resulting in the Treaty of Westphalia and making Münster known to the whole world.

"Bishop of the Cannon" C.B. von Galen

After the Treaty of Westphalia, Münster tried to become a Free Town of the Reich, i.e. to be directly subordinate to the Empire and the Emperor.

But the citizens of Münster did not reckon with Christoph Bernhard von Galen, ruling as prince-bishop from 1650 to 1678. He turned out to be an absolutist ruler, who wanted to make sure that the city's customary rights that had lasted for centuries, were transferred to the absolutist sovereign, i.e. the ruler directly appointed by God. After so many years of relative autonomy, the citizens of Münster naturally were not willing to accept these restrictions. So, from 1657 onwards, there was a war. With the help of the Netherlands, the attacks of the bishop's troops were at first successfully repelled. As the bishop's methods were sometimes quite drastic, and as he did not have any qualms about using force,

Christoph Bernhard von Galen was popularly called the "Kanonenbischof" ("Bishop of the Cannon"). Yet it was not the cannons but the gentle power of the water that led at last to the surrender of the besieged citizens of Münster. "Kanonenbernhard" simply dammed the River Aa in the area of today's Aasee (Lake Aa) to drain Münster's ditches and to be able to storm the city. During a thunderstorm, however, the dams broke and the water flooded the city. But, as better dams had been built behind the city, there was so much backwater that the city was under water and the citizens had to sail the streets in washing troughs. This is why in 1661 the proud and free city submitted to the prince-bishop Christoph Bernhard von Galen after a four-year siege. The result was the reduction of municipal rights, reaching its peak in the abolition of the election of the

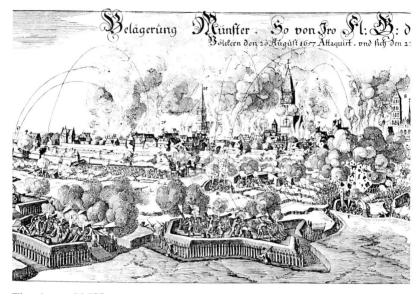

Belägerung Münster. So von Iro Fl: B: ð
Völckern den 20 August 1657 Attaquirt . vnd sich ðen 2

The siege of 1657

council. On a commemorative coin minted in the year of his victory, von Galen boasts of his deeds with the statement: "Monasterium Westfalorum ad obedientiam reductum" ("Münster in Westphalia led back into obedience.") Whether they liked it or not, the citizens of Münster were mere subjects again. By constructing a citadel, a fort in the western part of the town, which was specially protected by entrenchments and ramparts, the prince-bishop underlined his claim to power yet again. He himself, though, preferred to reside in Coesfeld, at a suitable distance from the unloved city. But he saw to it that the citizens of Münster could not lock him out for a second time. The citadel was equipped with a 4000-strong garrison. Besides, the citadel ('small town' in Italian) was special because, on the one hand, it was included in the ring of fortifications of the rest of the city, but, on the other hand, it was also protected from that same city by trenches and ramparts and thereby at the same time protected from Münster's possibly once more rebellious citizens. The prince-bishop purposely had an open field of fire, the glacis, put up between citadel and city and removed the western part of the city walls, now located within the overall fortifications. As a result, the city was left unprotected in the direction of the bishop's fortress. Today, we find the Hindenburgplatz on this spot, which is said to be Europe's second largest inner-city square after the Place de la Concorde in Paris.

The loss of the municipal rights and the debts accumulated during the siege resulted in a fall in trade and in city life becoming more and more unattractive.

Impoverishment and emigration followed, and the last outbreak of the plague in the years 1666/68, with about 600 victims, further contributed to the decline of the city.

But Münster would not have been Münster if it had not have got back on its feet again. The relative prosperity in the next decades and in the course of the 18th century can, however, mainly be put down to the fact that the nobility felt drawn towards the capital. Instead of getting bored in their moated castles in the surrounding area, the nobility wished to take part in social life and tried to outdo one another in the construction of magnificent noble residences, the remains of which can still today be admired in some places, e.g. on the Königsstrasse (King's Street). Especially during the reign of Clemens August of Bavaria (1719 - 1761), who had a craving for splendour, there was a lot of building work going on. For the most part, it was supervised by one person, the baroque architect of the Münsterland, Johann Conrad Schlaun (1695 - 1773), a pupil of Balthasar Neumann. Buildings so expressive and beautiful but also functional in their own way as the Clemenskirche (Church of St Clemens), the Erbdrostenhof or the Residenzschloss (Castle) were constructed. The latter, by the way, was erected in the area of the dismantled fortress grounds of the citadel next to the large shooting range, today's Hindenburgplatz. For other building projects the right time did not seem to have come yet. The remarkable attempt to build up a connection to the Netherlands and the North Sea with the Max-Clemens Canal failed in spite of initial successes because of lack of money and water, among other things. It was not until around 170 years later that the Dortmund-Ems Canal followed.

During the Seven Years' War, fought from 1756 to 1763 over predominance in Europe, Münster was on France's and the Emperor's side, against the Prussians, the Hannoverians and the English. Alternating occupations by different troops followed: in 1758 these were the Prussians and the English, who one year later were driven off by the French. After that the Prussian-Hannoverian troops besieged the city and bombarded it heavily - finally, the Prussians took over Münster again. The Seven Years' War revealed that the modern fortifications, which - up to that point - were regarded as extremely effective compared to the medieval fortifications, now no longer provided safety because of the advanced weaponry. Besides, in Münster the ideas of the Enlightenment also gained influence so that in 1764 the electoral minister Baron Franz von Fürstenberg ordered the dismantling of the fortifications - today only the Buddenturm and the Zwinger (Outer Court) on the Promenade remain of the fortified buildings. Mind you, following the Promenade and the entrenchments, like, for example, the Kreuz- and Engelenschanze, still today the visitor can easily make out the former course and the location of the walls and ramparts. But the dismantling of the city's fortifications and conversion into a promenade rampart had another motivation, too. With the restrictions of the city's fortification being eased, the population, whose number until then was li-

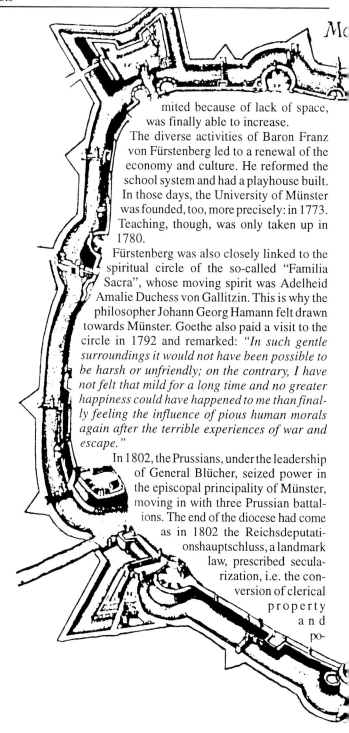

Mc

mited because of lack of space, was finally able to increase.

The diverse activities of Baron Franz von Fürstenberg led to a renewal of the economy and culture. He reformed the school system and had a playhouse built. In those days, the University of Münster was founded, too, more precisely: in 1773. Teaching, though, was only taken up in 1780.

Fürstenberg was also closely linked to the spiritual circle of the so-called "Familia Sacra", whose moving spirit was Adelheid Amalie Duchess von Gallitzin. This is why the philosopher Johann Georg Hamann felt drawn towards Münster. Goethe also paid a visit to the circle in 1792 and remarked: *"In such gentle surroundings it would not have been possible to be harsh or unfriendly; on the contrary, I have not felt that mild for a long time and no greater happiness could have happened to me than finally feeling the influence of pious human morals again after the terrible experiences of war and escape."*

In 1802, the Prussians, under the leadership of General Blücher, seized power in the episcopal principality of Münster, moving in with three Prussian battalions. The end of the diocese had come as in 1802 the Reichsdeputationshauptschluss, a landmark law, prescribed secularization, i.e. the conversion of clerical property and po-

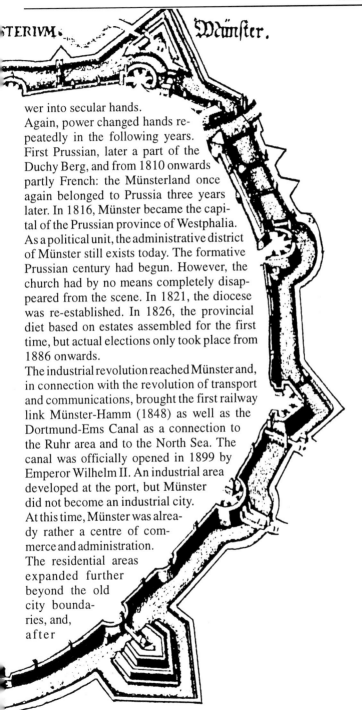

TERIVM. 𝔐ünſter.

wer into secular hands.

Again, power changed hands repeatedly in the following years. First Prussian, later a part of the Duchy Berg, and from 1810 onwards partly French: the Münsterland once again belonged to Prussia three years later. In 1816, Münster became the capital of the Prussian province of Westphalia. As a political unit, the administrative district of Münster still exists today. The formative Prussian century had begun. However, the church had by no means completely disappeared from the scene. In 1821, the diocese was re-established. In 1826, the provincial diet based on estates assembled for the first time, but actual elections only took place from 1886 onwards.

The industrial revolution reached Münster and, in connection with the revolution of transport and communications, brought the first railway link Münster-Hamm (1848) as well as the Dortmund-Ems Canal as a connection to the Ruhr area and to the North Sea. The canal was officially opened in 1899 by Emperor Wilhelm II. An industrial area developed at the port, but Münster did not become an industrial city.

At this time, Münster was already rather a centre of commerce and administration.

The residential areas expanded further beyond the old city boundaries, and, after

81

the First World War, the population reached the 100,000 mark in 1918. At the beginning of the First World War, Münster, as a garrison town and in view of the general mobilization, was seized by the same patriotic enthusiasm as other German cities. At the "Send" fair, "enemies on the gallows" could be bought for children! After the war, though, chaos reigned for some time. Workers' and soldiers' councils ruled, and in the course of time, all in all, more than one million soldiers passed through the city. The Ruhr area to the west was controlled by communist associations, but they did not reach as far as Münster. The city became a base of patriotically-minded associations and volunteer corps, congregating here in opposition to the French occupation of the Ruhr area. By the way, bank notes with Münster motifs dating from the

inflationary times can be seen in the exemplary City Museum. In 1930, a native of Münster became Chancellor of the German Reich: Dr Heinrich Brüning, freeman of the city of Münster.

If one believes the annals, there were as few Nazis in Münster during the Nazi period as everywhere else in Germany. Among the few who knew of their fundamental anti-Nazi attitude not only after, but also during the Nazi period, and who accordingly voiced their criticism, was August Count von Galen, who was consecrated bishop in 1933 and later became cardinal. In several sermons, he opposed the persecution methods of the Gestapo and the confiscation of monasteries and orders. From the pulpit he castigated arbitrary arrests of people and condemned euthanasia.

← *Model of the destroyed city (1945)*   ↑ *The City Hall destroyed in the war*

Post-war reconstruction (Prinzipalmarkt)

Especially in the two last years of the war, the destruction of the city by the allied bomber units was extraordinary. On April 2, 1945 - it was Easter Monday -, the first American tanks burrowed their way through the rubble of the Gau capital Münster. 63% of the buildings lay in ruins, the old town with the historic Prinzipalmarkt was the victim of bombs and fire to the extent of even 90%. Destroyed walls were the most harmless consequence of 12 years of Nazi rule. Münster became a British-American occupied zone. The appointment of a provincial government for Westphalia with its headquarters in Münster followed.

The inhabitants of Münster suffered from most serious housing and food problems, as did the rest of Germany. People had to live on around 1,000 calories per day; this corresponds to one third or a half of what today is regarded as appropriate for an adult. People lived in ruins repaired and insulated in a makeshift way. The monetary reform of the year 1948 was accompanied by a housing programme. Slowly, the amount of available living space increased, at first only in the number of buildings suitable for repair. Little by little, everything became more clear and well-ordered. People demanded culture, and the municipal theatre made use of the improvised stage in the castle gardens. But people also wanted to rebuild their historic Münster with the Hall of Peace, the Prinzipalmarkt and the baroque buildings. In spite of the well-meant advice not even to attempt such undertakings, Münster's old buildings were reconstructed according to original plans, as far as these plans were available. In 1958, the City Hall was restored. Other reconstruction work on historic buildings was still going on when Münster found itself right in the middle of the economic miracle. But it was not only faithfulness to original plans that guided the architects and city planners of the post-war years. Modern administrative buildings and the new Municipal Theatre on the Neubrückenstrasse were built. In view of the avant-garde design, the theatre was praised by experts as a milestone in city architecture. In 1949, the refounded Administrative Court of Appeal of the Land North Rhine-Westphalia was already moved to Münster, and in 1952 the Constitutional Court of Law of North Rhine-Westphalia followed. This, along with the re-establishment of many other institutions, once again restored Münster's importance as a centre of administration and helped Münster to become a city of commerce once again, too. After years of hunger and reconstruction, life in Münster finally returned to normal. In 1954, the last tram was removed from the streets, which is now being regretted in view of today's traffic problems. Perhaps a local rail traffic programme will be carried through in the future. Nowadays, even an underground system has been suggested for Münster, mostly, though, only on - er - April Fools' Day.

As far as the development of the population is concerned, Münster reached the 200,000 mark already in 1966. The university has increasingly gained in importance, and, from 1971 onwards, planning for the expansion ("Urban Development Plan 2000") of new parts of town began for the neighbourhoods Kinderhaus, Am Berg Fidel, and Gievenbeck, among others. Within the framework of the communal restructuring of North Rhine-Westphalia in 1975, the neighbouring villages of Albachten, Amelsbüren, Angelmodde, Handorf, Hiltrup, St. Mauritz, Nienberge, Roxel and Wolbeck were also incorporated into Münster, thereby quadrupling the population of Münster. In 1978, the city already had more than 275,000 inhabitants. In 1993, the citizens of Münster celebrated their 1200-year city jubilee. It was a time for looking back on a varied and interesting history, but also an orientation towards the future.

The Münster of the future ought to remain what it was and became again in post-war times: Metropolis Westphaliae and one of the most beautiful among Germany's beautiful cities.

The History of the University of Münster

The History of the University of Münster begins with the wish for a university, a wish which actually existed very early on and which was expressed time and again. This wish was expressed for the first time in the 15th century. In 1474, a writer regretted that his Westphalian home did not possess a university. It is true that in 1614 the University of Paderborn was already founded on East Westphalian soil, but not in the centre of the Münsterland, in Münster itself. Ferdinand of Bavaria, the prince-bishop of Münster, who reigned from 1612 to 1650, finally reacted to the strong desire for a university in Münster and made the necessary applications to the Pope as well as to the Emperor.

But in the confusion of the Thirty Years' War (1618 - 1648), the public announcement of the foundation charter, and thus the foundation of the university, was prevented. Furthermore, at this time there was a relatively large number of universities in Germany; but, as a result of the war, there were not enough students. Still, the Minister of Education for the Münsterland, Baron Franz von Fürstenberg, was able to found the university in 1773 after presenting the plans for a University of Münster to the Emperor and to the Pope again. But for the actual foundation - the constitution -von Fürstenberg took his time, making a meticulous choice of candidates for teaching because - if possible - they should all be of Westphalian ori-

Fürstenberg, founder of the University

gin. On April 16, 1780, the time had come: von Fürstenberg ceremonially inaugurated the University of Münster, and, in 1980, the 200th anniversary of the foundation was celebrated.

With the year 1802, the rule of the Prussians began in Münster. The Prussian statesman Baron von Stein introduced civil administration and was especially interested in the university. Von Stein was more liberally-minded than von Fürstenberg and had no interest in a Westphalian and denominational commitment of the university. He had a large German university in mind. In the university committee set up afterwards, there was then, of course, no place for von Fürstenberg. The population of Münster was more on von Fürstenberg's side and watched the dispute with mixed feelings. In 1806 -

in the Napoleonic era - the French took over from the Prussians and ruled for seven years. During this time, von Fürstenberg succeeded in installing "his university". But in 1813, with the return of the Prussian government, the university formed by von Fürstenberg was again dissolved.

Prussia's king Friedrich Wilhelm III initiated another important event in the university history of Münster: he faithfully promised his Rhenish subjects to set up a university for them. To the disadvantage of Münster, the University of Bonn was re-established in 1818 because in Berlin the government held the view that there was no need for two universities in the Westphalian provinces. The University of Münster lost her faculties of law and medicine and was converted into an establishment of secondary education (an academy) with two faculties as had existed before until around 1774. The Prussians let the citizens of Münster keep the faculties of theology and philosophy in order to avoid annoying the population and the church too much. But even this "rump university" remained attractive for many students and lecturers. Münster's academy was still able to compete with other, larger German universities.

In the following period, there were still some set-backs in spite of a constant progress especially in connection with the denominational affiliation of the university. Debates about this aspect reached their peak in 1830. The quarrels were settled in 1874/75 by the extension of the faculty of philosophy by seven new chairs and the

The twin towers of the University Clinics

Eldorado for the book-lover: The University & Regional Library

employment of Protestant professors based on a so-called "denominational simultanization", a quota system. After this was settled, the number of students increased continuously. The final breakthrough in the university's history occurred during the years 1901/2, when the then vice-chancellor succeeded in persuading the German Emperor and Prussian King Wilhelm II to authorize again a Faculty of Jurisprudence and Political Science in Münster.

The authorization of the new constitution by the king was enthusiastically received by the city of Münster. Rapid development of the university began, and, out of gratitude, it was named the "Westfälische Wilhelms-Universität", or WWU. The university not only survived the difficult years of war, but has built up a fine reputation, which reaches far beyond Münster.

It is not only in terms of figures that the WWU is currently among the five largest institutions of higher education in Germany. Münster today offers a range of around 100 different courses of study, ranging from Ancient Oriental Studies to Zoology. Research is mainly undertaken in special research fields: medieval studies, the pathobiology of cellular interactions, intra- and intercellular recognition systems, mechanisms of inflammation, nuclear physics and molecular chemistry. In the field of humanities and social sciences, the main focus is, for example, on New Testament text research, urban research, and Leibniz research. In the field of mathematics and natural sciences, there is biochemical sensor research, material sciences and polar research. Medical research goes on in the areas of arteriosclerosis, oncology and biomagnetism. For the practical application of its findings, the medical faculty also has at its disposal the large University Clinics, with their twin towers or "Bettentürme".

In order to ensure that basic as well as applied research will have consequences not only in medicine, importance is attached to the transfer of information between research theory and practical reality. The Centre for Research Transfer takes care of communication between university research and society in general, and, of course, industry in particular. For the latter, a technology centre has been set up, integrating innovative technology firms and establishing them near the university. Future plans even include an enormous technology park interlinking the university and industry even further, and heightening the attractiveness of the university as well as of the city of Münster as a location for high technology firms.

Apart from the lectures, the large university library enables the students to prepare themselves properly for their different subjects. For teaching staff and students, the library provides more than 2.2 million volumes. This amounts to - would you believe it? - about 55 kilometres of bookshelves. The eager student of statistics would now, of course, quickly calculate the thickness of the average book - we have done this calculation for you: it is roughly 2.5 cm. Every year another 1,125 metres of bookshelves are added, which corresponds to about 45,000 new volumes. Additionally, 9,692 newspapers and periodicals are subscribed to, catalogued and made available to readers.

Even students take a break (from time to time)

In addition, there is also a large number of important electronic databases. As it is also a regional library, it is an important source of information for Münster and the surrounding area. And still, hard as it is to believe, difficulties may arise concerning the supply of much-sought-after reference books. No wonder, as the number of students had increased more than ten-fold in the years between 1950 and 1985. During the same period, by contrast, the number of Münster's citizens had only increased by a little more than 200 percent. So, today, there are about 195 students for every thousand inhabitants. During the winter semester of 1997/98, 45,500 students were registered at the WWU, making the university the third on the list of the largest German universities after Cologne and Munich. If one includes the students of the

other colleges of higher education and the College of Applied Sciences, the impressive total comes to some 55,500 students, which then even corresponds to approximately 20% of the town's population. The university is having trouble coping with this unabating influx of students. During the university strikes in the winter semester of 1988/89, repeated demands for more funds, teaching staff and living space were made by and for the students.

In spite of this situation (other universities also share this fate), the University of Münster still today is a particularly popular university and alma mater for students. Certainly, another important contributory factor to this is the attractive urban environment with its varied cultural life, which makes Münster a true university town.

"After the rain" - Münster painting in the City Museum

Saved from grandma's time: corner shop from 1911 in the City Museum

EVENTFUL MÜNSTER: ART, BUSINESS, CULTURE

The City Museum Münster

"Culture is a thin varnish easily dissolved in alcohol."

Aldous Huxley

"It is the ultimate aim of all culture to make redundant what we call 'politics', but to make science and art indispensable to humanity."

Arthur Schnitzler

People travel to Mallorca and Sylt but nevertheless like to come to Münster. Why? Well, beach life alone is not enough for most people. They want more. But as everyone has a different idea of culture - and that is a good thing - we do not want to (and cannot) give a binding definition of Münster's culture.

Let us just yield to diversity and present to you in the next chapters with some examples of cultural life in Münster, which - so much still needs to be said - offers more than just a combination of the Kiepenkerl, Westphalian ham and Korn...

City history is "... presented against the background of general German and European history", states the museum brochure of Münster's City Museum. That does not promise too much. The new **City Museum (Stadtmuseum) (37)** (opened in 1989) offers a walk through history from Carolingian times to the present day with numerous selected exhibits, not just of local history. Through the integration of the city into general history, the special architectural features of the building itself as well as the didactic arrangement, a very interesting and entertaining exhibition has been developed.

Provincial narrowness is never felt as the objects relating mainly to local history are usually supplemented by additional exhibits like, for example, typical china, paintings or one of the first cars or radios, which exemplarily characterize each epoch.

Besides, local history and world affairs after all tend to overlap sometimes. This also applies to Münster: on the occasion of the signing of the Treaty of Westphalia in Münster's Hall of Peace (1648) all of Europe turned their eyes towards this city.

The central theme of the new City Museum is the development of the city's image in the course of the last 12 centuries, to which the individual exhibits, paintings, photographs, posters etc. relate. The main focus is - among many

Iconography genius loci -
Erbdrostenhof and City Museum

other topics - on "From Cathedral Castle to City", "Economy and Society in the Middle Ages", "The Anabaptists", "The Treaty of Westphalia", "City of Nobility", "Münster Painting in the 19th Century", "Biedermeier Period", "War of Bombs" or "Post-War Reconstruction". A permanent coin display may also be visited. Besides, apart from the collection on the first and second floors, alternating special exhibitions are presented, illustrating individual topics in a graphic way.

At the same time the selection of the exhibits and their form of presentation clearly show the praiseworthy aim of presenting history in a popular way so as to give everybody an understanding of it: for the youngest visitors there is the museum educationalist and the historic Punch and Judy theatre, for the older ones, for example, memories of their own youth: election posters, photographs and vehicles from the Adenauer era.

As the individual exhibits of the City Museum can best speak for themselves,

we would rather add a few words about the special architecture and lay-out of the new museum.

The combination of a museum and commercial interests under the same roof - on the ground floor of the museum there is an arcade of shops, the so-called Salzhof - is no less-than-ideal solution merely accepted for financial reasons, but the intentional confrontation or combination of things traditionally thought to be incompatible: the visitors come from the shopping area into the museum area and vice versa without noticing it. Here, of course, one could indignantly accuse the architect of currying favour with the world of consumption. But, on looking closely at the architecture, one quite soon realizes that here the architect has quite deliberately played with the juxtaposition of the world of the museum and the business world. For the actual exhibition rooms are located on the upper ("elevated") floors, therefore high above the short-lived world of fashion. In the rotunda, which allows the visitor to the museum to look down on the bustle from all directions, for moments even the pleasant impression of a certain independence from the glaring present downstairs may arise, an impression otherwise rather rare in view of the general commercialization and profanation. However, other visitors are already looking forward to the refreshing cup of coffee awaiting them afterwards while they are still strolling through the exhibition rooms. Regarded in this way, it really is successful architecture we are looking at here: inhibition levels are reduced without levelling off the differences between museum and business interests.

But in other respects the museum is also an architecturally delightful building. The rather unusual ground plan and the floor plan correlate with the baroque Erbdrostenhof directly opposite: the curved lines of the Erbdrostenhof's ground plan are mirrored in the foyer of the museum. In addition, the perfect Art-Deco façade of the former old department store was kept, thereby taking into account the mercantile character of the Salzstrasse as an historic trade route. These external dimensions are completed inside by an equally unusual floor plan. Together, they make the architecture of the museum appear like an intentionally laid out "stage" and not just simply as a depository.

On balance, one can therefore say that the museum is worth a visit for its original architecture alone. And if otherwise you tend to shy away from museums for fear of gloomy rooms and broadly extended topics: once you are here, you, too, will surely become quickly captivated by the bright premises with their varied and vivid testimonies to (city-) history. Where else can you get a view of an originally reconstructed air-raid shelter? Where can you still enter an old corner shop with original products from grandmother's time or comfortably get a bird's-eye view of the city with the help of enormous models? In Münster's City Museum!

Stadtmuseum Münster
in Salzhof/Salzstrasse 28, tel.: 4 92-45 03
Opening hours: Tue-Sun: 10 am - 6 pm
For those who are interested guided tours (on Sundays, 4 pm) and numerous publications are offered.

The Westphalian Museum of Art & Cultural History

You do not have to be a citizen of Münster to know that the **Westphalian Museum of Art & Cultural History (Landesmuseum für Kunst & Kulturgeschichte) (27),** located right in the city centre, next to the Cathedral Square, is worth more than just one visit. For many art lovers - from the immediate surrounding countryside as well as from regions further away - it has for a long time become a greatly valued destination.

One has made it one's business here to depict the interrelation between art and history. Medieval works of art are to be seen as well as works of Classical Modern Art and examples of most recent contemporary art.

In Münster it is already a valued tradition to combine art and cultural history in a way that is both vivid and worth seeing. In 1840, the collected treasures of the "Kunstverein" (Art Association) founded nine years earlier and those of the "Verein für Geschichte und Alterthumskunde Westfalen" (Westphalian Association of History and Archaeology) were combined to form the basis of the new museum. Another sixty-eight years had to pass before the museum collections could be housed in their own building. This Neo-Renaissance building, the so-called "Altbau" (old building), was designed by the architect Hermann Schaedler and is undergoing renovation at the moment. During the summer of 1997 it was temporarily opened for the exhibition "Sculpture. Projects in Münster 1997". But you do not have to miss a still worthwhile visit to the museum as there is still the new building, which, since 1972,

*"Adoration of the Child", altarpiece by Derick Baegert (around 1480)
in the Westphalian Museum of Art and Cultural History*

"Fashion shop", August Macke (1913), Westphalian Museum of Art & Cultural History

has been supplementing the "Altbau", which was damaged in World War II and renovated afterwards. A necessary project, as it soon turned out that the collections of old and contemporary art actually took up more and more space. In the new building both works of old art from the Middle Ages to the Baroque Age and modern works are shown in a condensed form. Since October 1995, the branch Schloss Cappenberg near Dortmund has been showing art and products of craft industry from the Baroque Age to Art Nouveau.

There was no doubt that the work in and on the museum over the last years had indeed been worthwhile, but during the internationally renowned three-month sculpture exhibition 1997 it again became very obvious what the flagship of the Westphalian museums has on offer. The renovation work will be completed in 1998, in time for the Council of Europe exhibition "War and Peace in Europe - 350 Years Treaty of Westphalia". This museum enjoys a good reputation - not only among art historians. A visit can be recommended for every Münster tourist. One should, though, take enough time. A tip: ask for current exhibitions and pedagogical museum programmes.

Westfälisches Landesmuseum für Kunst und Kulturgeschichte: *Domplatz 10, tel.: 59 07-01; Opening hours: Tue - Sun 10 am - 6 pm; Museum shop, Café*

"Red Dog for Landois", Keith Haring (1987)

Sculpture in Münster:

Of Pool Balls, Will-o'-the-Wisps, and a Red Dog ...

The great importance attached to art in Münster does not only show in the costly and carefully thought out exhibition concept of the Westphalian Museum of Art and Cultural History. In Münster, art does not only exist in small, closed rooms. Here, art is also a widespread phenomenon and is fairly common in the so-called "public spaces".

An essential reason for the fact that so many and so very different pieces of sculpture can be found in the city and the surrounding areas is the big and now also internationally renowned open-air exhibition "Sculpture Projects", which took place in 1977, 1987

and 1997. City purchases and loans of the works of art, which have mostly been developed from the analysis of specific aspects of Münster's urban features, enable both the local citizens and the tourists to maintain a steady contact with plastic art.

An especially striking example of this "location art" is the "Giant Pool Balls" (see 46) by the American artist Claes Oldenburg, completed in 1977 during the first "Sculpture Projects".

In 1975, Claes Oldenburg was invited to develop and present a work of modern sculpture in Münster. Thereupon, he developed the idea of the colossal ball constellation of a pool game. The lawn on the shore of the Aasee plays the role of the pool table's green felt cover. Because of their place above the eastern Aasee terraces, the concrete balls, 3.5m in diameter, are called "The Aasee balls" by the citizens of Münster. Today, they are a fixed component of the city landscape. Their in-

"Vertebrae", Henry Moore (1968/69)

stallation more than twenty years ago caused the most varied reactions - from strict disapproval to pronounced enthusiasm. In the meantime, unknown graffiti artists regularly provide the "Giant Pool Balls" with innumerable works of art, which are time and again removed by the city authorities. Of course, this only provides fresh "canvas" for the young artists. And thus, the balls are - as virtually a new form of advertising columns - important examples of the idea that contemporary plastic art again and again embodies new challenges - not only for passionate museum visitors.

Another group of works installed for the Sculpture Project '77 are the distinctive triangular granite wedges. The cut-to-size elements carry on a dialogue on form and measure with the Church of St Peter, opposite. Once very controversial, Professor Ulrich Rückriem's sculpture "Dolomit zugeschnitten" (Dolomite Cut to Size) **(see 23)** is today an undisputed masterpiece. It is located between the River Aa and the Westphalian Museum of Art and Cultural History in the immediate vicinity of the Juridicum, the main building of the Institutes of Law and Economics.

From 1987 to 1997, Keith Haring's "Red Dog for Landois"**(see 17)** served as a reminder of the old zoo and its dynamic founder, Professor Landois, whose zoo had to give way to the new building of the WestLB bank building. Sadly, the privately owned creation of the late New York "pope of graffiti" was removed from the Himmelreichallee, near the old zoo, in the autumn of 1997 and given as a loan to the "Zentrum für Kunst und Medien-

technologie" in Karlsruhe. So all we can show you is a photo of this truly original sculpture (see p. 96).

In conclusion, the cherry column by Thomas Schütte on the Harsewinkelplatz not far from St Ludgeri should be specially pointed out. "Symbol Treating Appearance and Reality ironically" could be the title for the crisply draped pair of cherries. Colour and shape suggest sensuality and eroticism, but at the same time give rise to the impression of modern artificiality and urban superficiality. The symbol, raised onto the pedestal: does it not gain an all-too-pedagogical character when it is presented like this? Certainly, we may assume here a winking roguishness on the part of the artist. Further interpretations may be taken from the excellent guides of the Westphalian museum. There are also quite a number of important works of sculpture that arouse enthusiasm straight away without all the onlookers being proven specialists. The three memorable "Will-o'-the-Wisps" in the cages of St Lambert's Church (Lothar Baumgarten) **(31)** can still be seen at night. And the "32 Cars for the 20th Century: Play Mozart's Requiem Quietly" by Nam June Paik (1997) really turned out to be extremely popular with the public.

At this stage, we would like to ask you, dear reader, to follow the development of sculpture in Münster. Measured by the class of many a piece of sculpture, Münster is an enviable city. By the way, further suggestions for an "art walk" can be found on the **sculpture list** in the chapter "Münster at a Glance".

The Municipal Theatre

Münster's **Municipal Theatre (Städtische Bühnen) (9)** was already something special before an artist, a dancer or a singer ever stepped on stage. When the theatre was opened to the public and the artists in 1956, there was nothing but praise for the interesting architecture and the integration of the ruins of the 18th-century Romberger Hof into the building complex. Nevertheless, it is not only the architecture that draws theatre-goers to the "Grosse Haus" (955 seats) and the "Kleine Haus" (350 seats). There is a fresh wind blowing in this "established' company as the ensembles of both houses have devoted themselves to innovation and a concept of liveliness. The programmes are extraordinary: each theatre project is linked to a special motto,

for example '200 Years French Revolution', '50 Years World War II' or 'Theatre as a Condensing Mirror of the World'.

Other strengths of the Municipal Theatre are, of course, opera, operetta (musical comedy) and the symphonic orchestra - the classic sections of the theatre, which take up much of the programme in the "Grosse Haus". Performances of world-famous operas and plays such as 'Tosca' by Giacomo Puccini or Richard Wagner's 'Parsifal' enable the opera lover to compare Münster's performances with those of other big theatres. However, recent productions such as 'Heimatlos' (Theater in der Kneipe), 'Das Fest des Lammes' or Tony Kushner's play 'Angels in America' (started in the 1997/98 season and deals with the turn of the millennium) convincingly show the originality and creativity of Münster's Municipal Theatre. One should not forget to mention the regular guest performances of the American Drama Group, who present a wide range of plays with different ensembles. Unfortunately, the theatre's divers range of productions cannot be described in the detail it deserves. Therefore, we would strongly recommend that you take a look at the current programme. Thus, anyone can inform himself and see his favourite plays or risk one experiment or the other - as does the Municipal Theatre.

Städtische Bühnen Münster
Neubrückenstrasse 63
Advance Booking Office:
tel.: 414 67100
fax: 59 09-205

The Wolfgang Borchert Theatre

Right at Münster's central station, there is a small theatre, which has been offering much more than Shakespeare and Schiller for 30 years.

Back in 1956, the **Wolfgang Borchert Theatre (51)** started in a room on the Prinzipalmarkt above the (no longer existent) Café Schucan. After only six months the company had to move to their present location. Since that time, this private and literally "one-room theatre" has been developing enormously. The small stage - with only 99 seats - has a fixed repertoire, a fixed, professional ensemble, and also presents guest performances. The combination of professional skill, personal contact to the audience together with the mandate to pay particular attention to "the modern, literary committed, contemporary, sometimes even unusual plays from new and in some cases less well-known German and foreign playwrights" helped the Wolfgang Borchert Theatre to acquire fame well beyond Münster.

Of course, a theatre named after the German writer Wolfgang Borchert is pledged to him. Naturally, his well-known play about a returned soldier entitled "Draussen vor der Tür" is part of the repertoire as it is important to the actors to work in accordance with Borchert's ideas. It is their claim to present critical, committed theatre showing man's struggle with his environment, history and society. In pursuing this aim, conflicts may arise, some of which cannot be forseen at all.

This happened when the play "Wasch-tag" (Wash-day) was to be performed. The drama was meant to "attack ironically the relics of the Third Reich". However, it was not the play itself that became the stumbling-block, which nearly ruined the theatre financially, but the poster which was to advertise the play. It showed, as the unmistakable emblem of the Nazi period, the swastika, whose left half was covered by the partly torn symbol of the consumer society, the Coca-Cola logo. Strictly speaking, this was a clear message: the suppression of the German past was meant to be illustrated. The swastika was covered by the symbol of the modern, positive attitude towards life, which was propagated by advertising. "Our poster puts these two symbols in contrast with each other, which is expressed by the act of tearing: the symbol of the 'new' present is partly torn and the relics of the 'old' past become visible again", said the manager of the theatre. However, Coca-Cola thought that they were depicted in disagreeable company and instituted legal proceedings against the theatre. A potential fine of 500,000 marks, the payment of which would have ruined the Wolfgang Borchert Theatre, made the organization of supporters ("Förderverein") refrain from lodging an appeal, and the poster was pulped.

Fortunately, this unhappy affair had a happy ending: the incident met with a lively response in the German media, and thereby provided free publicity for the Wolfgang Borchert Theatre, which is reflected in the number of theatre-goers.

Wolfgang-Borchert-Theater
Berliner Platz 23, tel.: 4 00 19

Theatre in the Pump House

Apart from Münster's established theatre scene, there also exists an "alternative" one. "Alternative" in this case refers to the possibility of carrying out theatrical projects in those fields that cannot be covered by the so-called "established temples of culture". In the beginning, the innovative companies flourished in obscurity. Twenty years ago, the independent companies called themselves "Plöp", "Dingsbums", "Sumpftheater", "Syphon" or "Wahnsinn".

In most cases, their members were semi-professional actors, who devoted their leisure time to the alternative cultural scene. Tainted with the blemish of dilettantism, they all had to suffer from the fact that their work was hardly noticed by the public.

All of a sudden, things started to change. "Münster's First Festival of Independent Theatre Groups" in May 1981 was such a great success that all the independent companies joined together in accordance with the motto "unity is strength" to form the "Theater Initiative Münster e.V.", called TIM for short. This very promising start was soon followed by a long struggle to find a suitable location. Finally, the company was allocated the old sewage pump house in the Gartenstrasse.

Since then, the motley troupe has been working much more professionally and with obvious success. Many full-length plays have been produced in co-operation with internationally known stage directors. In addition to this, guest performances of national as well as international experimental companies are part of the programme.

Besides the cultural programme the "Theater im Pumpenhaus" is also involved in special pedagogical projects, such as theatre and play groups for socially and culturally isolated persons, e.g. deaf children and teenagers. Moreover, they also offer further vocational training for actors.

This commitment has obviously paid off - nowadays, it is impossible to report on Münster's cultural scene without mentioning the "Theater im Pumpenhaus".

Theater im Pumpenhaus
Gartenstrasse 123
tel.: 23 34 43

Boulevard Münster

The **Boulevard Münster** in the Königspassage (not far from **45**) was opened in December 1997 and is dedicated to Boulevard drama. Today, it is rather unusual that an ensemble aims at entertaining the audience by presenting solely domestic comedy or farce. In this day and age, when each form of artistic expression is expected to contain a certain amount of social criticism, the explicit commitment to Boulevard drama might almost be regarded as a provocation. However, this new theatre follows an old tradition, which developed in the French theatres in the 19th and at the beginning of the 20th century. The interior of the theatre, which was designed by Dieter Sieger, takes up elements of the "Boulevard", the wide city street of Paris, after which this theatre was named. The auditorium is lined by two stylised façades, which creates the atmosphere and the impression of width typical of a Boulevard. In addition, you find elements of famous theatres like the Teatro La Fenice in Venice, which were given a modern interpretation by the designer.

There are daily performances (exc. Tue) over a period of two months with a changing ensemble. Late in the evening, there are (musical) Midnight Specials. Founder and director is the former actress of the Municipal Theatre, Angelika Ober, who also acts in almost every production. One has certainly to admire her courage in establishing a theatre of this kind in view of the general financial problems. But maybe it was the right decision as "Boulevard" originally referred to ramparts. And maybe we all need the kind of protection against the problems of everyday life that the Boulevard Münster can offer us and which was originally one of the important aspects of art.

Boulevard Münster
Königspassage / Königsstrasse 12-14
tel.: 5 45 64 / fax: 4 14 00 71

Münster for Music Lovers

In a city like Münster, where tradition is highly valued, there exists of course a wide variety of different styles of music. Let's have a look first of all at the so-called serious music. There is a wide choice of classical concerts, chamber music recitals, matinées and baroque concerts, so that each music lover will find something to suit his or her personal taste.

Firstly, one has to mention the Municipal Theatre (Städtische Bühnen). Every season, Münster's symphony orchestra is very busy in the Municipal Theatre. Anybody who wants to listen to its musicians more often ought to take a look at the current calendar of events; they also play quite often every year in St Lambert's Church. They give a serenade concert at the Castle's garden pavilion or even stage an open-air concert in the theatre's inner court. And, anyway, who says that music always has to be performed in the concert hall of the Municipal Theatre?

Local concert agencies provide further interesting and enjoyable musical events. The rich diversity ranges from piano concerts, brass chamber music from four centuries, lieder recitals with songs by Schubert, Brahms or Strauss or classical guitar concerts to saxophone concerts and organ recitals in the Church of St Clemens and many other events.

The church in Münster is known for its love of music, too. No matter whether the music is played and enjoyed in festival halls, churches, assembly halls or somewhere else - the variety is wide.

Lovers of baroque music can hardly wait for the middle of June as that is the time when the Erbdrostenhof changes from a monument of baroque architecture into a splendid venue for the annual Baroque Festival. Numerous cultural events taking place inside this old aristocratic residence have ensured that this summer festival has become a fixed date in the diaries of music lovers. Each year, the festival's special highlight is the display of original baroque fireworks to the sound of appropriate baroque music. Münster's students of music also insist on having their chance to demonstrate their skills in different styles of serious music. Let yourself be surprised by the virtuosity of these young musicians - the dates of the concerts can be obtained from the university.

Street musicians

No matter what your favourite style of music is, you will always be faced with the same problem: the wider the choice, the greater the difficulty in choosing. The choice will be much more difficult if you also have a great affection for light music and modern live music as Münster has a lot on offer in this field, too.

In Münster, the expression "jovel" is used for everything that is somehow "good". A movie or a party can be "jovel". Even a person can be described as "jovel", but this does not necessarily mean that the person concerned is a "good man" in the biblical sense but rather an interesting, amusing and nice person.

And - nomen est omen - "Jovel" is also the name chosen by Steffi Stephan, former bass player with the well-known German rock stars Udo Lindenberg and Peter Maffay, for his disco with a stage and a large pub on the premises of the former "Germania" brewery - after the former smaller venue had to be closed. Since then, Münster houses - in addition to the Halle Münsterland - a second place where stars can perform in front of their fans. The list of visitors proves that this venue is widely used as internationally known musicians such as Marius Müller-Westernhagen, Miles Davis or Die Toten Hosen have appeared live on stage in the "Jovel".

In the much smaller rooms at the "Odeon" the fan can listen to excellent musicians, too. Since the opening in 1977, famous musical performers played there. The Godfathers, John Cale and the German band Die Einstürzenden Neubauten have been on stage at the "Odeon". This club has become the third venue in Münster where musical events can take place in grand style.

The Halle Münsterland - a large multi-purpose hall - is long-established and known for a wide range of events. Situated on the Albersloher Weg, only a fifteen minute's walk from Münster's city centre, such a large hall for trade fairs, congresses, concerts and other events has certainly found an outstanding location. It is not possible to list every single event which has ever taken place there, but it is a fact that the performances can be watched by as many as 12,000 people. Riding tournaments, gala balls, German folk music (Original Oberkrainer), André Heller, BAP and other German bands - nearly everyone who is celebrated in entertainment, sports, music or the theatre has already been at the Halle Münsterland.

The "Destille" (on the corner of the Jüdefelderstrasse and the Kuhstrasse) is the hot tip for the lover of jazz and blues. There, a good many jazz stars have appeared as guest musicians in this informal and friendly circle. Then, every other year *the* jazz happening - the Münster Jazz Festival - takes place and can unhesitatingly be compared with the Moers Jazz Festival. For three days, stars like Chick Corea or Jan Garbarek, as well as genuine local matadors meet on stage.

In case there is no big event, music is played in a number of well-known pubs and discos. Where exactly? Well, again you are faced with a difficult choice. Some selected meeting places and further venues for live music are to be found in the service section of this book. Details about current programmes and events can be found with the help of the dailies, but more conveniently with the help of the "alternative" journals *Ultimo*, *Gig* and *Na dann*.

It's Fair-Time

For once, a sword becomes the bearer of good news. As soon as it is fastened to the left-hand wall of the City Hall, Münster's citizens know that it is "Send" time again. Vast crowds of people from Münster and its surrounding villages and towns meet on the Hindenburgplatz.

Since 1578, the "Send" sword has been used as the symbol for the right to hold markets, but it also reminds people of the special laws in force during these "Send" days.

After the episcopal synods, which attracted people from near and far, a lively trading activity ensued. This market was called "Send" (derived from "synod"). During this time, particular attention was paid to the observance of law and order. Whenever quarrels ended in bloodshed, the troublemakers could easily be faced with the death sentence.

It is the other side of the coin that during the five days of "Send" it is almost impossible to park your car in the city. Because of the fair, the Hindenburgplatz cannot be used as a parking lot as is normally the case. Moreover, visitors from outside arriving by car need additional parking space. In spite of these problems, Münster enjoys the special lively atmosphere, with good-humoured people strolling everywhere through the city, over the fair-ground and late in the evening visiting those city quarters where most of Münster's pubs are located.

In 889, the earliest documented synod took place. The "Send" slowly developed during the first half of the 11th century. In those days, trading was most impor-

103

tant. Merchants from afar travelled to Münster in order to sell their goods and cattle. Originally, the "Send" was held in the cloisters of the cathedral, but, because larger crowds were attracted each year, it had to be moved to the Domplatz (Cathedral Square) and finally to the Hindenburgplatz. The concentrated spending power of the visitors did not only attract traders of useful goods but also merchants dealing in those useful amenities no one can really do without: candy-floss, gingerbread, oracles, beer, flowers, trash and kitsch.

The "Send" takes place three times a year: in March, June and October. It is interesting to listen to the talkative florist, who - according to his own statement - sells all his flowers at a loss.

Or you can listen to the seller of traditional Westphalian meat products, whose naughty comments sometimes make anxious mothers take their small children quickly out of earshot. Such characters, in combination with numerous stalls, have turned the "Send" into much more than a simple fair. Over the years, it has become a distinct element of Münsterland culture. Needless to say, among the approximately 200 fairground stalls you can find the obligatory chairoplane (merry-go-round), the swing-boat or the Devil's Wheel. A ride on the Ferris Wheel offers the unique opportunity of leaving firm ground behind you and enjoying a magnificent view of the "Send" and Münster at the same time. Those moments when the wheel stops right at the top just before it moves slowly downwards to solid ground again are indescribable. This also symbolizes the main purpose of the "Send" - to leave everyday life behind and enjoy oneself.

The Economy of Münster

Münster is known as an episcopal residential town, Prussian provincial capital and university town. Not even all of Münster's citizens realize that their city became an important economic centre a long time ago. Münster has experienced a remarkable economic boom during recent years and thus it is not surprising that the city belongs to the top group of all the cities of a fair size in Germany. Since 1983, the number of jobs in all economic sectors has increased continuously. The biggest growth rate by far has been registered in the "tertiary" sector, that is the service industries. More than 22% of Münster's citizens have found a job in them.

Münster is regarded as the "office of Westphalia". Being the administrative capital, it houses numerous important institutions such as the administrative centres of insurance companies, banks, boards and chambers. Moreover, the city is the seat of the District President, the Regional Association of Westphalia-Lippe as well as the Constitutional Court of Law of the Land North Rhine-Westphalia and the Administrative Court of Appeal of the Land North Rhine-Westphalia. Therefore, it comes as no surprise that the majority of the working population are civil servants and salaried employees.

In general, Münster's economic structure is also characterized by a stable "secondary" sector with many medium-sized businesses as well as quite a few important industrial enterprises.

Münster is, of course, also *the* "shopping centre" for the whole of the Münsterland in general and even beyond its borders. In contrast to many other regions, Münster's ecomomy has been booming. What are the reasons? Can it be due to the so-called "secondary" advantages of the location (good life quality, a lot of green, the fairly intact environment, the wide cultural diversity and the attractive old part of the city), or is it due to the so-called "primary" advantages, e.g. a good traffic network? You can reach Münster by car (via motorways A1/A43), by train (intercity rail link), by plane (Münster-Osnabrück International Airport (FMO) at Greven) and by ship (Dortmund-Ems Canal).

No doubt, apart from the advantages mentioned above, many businesses tend to favour Münster as a suitable location when they think of the university and the College of Applied Sciences nearby. Because of the ready availability of highly qualified staff, the future of Münster's and the region's economic growth is likely to be secure.

There are plans to make the city even more attractive as a venue for conferences and congresses. The necessary infrastructure to realize such plans already exists. In addition, the Halle Münsterland is to be enlarged, and a special congress hotel is planned. However, the additional traffic will cause many problems if you think of the approximately 1.5 million people living in Münster and the immediate area. The Chamber of Industry and Commerce has found out that 95% of conference and congress participants come to Münster by car. This is the reason why the Chamber supports the cause of private traffic, which mainly involves combatting the lack of parking space. However, in doing so, they fail to notice that there is hardly a possibility to create much more parking space and driving space inside Münster because of

urban development in general. In other words, it is, of course, possible to widen the streets and to build additional parking lots, so that anybody can come to Münster by car. But then there will no longer be a city centre, which is after all a major part of Münster's attractiveness. Perhaps the idea of a tramway, which tinkled through Münster in the mid 1950s, integrated into a park-and-ride system, will be reconsidered as one possible alternative. The German weekly *Die Wirtschaftswoche* has awarded Münster the title of "most employer-friendly city in Germany". For the future, Münster believes in establishing firms from the sector of the "new technologies" and the ensuing exchange of knowledge and research between university and economy. Thus, the "Technologiehof", a landmark for this concept, was established. There are further plans for a large-scale technology and science park to be built near the university. Of course, it is the hope of the city council that they can be proud of their city's economy in the future, too.

Beginning of the Semester

The first-year student - the fresher - experiences the wonderful feeling of complete independence for the first time when he or she is looking for a flat or room ... And they usually lose that special feeling almost immediately ... There were times when suitable accommodation for students was so rare that the vice-chancellor of the university had no other choice but to allow the students to camp in front of the Schloss. In other words, the first thing that freshers on the look-out for living quarters had to learn about the Westphalian character was its business acumen, which is certainly not always beyond all doubt.... There might be only a few landlords who try to offer you a room of 8m² without a window for a "mere" 300 Deutschmarks, but rents of fifteen or twenty Deutschmarks (or even more) per square metre can be expected.

However, it's also quite difficult to get one's bearings in this city. Usually, you can easily spot the fresher roaming the campus and the city by the map clutched in his or her hand. Sometimes, you find them standing at the corner desperately trying to shelter from the wind so as to be able to fold the large map afterwards (at least in theory).

In Münster, the different buildings of the faculties are scattered all over the city; thus, the newcomer simply has to get to know Münster quickly if he or she intends to attend to the chosen subjects in earnest. In addition, the situation is further complicated by the rather exaggerated love of abbreviations in general, which - on this scale - you usually expect in the Armed Forces.

Nevertheless, once the first-year student has managed to cope with these pitfalls of student life, he can enjoy life in Münster, too. For starters, one can check out the local pub scene, which is characterized by its informality. When going to one of the pubs usually frequented by students, customers under thirty should be prepared to be addressed by the landlord or staff with the familiar German "Du" instead of the more formal "Sie" normally used when talking to strangers. Since more and more older people are beginning their studies at the university and insist on being treated the same as all the younger students, the younger

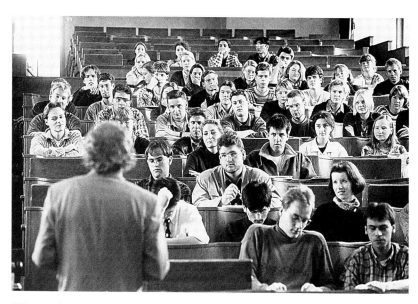

"Non scolae ..."

The bicycle, a reliable friend - if you manage to find it

fellow students have grown accustomed to using the informal "Du" with older persons, too (if they look like students). Students work hard - but from time to time it's also most enjoyable to skip lectures and seminars and go down to the Aasee to get a bit of sunshine and generally forget about work for a while. Less enjoyable, however, are the many problems caused by the vast number of students in Münster. In the summer term of 1988 the then fourth largest university in Germany was - contrary to all predictions - faced with much more newly registered students than were expected. Consequently, not only the a-bove-mentioned housing problems but also severe problems caused by lack of room ensued. 45,000 university students plus another 10,000 from the College of Applied Sciences have been causing constantly overcrowded seminars ever

since. Lectures held in auditoriums intended for 400 listeners are filled with up to 800 students. Standing close to each other with hardly any space left, some of them actually try to take down notes as they need the certificate of attendance for the "BaföG-Amt", the institution responsible for the payment of grants for higher education in Germany. No matter how many tales are told about the free and independent student life - though some of them might certainly be true - today's students are without doubt faced with many problems. On the housing market, in the university, in the university library - the masses of students make themselves felt simply everywhere. If hundreds of students need the same books to write their term papers, not even the large University and Regional Library can provide enough copies. Thus, some of the stu-

Some try to find a tenant student for everything

dents won't get the necessary material to hand in the paper on time. You can only hope that they do not rely on grants, which are only paid if you get all the necessary certificates each term.

But there are also nicer lessons to be learned, for example sharing a flat with a group of fellow students, which was rather a "revolutionary" idea twenty years ago. Still today, it's more than just an economic necessity: though it is true that rents are generally lower the larger the flat is, it is also a positive experience for many people. Although problems do not miraculously disappear just because you share a flat, it certainly helps a lot to be able to share these problems with two, three, four or even more people. You learn to accept different personalities and to stand up for your own wishes. You have discussions about political views, art, culture and everything under the sun - and, last but not least, you learn to pay the telephone bill.

Sharing a flat and meeting other students is quite helpful in other respects, too. Scholars often fail when it comes to interdisciplinary research, and they are not always prepared to impart their knowledge to the young students, who have just started on their way to becoming scholars themselves. So lively discussions very often take place among roommates or in the student community in general. Münster can definitely be rather grateful to be called one of the centres of the Humanities, where such a climate of open discussion can develop. And the city should try to keep that reputation and support the Humanities, even though they cannot produce verifiable results as quickly as the other subjects, which is why critics like to describe the Humanities as such as an encouragement to idleness.

Let's Go to the Kuhviertel

What makes a normal man, who is happily, and above all in quite a stress-free way married to his typewriter, write a city guide to Münster? Well, he knows that at some time or other he will necessarily have to deal with the variety of Münster's pubs. Then he has to give everything. Journalistic virtues such as thorough investigation and the stubborn search for information can be perfectly applied under these circumstances. Each pub, each brand of beer and each drink has to be tested with the greatest care before you can recommend it with a clear conscience. How does the "Altbier" (= special brand of beer) taste in the pub on the fringe of the city? Is the "Krefelder" (= beer mixed with Coca Cola) in the city centre as good as in the outskirts? It's really an exhausting job,

but someone has to do it, and it satisfies the investigator. Once again, the Prinzipalmarkt is the starting point for our stroll. The way to the tap follows the Prinzipalmarkt. On the right, we pass St Lambert's Church. It takes at least a ten minute's walk, but who knows what the breath of fresh air is needed for later on? At the end of the arcades, you keep walking straight ahead all the time, pass the Kiepenkerldenkmal on your right, cross the Aa bridge and walk to the Rosenplatz, where you enter the Kuhviertel with its enormous variety of pubs situated close to each other.

Two "pub miles", the **Kreuzstrasse** and the **Jüdefelderstrasse**, are particularly attractive to the visitors. The latter runs parallel to the Hindenburgplatz and houses a handful of pubs and thus suits different tastes. The **Destille** is a jazz pub with a unique tradition. Here, well-

The "heraldic animal" of the popular pubmile

On the Kreuzstrasse

known jazz and blues stars appear on stage regularly, and local musicians have their turn as well.

Nevertheless, the Kreuzstrasse is the better-known "pub mile". It branches off right from the Rosenplatz and cannot be missed. By the way, at certain times of the day you can simply sniff the air to find out whether you are on the right track. This is possible because directly to the left of the Kreuzstrasse the beer-supplies for the neighbouring pub are brewed. The small and last existing "Altbier" brewery in Münster, **Pinkus Müller**, produces a beer, which is sold in the pub of the same name next door, which is known well beyond the borders of the Münsterland. The brand "Pinkus-Alt" is distributed world-wide and can even be bought in the U.S. A visit to Pinkus is an absolute must for the sight-seer - the pub's "Altbierbowle" (= Alt-

bier mixed with fruit) is the speciality of the house.

The Kreuzstrasse consists mainly of old gaily coloured half-timbered houses - nearly all housing pubs. Here, thirsty or sociable people of all ages - but especially students - stroll about from pub to pub. By the way, the pub **Cavete** is the centre of social life here, which unfolds most splendidly in fine weather, when tables, chairs and benches are placed outside all along the street and when friendly guests leave at least a small path in the middle enabling them to move freely from pub to pub.

The "Cavete" is the result of a dissatisfied student's lament. In the 1950s this student wrote an essay, which climaxed in the recommendation "cavete Münster!" - Latin for "beware of Münster!". Why? Because at that time there were no special pubs for students, which is certainly not the case today. Therefore, a separate chapter deals with the pub "Cavete".

For the time being, we enjoy the beer or - each to his or her own taste - the other delicacies a street full of pubs has to offer. The exact observance of the closing time is the sole drop of bitterness. So let us drink to the transitoriness of the world's pleasures: Cheers!

Cavete? Gaudete!

"It is a year today since the term when I was driven by a wretched fate to Münster. Münster - this enclave of bleak dullness, where I have been forced to live ever since. What a fate!". This is how Wilfried Weustenfeld, a student of law, started his lament. It was written in 1958 and published in the *Semesterspiegel*, a students' paper, which still exists today. "Münster is an El Dorado for Philistines. The type of the proverbial soberside or ultra-Philistine - here is where he has found a second home. Conventional and replete and always trying to keep up appearances, he sits in the café or the "VHS" lecture (= Adult Education Centre). No "Send" that would not close its gates at 11 pm, where you would find any other visitors than teenage girls and grown-up daughters accompanied by their mothers". In the same negative way he commented on the students at that time: "wanderer, if you come to another town, report there that you saw them attending lectures, as their duty demands". In fact, the situation in Münster was not much different from that of other student strongholds in Germany in the 1950s. But in cities like Marburg, Munich or Heidelberg there

existed at least something like a "pub-culture" and not only an "antiquated cosiness like 100 years ago". In his essay, Weustenfeld advised everyone: "Cavete Münster!" - that is "Beware of Münster!"

This controversial text met with a lively response. The essay was not only passionately discussed in Münster, but even such well-known supra-regional newspapers as *Die Zeit* and *Die Süddeutsche Zeitung* dealt with "cand. jur. Weustenfeld" and his writings. Reactions ranged from joyful agreement by way of a permissive shaking of the head ("Well, he's not wrong, but couldn't he put it more moderately?") to flat refusal and the speculation that one of the Anabaptists' cages was already being lowered for him. Despite this uproar: until then, this incident would have been sufficed at best to become a humorous footnote in Münster's history. But it is due to two students of philosophy that it has become much more. The two of them undertook a study trip financed by the then rector of the university (!) in order to explore extensively the "pub scene" in other university towns. They came back to Münster with an assortment of impressions. After a great announcement tour with a brewer's dray cart through Münster and accompanied by the lively interest of the regional and supra-regional media, the students opened an "Academic Beer Institute" in the Kreuzstrasse on April 29th, 1959. This pub was given the name "Cavete" in honour of its spiritual father. In order to show that this pub was meant to be an alternative to the 1950's tedium, it was painted in an extreme lilac colour, which really caused a stir in the street. The story goes that the house-owner next door - a resolute lady named Sophie Niehüser - was asked by her neighbours why she tolerated this unsuitable colour in her vicinity. Her answer is said to have been: "Why not, anyone can do what he likes with his property." Having said so, she had the painter come to paint her house glaring red. Subsequently, Aunt Sophie, the "benign spirit of the street", went regularly to the "Cavete" even in old age, to take "the medicine prescribed by the doctor - two glasses of gin" - as the *Münstersche Zeitung* reported on the occasion of her 83rd birthday. No doubt, the doctor had really prescribed the lady the gin because he knew how much she needed the contact to "her" students.

The only other possibility for students to enjoy themselves was the tea dances organized by the ASTA (General Students' Committee), but they took place only at long intervals. The "Cavete" represented somewhat of a revolution in Münster's "pub scene". However, even a revolution has its physical limits: although there is space in the smallest hut, there is unfortunately not enough of it for everyone. Consequently, the "Cavete" was so besieged by thirsty people waiting outside that only a resolute door-keeper could guarantee a minimum of oxygen and space for the guests inside.

The "Cavete" was not only the "drinking centre" of the Westfälische Wilhelms-Universität but also a meeting place for artists and quarrelsome intellectuals. If you believe the older regulars, important developments in world politics and philosophy have been anticipated here ever since 1959.

Those guests soon became a fixture in the "Cavete" just like Uncle Hans, whose surname remains a secret. For more than 10 years, he has accompanied "pub life" in the Kreuzstrasse on the grand piano with music by Liszt, Chopin and favourite pieces of the regular guests. And, when he was in a good mood he performed his not quite respectable "Song of the Porcupine". Jazz bands performed when Uncle Hans had a day off. Even today, the present owner likes to tell the story of how they once managed to attract jazz star Benny Goodman to come to the "Cavete" directly after a concert in the Halle Münsterland. Here, after he had been worked on and given some delicious beer, he agreed to show the musicians present what could be got out of a clarinet. A signed photo of this great musician testifies to the truth of this story. After the enormous success of this first "students' pub" in Münster more and more pubs were opened. Today, you can find pubs like the "Blaue Haus", "Pulcinella", "In'n Holsken", "Biergalerie" and the "Ziege", which is probably the smallest pub in Germany, in this "beer-avenue".

Today, there is a great number of students' pubs in Münster. The run on the "Cavete" has receded to a normal level, although it is still better to come early in order to be certain of getting a seat. If you go to the "Cavete" today, please do not behave as if you are entering a museum. It is a pub - neither more nor less. And do not be surprised if you become aware of a man with a rather dignified demeanour, who drinks plenty of beer and who leaves without paying. This man was granted a document which guarantees him "free schnapps and beer". His name is Wilfried Weustenfeld, and he studied in Münster in the late 1950s.

Façades in the "Kreuzviertel"

Two façades of one house

Detail of a façade

The Haus Hülshoff, a moated castle

Parlour in the Haus Rüschhaus

DISCOVER MÜNSTER'S SURROUNDINGS

In this chapter, we want to draw your attention to some places outside Münster that are worth visiting. Of course, there are many more and some of them are listed on p. 150ff. Not without reason, one tour is called "100-castles route". The flat Münsterland area is the ideal region for moated castles. Many guided castle tours by bus or by bike are on offer. For detailed information, contact: *Stadtwerbung und Touristik, Klemensstr. 10, tel.: 02 51 / 4 92 27 10*, or the *Fremdenverkehrsverband Münsterland Touristik "Grünes Band", Hohe Schule 13, 48565 Steinfurt, tel.: 0 25 51 / 93 92 91.*

The Baumberge (west)

Take the road to Roxel, and then drive straight ahead to Havixbeck: this is how you get to the Baumberge. You can go there by car, but the approximately 20 km can easily be covered by bike, too. The Baumberge stretch from Havixbeck in the north to Nottuln in the south. Here, the Münsterland shows some features not at all typical of the area. While the Münsterland is usually as flat as a pancake, which pleases every cyclist, the area of the Baumberge suddenly presents itself with hills covered with dense forest. The highest hill is 186 metres high and guarantees a free view across the western Münsterland if the weather is fine. Here, Baumberge's sandstone was quarried in former times. It was required as material for various buildings, including Münster's Cathedral and the Castle where it was skilfully utilized.

The newly-opened Sandstone Museum describes the use and history of unique building material. Not onl' you visit the permanent exhibiti the thousand years of mining and the artistic working of the sa but you can also watch a pro stone-cutter at work.
Baumberger Sandstein Mus nerich 9, 48329 Havixbeck, t 02 507/ 3 31 75, open: Tue - Sun, N am - 6 pm, Nov-Feb: 1 pn 6 pm, ad mission free, café.
By the way, after your ex the Baumberge, a gast nearby awaits you: Ha usual combination of brewery museum. Wi de cakes, you can dri have a taste of their home-afterwards.
Haus Klute, Poppenbeck 28, 48329 Havixbeck, Tue - Sun: 2 pm - 7 pm, tel.: 0 25 07 / 29 55 or 29 58. Historisches Brauhaus Klute: Mon - Sun: 11 am - 12 pm, tel.: 02507/ 9 8390.

Haus Hülshoff and Haus Rüschhaus (north-west)

Haus Hülshoff - a two-winged mansion to the west of Münster - is the house or, to put it more precisely, the moated castle where Annette von Droste-Hülshoff grew up. That is why one of two existing "Droste museums" is housed here.
We suggest you go for a walk around the moated castle; the well-kept gardens are

certainly worth seeing. When you follow the Sentruper Strasse from Münster, you'll find Haus Hülshoff to the north-west of Münster. The distance can easily be covered in a relatively short time. After reaching the older part of Roxel, you have to orientate yourself by the church, then turn right and go straight ahead, after approx. 3 km, you'll reach Haus Hülshoff.

From there the way to the Rüschhaus, another aristocratic residence in Nienberge, is signposted. The poetess Annette von Droste-Hülshoff spent more than 20 years of her life here and produced some of her most beautiful literary works in Haus Rüschhaus. If you visit the house with its romantic gardens, you will immediately understand why inspiration came easily to a poetess in such a place. In former times, the Rüschhaus had been the country residence of the architect J. C. Schlaun, who designed it himself in the baroque style on the location of a former manor-house. Inside, in the second Droste Museum the visitor can see not only pictures, manuscripts and treasures but also the almost complete original interior decoration dating from the 18th and 19th centuries with its valuable furniture and impressive wallpaper decorated with landscape scenes.

Droste-Museum Burg Hülshoff
48329 Havixbeck, tel.: 0 25 34 / 10 52 or 6 57 21; opened from Mar 13th - Dec 20th, opening hours 9.30 am - 6 pm

Droste-Museum Haus Rüschhaus (60)
Münster-Nienberge, phone 0 25 33 - 13 17 Opening hours: Mar 1st to Apr 30th & Nov 1st to Dec 23rd: Tue - Sun: 11 + 12 am/ 2 +3 pm; May 1st to Oct 31st: Tue - Sun: 10, 11, 12 am / 2.30 pm - 4.30 pm half-hourly.

Rieselfelder (north)
(sewage fields)

The area between Coerde and Greven lies on the way to Africa - if you come from Scandinavia. This is perhaps less important for the reader, but of great importance for the vast numbers of migratory birds flying in from Scandinavia.

Originally, the Rieselfelder covered an area of 500 ha (1235.55 acres). Since the opening up of the area at the beginning of this century, they have been used for the purification of sewage. The fields were covered with sewage - hence the name - and then the water seeped away into the soil and was cleaned in this way. Until 1975, the Rieselfelder had been a natural sewage plant, but then they were replaced by a regular one.

As early as the 1960s, many birds, also rare ones, found ideal living conditions in the Rieselfelder. Common snipes or becassines, greenshanks, common sandpipers and shovellers are some examples of birds living in marshlands. As such areas have these days become very rare in Germany, these species have found a place of refuge here. Soon, the birds had taken possession of this area, and in 1977 the North Rhine-Westphalian government gave this occupation its blessing by taking on lease approximately 230 ha (= 568.353 acres) of the Rieselfelder and by provisionally declaring it a wildlife sanctuary for a period of 20 years.

This wet paradise for birds is a much needed resting place for the migratory birds mentioned above, a home for rare birds, where they can brood and moult comparatively undisturbed. In the same year as the government decided to protect the Rieselfelder, the city was plan-

A paradise for birds - the "Rieselfelder"

On the River Werse

The Rüschhaus

ning to use a part of this land as an industrial area. This plan caused vigorous protest. The city planners did not care a lot about this protest, but eight years later they had to accept the veto of the government of the Land. Today, the area is classified as a "European Reserve - Marshland of International Importance" and consequently enjoys special protection. The "Biological Station 'Rieselfelder'", which was established in 1980, offers guided tours to special bird-watching stations as well as a nature trail and a small museum.

Today, the Rieselfelder are one of the most popular recreational areas in Münster's surrounding area. Coming from Münster, it is best to drive up the Kanalstrasse, then turn right to Coerde and follow the signposts.

The ornithologists of the "Biological Station 'Rieselfelder Münster'" request visitors not to leave the asphalt paths under any circumstances in order to avoid disturbing the birds or even dama-

ging their nests. Enjoy your bike ride or walk through the Rieselfelder - and help to preserve this nature reserve.

Biologische Station Rieselfelder
guided tours through the bird sanctuary by special appointment, tel.: 161760

Handorf (north-east)

Even at the turn of the century, the small River Werse was a popular destination for a weekend trip. People promenaded in their Sunday best and met lots of fellow citizens from Münster, went rowing or swimming. After that, they had coffee and cake in Handorf. Even today, Handorf is still called the "village of the big coffee-pots" because here on the banks of the River Werse several good cafés and restaurants are to be found, which carry on this tradition. A boat trip on the River Werse is an experience because weekend domiciles line its banks, so that from time to time you may feel obliged to sigh "I would like to have a weekend-house here myself". Today, swimming in the river is not to be recommended, but there are three alternatives in Handorf, among them the open-air swimming pool with artificially produced waves. Nevertheless, a walk along the banks of the Werse guarantees an extremely relaxing afternoon - provided that the weather is fine.

The Meeting at Telgte (east)

For the German writer Günter Grass, Telgte was interesting enough to choose it as setting for his story entitled *Das Treffen in Telgte (The Meeting at Telgte)* (1979). In this story, he describes a fictitious meeting of a group of famous poets of the baroque period, which is nevertheless important for the present. However, not only for these fictitious poets but also for a real group of people Telgte is a chosen destination. Every year, more than one hundred thousand people make a pilgrimage to the former Hanseatic town, which - as early as 1455 - became a place of pilgrimage devoted to the Virgin Mary. Telgte possesses a hexagonal pilgrimage chapel, which Prince-Bishop Christoph Bernhard von Galen had built in the middle of the 17th century. However, there is also a very different group of pilgrims which streams into the town: those who have devoted themselves to the ideals of the Montgolfier brothers - that is to send up a hot-air balloon with passengers in a basket. Once a year, at Whitsun, the great "Montgolfiade" (= festival of hot-air ballooning) takes place.

Drostenhof Wolbeck (south-east)

In Wolbeck, another part of Münster, an aristocratic residence with a lovely park attracts visitors: this is the Drostenhof Wolbeck. The manor-house, in particular, is a representative building of the Renaissance period. The façade is particularly attractive. The typical stepped gable with half-rosettes which are decorated with spheres on the gable-steps remind the visitor of two houses in Münster's city centre: the Krameramtshaus opposite the Church of St Lambert and the house No. 44 on the Rothenburg, which both have similar façades - especially as regards the design of the gables. On the upper floor of the Drostenhof the West Prussian State Museum with its important West-Prussia Collection has found its location.

The Drostenhof in Wolbeck

__Westpreussisches Landesmuseum (Drostenhof)__, Münster-Wolbeck, Am Steintor 5, tel.: 0 25 06 / 25 50. Admission free, opening hrs: Tue - Sun: 10 am - 6 pm.

Schloss Nordkirchen (Nordkirchen Castle) (south)

The "Westphalian Versailles" is situated approx. 45 km south of Münster. Covering this distance by bike surely requires some training. The last 10 km from Ascheberg to Nordkirchen Castle are not as flat as people from Münster are accustomed to it being. Anyone who thinks that he can do this tour by bike should get one of the special maps for cyclists available in the shops.

The "Pättkes" (narrow paths) to the side of the roads cannot be found without their help, but cycling on those paths is certainly nicer and more eventful. The reward for the long ride, however, is magnificent. Unsuspectingly, you turn left -

shortly after reaching Nordkirchen - and then you see a delightful and spacious park in the centre of which Nordkirchen Castle is situated. A well-guarded moated castle stood on this land before the famous architects Johann Conrad Schlaun and Gottfried Laurenz Pictorius started to design this magnificent building by order of Prince-Bishop Friedrich Christian zu Plettenberg about 1703. This moated castle had been given the name "Morrien", and it is still to be seen on a painting inside Nordkirchen Castle. The two architects bridged fords with solid stone constructions and then created a representative baroque castle in the style of the French Versailles. The similarity can be proved if one compares the interiors of the buildings. Just as in Versailles, the doors to the different rooms in one wing have been put exactly in a straight line. The result is a 60-metre-long view through seven rooms. As the Castle is still used today, many rooms are closed to the public. The North Rhine-Westphalian College of Finance has chosen this suitable location for the training of their future senior tax officials.

The extensive park tempts you to go on long and leisurely walks. After all, the north-south axis of this park has a length of 10.5 kilometres, and new building projects in this area are prohibited.

Schloss Nordkirchen
59394 Nordkirchen, phone: 0 25 96 / 91 71 37 or 93 34 02
opening hours: park and exterior accessible any time; interior accessible: Sun: 2 - 6 pm, guided tours by appointment, daily 9 am - 6 pm.

Borderland Region (west)

J.w.d. "janz weit draußen"- really far away, at least for cyclists, but nevertheless to be recommended is a visit to the village of Zwillbrook near Vreden and the nearby Zwillbrocker Venn. Both are located on the Dutch border. This region is one of the largest wildlife sanctuaries in Westphalia and covers nearly 160 ha (= 395.38 acres). This moorland is the home of thousands of rare birds and hundreds of different species of birds, which are not necessarily typical inhabitants of marshland biotopes. The reason for this is quite obvious: in the middle of the moorland there are a number of heather "islands", which cannot be reached by the enemies of the moorland birds. Therefore the presence of these birds is natural for the ornithologists, but the experts are unable to explain the huge flocks of black-headed gulls coming to the Venn at brooding time in the spring. There is no evident reason why so many of these birds choose the Venn of all places. The visitor even finds flamingos here. Whether they have escaped from a zoo has remained unclear to the present day.

At Zwillbrock itself the admirer of the baroque period will find something to suit his taste: the Church of St Francis (Franziskuskirche) (first half of the 18th century) is considered to be a jewel of baroque architecture. Moreover, the nearby Netherlands attract visitors with numerous leisure-time activities and great shopping centres.

Biologische Station Zwillbrock
(Moormuseum),48691 Vreden, Zwillbrock 10, tel.: 0 25 64 / 46 00 or 8 71
opening hours: by appointment

Nordkirchen Castle

Wilkinghege Castle

Festival of hot-air ballooning - "Montgolfiade" in Telgte

The Münsterland, paradise for horse lovers

SPORTS & LEISURE-TIME ACTIVITIES

Here are some suggestions for leisure-time activities in Münster and the Münsterland:

angling
ballooning
boule
camping
canoeing
clay pigeon shooting
covered wagon tours
epicurism
farmhouse holidays
gliding
golf
hiking
ice-skating
jogging
keep-fit trails
lazing around
moated castles tours
observation of nature
open-air theatres
paddling
"Pättkestour" (bicycle tours)
pedal boating
picnicking
riding
rowing
sailing
sculpture exhibitions
sightseeing flights
sky-diving
soccer
"Speckbrett"
surfing
swimming
tennis
visiting museums
water-skiing

On the following pages you can read about typical sports in the Münsterland.
You'll find further information on the different items in the chapter "Sought and found: Münster from A-Z" at the end of this book.

Let's Talk about Horses

It's no exaggeration if you describe the Münsterland as a paradise for horses and horsemen. It is a region known for its long tradition of horse-breeding and riding and the promotion of these activities. If you look around when you try out the "Pättkestour" we recommended earlier in this book, you will see horses nearly everywhere: Westphalian riding horses and ponies as well as "exotic species" like Arab and Andalusian horses and Icelandic ponies. They frisk about on the green meadows and pastures of the rural estates, stud-farms and riding clubs.
Münster and the surrounding villages alone provide a number of private and public institutions which are concerned with both amateur and professional equestrian sport.
The "Westerholt'sche Wiese" next to the Promenade is the place where many horse lovers regularly meet to watch the "Turnier der Sieger" (Tournament of Champions), which is held there.
Dr. Reiner Klimke - actually a lawyer - is without doubt Münster's most famous horseman. He has several times won the World Dressage Championship.

123

Sailing on the Aasee

In his riding club ("Reiterhof St. Georg") near the Aasee he has brought together some of his best horses as well as a number of young, talented riders. You can watch them at their morning training - by appointment only, of course!

The four-day riding competition at the Halle Münsterland is the official meeting-place for interesting show jumping and dressage specialists and for the well-informed audience, who are fairly spoilt as far as top-class riding events are concerned. This riding competition takes place in January and is the start of a series of equestrian events in the Westphalian metropolis.

For true horse lovers with a little more time on their hands we can recommend two interesting trips. It is only a 30 minute's drive from Münster to Warendorf, a small town traversed by the River Ems. This town is generally known as the "Town of the Horse".

The annual "Warendorfer Hengstparade" (Warendorf's Stallion Show), which takes place at the end of September and the beginning of October, is the main attraction in this Westphalian provincial town.

The second trip takes you to the Merfelder Bruch, a very attractive area near Dülmen. Here we find a big herd of wild ponies. On the last Saturday in May they are rounded up for the famous "Wild Horse Round-Up at the Merfelder Bruch" - which is the true highlight horse lovers eagerly await in the "equestrian paradise", the Münsterland!

And what is missing in this paradise? Exactly, a Horse Museum! This museum has been in the planning stage for a short time now and will be built in the grounds of the All-weather Zoo. One can safely assume that such a museum will attract lots of visitors. Let's wait and see!

"Fair Winds...

and always a handbreadth of water under the keel" is a familiar slogan among yachtsmen, and anyone strolling around the Aasee (Lake Aa) might well hear it. The "Westfalicus Munsteranensis" not only has a well-known weakness for smoked ham, "Korn" (= grain spirit) and "Töttchen" but also a less well-known weakness for sailing close to the wind on "Münster's biggest puddle", the Aasee. After the long winter break it's a lovely sight to watch the hobby skippers make their boats ready as soon as the first warmer winds are blowing. They lash down heaving and log lines and - with a strong breeze from behind - they finally sit on the planks of their small boats, which impetuously, under full sail, describe circles on the lake. Perhaps the onlooker himself by now wishes to board one of the heeling boats for a little trip, too. If you really want to, you can make this wish come true.

Münster's yachting club has successfully navigated many beginners through the theoretical and practical pitfalls of winds, current and various knots so that they have attained the goal they aspire to - the sailing licence, which is obligatory in Germany.

Those who cannot spend so much time can always try one of the many pedal boats, canoes and rowing boats which are on hire at the Aasee.

Up and Away with Hot Air

The disciples of the Montgolfier Brothers never tire of explaining it: anyone standing in a basket attached to a large and brightly-coloured bag, which he fills with hot air by burning gas to make it rise in the air, neither flies nor floats but rides a balloon! Münster is considered one of the centres of ballooning.

As soon as the weather permits, they are in the air and hovering quietly and gently in the sky above the city. Or they take part in a sporting competition and try to reach a fixed landing point by anticipating the moods of the capricious winds and skilfully changing heights to use the different air currents to get there first.

Every year at Whitsun amateur flyers - sorry - amateur balloonists from all over the world come to Münster to take part in the "Montgolfiade", a festival of hot-air ballooning and the biggest international sporting event for balloonists in Germany. During the event about eighty gently moving spots of colour can be seen in the sky over Münster.

By the way, ballooning is far from being an élitist hobby. As a passenger in one of the balloons even the curious visitor can experience the feeling of floating - under the clouds, though, but still above the tree tops.

For further information contact: *Stadtwerbung und Touristik, im Stadthaus 1, Klemensstr. 10, tel.: 02 51/4 92-27 10* and *Freiballonsportverein Münster-Münsterland e.V., tel.: 02 51/6 04 48*, who will gladly help you to go on your maiden voyage with a "champagne baptism".

"Speckbrett"

True, it is possible: someone swinging the tennis racket in an elegant sports dress, someone who likes the quiet and concentrated manner of playing golf or someone whose favourite recreational activity is perfecting the art of sailing will perhaps turn away from the "Speckbrett". However, anyone who considers himself a true citizen of Münster chooses not the tennis racket but the "Speckbrett".

It is true that this game was only invented long after the discovery of tennis. About forty years ago the idea emerged to replace the far too complicated

Skateboarder in action

"Speckbrett" before it becomes a mere part of folklore. As "Speckbrett" is probably only played in and around Münster, you can call yourself "world champion" as soon as you have beaten the well-known local champions.

Skateboarding

It is not a dance but nevertheless the onlooker is impressed by the elegant movements. It is not hectic though very fast-moving. It is not officially considered an artistic skill, yet the onlooker tends to describe the people doing it as artists: we are talking about skateboarding, the art of balancing on this rather narrow board made of wood or plastic with two pairs of roller-skate wheels fixed to it, which is manoeuvred by shifting your weight.

When the first boards rolled from the U.S. to Europe more than fifteen years ago, no one expected Münster of all cities to become a centre, if not *the* European stronghold of skateboarding. Germany's first "half-pipe", a special track for daredevil skateboarders was built in Münster. Therefore, the city was the venue of the first international skateboarding championship in Germany in 1982. This event met with such extraordinary response that Münster was chosen as the venue of the world championship. The organizers proudly reported that "skateboarders all over the world were looking towards Münster." In 1988, about 10,000 spectators came to Münster to watch the breathtaking performance of the world's best amateur and professional skateboarders in the Halle Münsterland.

design of the tennis racket with its strong strings and its carefully worked out static by the much simpler all-wood racket. And because of its striking similarity to the kitchen utensil of the same name it was called "Speckbrett"(= a board used to cut bacon).

The game is played as long as you like - following rules that are somewhere in between those of tennis and table tennis. "As long as you like" could have taken quite a while. And during a game it must have occurred to one of the players that it would be less tiring and much easier to handle the racket if it had less air resistance and less weight. Consequently, he drilled a number of holes through the wooden racket, giving it its final shape.

Though there are several "Speckbrett" courts in Münster, this unconventional game is falling more and more into oblivion. You should play a round of

FAMOUS CITIZENS OF MÜNSTER

The Master Architect: Johann Conrad Schlaun

One of Münster's famous personalities is the baroque master architect Johann Conrad Schlaun. Born on June 5th, 1695 in Nörde (Westphalia), he was later to enrich the world with many masterly baroque buildings.

At the age of 25, the pupil of the famous architect Balthasar Neumann travelled by order of Prince-Bishop Clemens August of Cologne to the capitals of architecture at that time: Paris, Rome and Würzburg. Five years later, this educational tour ended, and Schlaun was able to make use of the newly gained knowledge when he designed Schloss Augustusburg in Brühl for the Prince-Bishop.

His work in Münster began in 1724. During this year, among other projects, the Church of the Capucin Order (Kapuzinerkirche) (today St Aegidii) with a remarkable sandstone front was built according to his plans. Afterwards, he gradually created the most important buildings of the "Westphalian Baroque period". First, the Church of St Clemens, a cylindrical domed building with an impressive fresco in the cupola, and the neighbouring Hospital of St Clemens were built (1745-1754). Then the "Erbdroste" Adolph Heidenreich von Droste-Vischering commissioned him to build a three-winged representative building on an extremely confined site. Schlaun managed to find a brilliant solu-

tion to this problem by choosing a concave front for the Erbdrostenhof (1753-1757) and by erecting the building diagonally on the corner site. The interesting contrast between sandstone elements and red brick as well as the unique curvature of the residence creates the special kind of dynamic that is typical of the baroque period. The interior decoration was chosen to meet the requirements of representation, which today enhances the overall impression when the Erbdrostenhof is used as a venue for concerts.

In addition to these large buildings, Schlaun also undertook a number of smaller and quite different projects ranging from the conception of firework displays to the design of sepulchres and bridges or the new spire he had added to the church tower of St Martin's Church

Johann Conrad Schlaun

Annette von Droste-Hülshoff

(1759/60). Even more practical problems such as the conversion of the medieval outer court near the Promenade into a prison (1732) were solved by Schlaun. However, the Prince-Bishop's palace residence (1767-1787) is considered to be one of his most important works. Today it is part of the university. The three-winged building is characterised by the stark contrast between the light-coloured sandstone from the nearby Baumberge region and the red brickwork and the dominant central wing decorated with ornaments and statuary, which is typical of the baroque period. Münster's Schloss went down in the history of architecture as the last baroque residence. Schlaun himself, however, did not live to see the end of the construction work.

Someone who designs magnificent buildings for other people certainly does not want to live in a small hut. But Schlaun was not allowed to do what he could have done as far as his own home was

concerned. A commoner, someone who worked for members of the nobility, was not permitted to build a moated castle or a residence which could be mistaken for an aristocratic mansion. This becomes quite apparent if you look at the Rüschhaus (built 1745-1749): Schlaun's former domicile is a very clever combination of elements typical of Westphalian farm-houses and elements taken from noble residences.

Unfortunately, Schlaun's town house in the so-called "Kuhviertel" can no longer be visited. It was destroyed by bombs in World War II.

Schlaun died on October 21st, 1773. The Münsterland and Münster, in particular, became famous for his buildings. In the whole of northern Germany Münster has the highest number of baroque buildings.

Annette von Droste-Hülshoff

If you want to talk about famous sons and daughters of Münster, you should by no means forget to mention Annette von Droste-Hülshoff. The famous poetess of the "Biedermeier" period - usually simply referred to as "Droste" - was born as Anna Elisabeth Freiin (Baroness) von Droste zu Hülshoff on January 10th, 1797 at Burg Hülshoff, a moated castle near Havixbeck, as the second of four children. Her father, Clemens August von Droste, a retired cavalry captain, did not only take pleasure in strategic games but - like his daughter - also had a great affection for music and nature. Her mother, Therese Luise von Haxthausen, seems to have been a dominant woman. Even though she could not make anything of her daughter's literary work, she nevertheless supported her daughter simply through the fact that she herself liked to be surrounded by intelligent and cultured people, which certainly helped to broaden young Annette's horizons. Among the regular guests were Adele Schopenhauer, the sister of the philosopher Arthur Schopenhauer, and Professor Matthias Sprickmann, who at that time was Master of the Münster Freemasons' lodge. They were to become close friends of Annette von Droste-Hülshoff.

Annette's first love ended in complete disaster. At the age of 23, she felt torn between August von Arnswald, who was the son of a minister, and the student Heinrich Straube. When she had finally made up her mind as far as her feelings were concerned, she could not summon up the courage to express them openly. Thus, her love affair with Straube ended before it had really begun. At that time, she had already written the tragedy "Bertha" and her romantic epic "Walther".

From early youth, her health had been extremely delicate. It is thought that any feeling of uneasiness was soon reflected by a strong reaction of her body. In July 1826, while she was away on a trip to restore her health, her father, of whom she had been very fond, died. Her mother then moved with her two daughters to the Rüschhaus, the former country house of the architect Johann Conrad Schlaun. As her mother and sister travelled quite a lot, Annette was often alone. Her literary work at that time progressed only slowly. This seems to have changed when she gave up her secluded life and started to visit some people, among them her friend Adele Schopenhauer. Her head full of new impressions, she came back to Haus Rüschhaus, but soon her delicate health troubled her again and kept her from writing.

The following years brought several severe strokes of fate for "Droste": in 1829, her brother Ferdinand died, and, in November 1831, she lost her friend Katharina Schücking. Nine months later, her cousin died, and, finally, in November 1833, Sprickmann died, whom she had admired very much.

In spite of these sad events, she managed to go on with various projects. During the following years, she continued with her cycle of poems "Das geistliche Jahr" ("The Spiritual Year"), completed the long narrative poems "Das Hospiz auf dem großen St. Bernard" ("The Hospice on the Great St Bernard") (1833),"Des Arztes Vermächtnis" ("The Doctor's Legacy") (1834) and "Schlacht im Loener Bruch" ("The Battle of Stadtlohn Moor") (1838).

In 1835, Annette travelled with her mother to her sister's in Switzerland, where she wrote several nature poems.

In 1841, she moved to Meersburg Castle on Lake Constance - the new home of her sister and her family. She was accompanied by her friend Levin Schücking, son

Droste in everyone's hands - 20 DM note

Spätes Erwachen (Mai 1844)

Wie war mein Dasein abgeschlossen,
Als ich im grünumhegten Haus
Durch Lerchenschlag und Fichtensprossen
Noch träumt' in den Azur hinaus!

Als keinen Blick ich noch erkannte,
Als den des Strahles durchs Gezweig,
Die Felsen meine Brüder nannte,
Schwester mein Spiegelbild im Teich!

Nicht rede ich von jenen Jahren,
Die dämmernd uns die Kindheit beut
Nein, so verdämmert und zerfahren
War meine ganze Jugendzeit.

Wohl sah ich freundliche Gestalten
Am Horizont vorüberfliehn:
ich konnte heiße Hände halten
Und heiße Lippen an mich ziehn.

Ich hörte ihres Grußes Pochen,
Ihr leises Wispern um mein Haus,
Und sandte schwimmend, halb gebrochen,
Nur einen Seufzer halb hinaus.

Ich fühlte ihres Hauches Fächeln,
und war doch keine Blume süß;
Ich sah der Liebe Engel lächeln,
Und hatte doch kein Paradies.

Mir war, als habe in den Noten,
Sich jeder Ton an mich verwirrt,
Sich jede Hand, die mir geboten,
Im Dunkel wunderlich verirrt.

Verschlossen blieb ich, eingeschlossen
In meiner Träume Zauberturm,
Die Blitze waren mir Genossen
Und Liebesstimme mir der Sturm.

Dem Wald ließ ich ein Lied erschallen,
Wie nie vor einem Menschenohr,
Und meine Träne ließ ich fallen,
Die heiße, in den Blumenflor.

Und alle Pfade mußt' ich fragen:
Kennt Vögel ihr und Strahlen auch?
Doch keinen: wohin magst du tragen,
Von welchen Odem schwillt dein Hauch?

Wie ist das anders nun geworden,
Seit ich ins Auge dir geblickt,
Wie ist nun jeder Welle Borden
Ein Menschenbildnis eingedrückt!

Wie fühl' ich allen warmen Händen
Nun ihre leisen Pulse nach,
Und jedem Blick sein scheues Wenden
Und jeder schweren Brust ihr Ach.

Und alle Pfade möcht' ich fragen:
Wo zieht ihr hin, wo ist das Haus,
In dem lebendge Herzen schlagen,
Lebendger Odem schwillt hinaus?

Entzünden möcht' ich alle Kerzen
Und rufen jedem müden Sein:
Auf ist mein Paradies im Herzen,
Zieht alle, alle nun hinein!

Annette von Droste-Hülshoff

of her late friend Katharina. Schücking, a fairly successful writer, had been offered the post of librarian at Meersburg Castle. Moreover, he followed Annette's literary activities with interest. Above all, the congenial Schücking helped "Droste" regain her self-confidence as a writer, which had taken quite a blow when the publishing of her "Gedichte von Anna Elisabeth von D.H." in 1838 had turned out to be a total failure. The company of Schücking proved to be rather inspiring. Among other texts, the well-known novella "Die Judenbuche" ("The Jew's Beech-tree") was written during this period, which came to a sudden end in the spring of 1842 when Schücking left the castle to work somewhere else. Annette von Droste-Hülshoff never got over this shock completely. Her disappointment at losing her friend was alleviated by the comfort she was able to find in the appreciation with which her literary work was greeted in 1844, when the publication of her second collection of poems was a success.

In 1846, she fell seriously ill during a stay with relatives at Haus Rüschhaus. Two years passed, but she never quite recovered, and she finally died at Meersburg Castle on May 24th, 1848.

Her literary work has always been noted for its sensitive and very detailed yet quite realistic description of nature, which to some extent tended to exclude the poet's subjectivity. In a time of secularization, she wanted nature to be regarded as a part of divine revelation. Thus, in her work realistic description is interspersed with the supernatural, thereby adding allegorical meaning to the surface description of nature. We have chosen her poem "Late Awakening" to give you an idea of her work.

Professor Hermann Landois

"For a long time his stocky Westphalian figure in a black frock-coat, on his head the inevitable top-hat, in his mouth the equally inevitable pipe and with the gnarled stick in his hand had been a well-known sight in Münster. Every child knew him and every visitor hoped to catch a glimpse of him. (...) Although he was one of Münster's notorious revellers - Nikolaus and his pony Philipp drank the beer straight from the bottle just like he did - neither his productivity nor his robust health nor even his reputation with the citizens seems to have suffered."

This is how Joseph Otto Plassmann describes Professor Hermann Landois in the fourth volume of his *Westfälische Lebensbilder* (*Westphalian Biographies*), a man who - full of self-confidence but obviously also with some justification - considered himself to be a typical and ideal Westphalian. Landois wrote several books on zoology and biology, but he was respected not only as a scientist, as he also wrote light fiction and satirical texts in the vernacular and - incidentally - founded Münster's zoo. Today, he is seen as the image of the proud Westphalian: he is said to have been moody, merry, stubborn, earnest and very accurate as well as spiteful and malicious. People never knew which character trait predominated at any given time. Hermann Landois was an anarchic character full of esprit and with a ready wit, with whom people dreaded arguing but with whom they loved to chat. He represented the proverbial Westphalian stubbornness (maybe it has become proverbial because of Landois ...)

and had an almost legendary ability to hold his drink. He was a hard-working yet merry man, an obstinate and clever opponent - in short, a true Westphalian character.

Of course, an original is also characterized by his or her unusual biography. Landois was born on April 19th, 1835 in Münster. Soon he could be listed among those who achieved something in life despite having problems at school. He passed school-leaving exams only at the second attempt in 1855. In 1859, after studying theology, Landois was ordained a priest, but soon his love of nature prevailed: in 1863, his thesis on the nervous system of insects was awarded the degree "magna cum laude".

Soon after that, he passed further exams that allowed him to teach at grammar schools. He then taught at his old school, the prestigious Paulinum Gymnasium, the very school that had years ago expelled him. However, life as a teacher was soon not enough for this man, who always aimed at gaining more knowledge. In 1873 - by now he was known all over town - Landois was appointed associate professor, and as of 1876 he held the chair in zoology at Münster.

His first important act as a lover of nature and conservationist was the foundation of the "Westphalian Society for the Protection of Birds, Poultry Farming and Breeding of Song-Birds", which soon became very popular.

After this encouraging start greater projects followed, for example a zoological garden housing animals native to Westphalia. After a fairly successful though quite daring campaign to raise money for this new project Landois founded the "Westphalian Zoological Garden of Münster" on February 14th, 1874. Through clever public relations and personal efforts he succeeded in supplying the zoo time and again with money or goods and food. Plassmann reports that Landois "... on highly-official occasions used to stuff all the pockets of his inevitable frock-coat with pastry. 'Dat is för minne Apen' (For my apes)..." he used to explain. Indeed, Landois was always quite unwavering and amusing when he wanted to get his own way. Moreover, he seldom missed an opportunity to play tricks on unsuspecting fellow citizens. On one occasion, Landois is said to have helped Baron Giesbert von Romberg, who became known as the "Crazy Bomberg" in the stories of Josef Winckler, when he had thought up a nasty trick. When Romberg was invited to a social gathering, that was bound to be extremely boring, the Professor supplied Romberg with several dozens of fleas to put them on the ladies present. The poor women hardly managed to control the itch and show their usual composure and finally could not help contorting themselves in front of the gentlemen. The gentlemen, however, were convinced that their witty conversation was the cause of the high-spirited atmosphere.

But Landois was mainly occupied with financing his zoo. He was up to all sorts of tricks and dodges to secure the money for his zoo. He organized card-games, lotteries and bets to raise money to feed his animals.

As was the case with his congenial predecessor "Till Eulenspiegel", certainly not all the stories told about Landois are true. Quite a few of them may have occurred only in the heads of their narrators, and others were embellished with exaggerations.

So one has to stick to the general rule that, if many stories are centred around a person, truth will often not be found in the details of the story itself but in its intention.

Landois became known as a fairly coarse and whimsical man and also as a Low German poet. But numerous scientific studies also originated from his pen. *Das Studium der Zoologie* (*The Study of Zoology*), *Das Lehrbuch der Botanik* (*A Manual of Botany*), *Tierstimmen* (*Animal Voices*), *Das Lehrbuch der Zoologie mit besonderer Rücksicht auf das Zeichnen der Tierformen* (*Manual of Zoology with Special Emphasis on Drawing the Different Species*) - all of them works of a dedicated scientist. His ability to put theoretical knowledge into practice led to the foundation of a zoo. He was able to describe animals very accurately, he knew how to feed them appropriately in his zoo, and he developed a method of taxidermy. Incidentally, Landois - true to his character - did not forget to erect a monument commemorating himself five years before his death. Professor Hermann Landois died on January 29th, 1905, aged almost seventy.

Whoever wants to see him just as he lived and worked nearly a hundred years ago, should have a look at his memorial on Landois-Platz in front of the Zoo. There he stands in his best frock-coat, with a walking-stick, top-hat and his pipe, and watches over his life's work. And woe betide anyone who tries to shake him. The "unwiese Profässer" (crazy professor) would

Professor Landois and his own memorial

certainly find a way of stealing away from the beyond to take radical measures against the offender.

The Crazy Bomberg

Just married, the "Crazy Bomberg" - our hero - had nothing but nonsense with his wife on his mind. He said that he wanted to show her the whole wide world, then put her in his carriage, which drove four times all around Münster. In each little village they passed, the young bride was given a bird; in the last village, then, even a stork was put on her lap. Thus, the coach soon housed almost as many specimens of the feathered species as the zoo of Professor Landois. Back home again, the "Crazy Bomberg" led his Sophie into the castle and told the poor girl: "And this is your nest, my little dove."

The real name of the "Till Eulenspiegel of the Münsterland" was Giesbert Freiherr von Romberg, and he was born on July 20th, 1838 at Buldern Castle near Münster. It was the author Josef Winckler (1881-1966) who turned Romberg into the "Crazy Bomberg". Winckler investigated all of Romberg's activities very carefully and untiringly. He talked to those who had witnessed Romberg's pranks and to those who had become the butt of his jokes and then commemorated the Baron, who had been the terror of both middle-class citizens and aristocrats in his picaresque novel *Der tolle Bomberg* (1924).

One day, a group of gentlemen had the fervent wish to enjoy a bit of carousing now and again without being supervised by their better halves. They concluded this could best be achieved by staging a hunting trip. Again and again, they badgered the Baron with their request until he finally gave in and invited them to form a hunting party. As it was fairly obvious that the happy party was at best able to shoot one of the beaters rather than any game, Romberg gave each of them two hares. As was to be expected, the hunters did not shoot anything, so they went home with the two hares and passed them off as their bag. Everyone at home was duly impressed, until the cooks started gutting the hares and found the strangest offal: in each hare they discovered a sucked egg filled with suet.

The Baron thought up many of his pranks together with his like-minded friend Professor Landois. And soon the two men started competing with each other. One day, a magician and conjurer named Bosko was in town. The crazy Professor Landois was the first to notice the arrival of the rival. He walked up to the magician and challenged him to a duel of tricks. Their chosen task seemed impossible to perform. Which of them could reduce one of the extremely rough market wives, whose stock of swearwords alone was larger than the vocabulary of common people, to astonished silence for ten seconds. Soon, Romberg, or rather the "Crazy Bomberg", came to know about this wager and joined the competitors. Within a short time, they had found their "victim", and Professor Landois was to make the first move. He poked his walking-stick into a big bowl of curds offered for sale, slowly pulled it out and then tasted the curds sticking to the tip. "Sour", he judged. The market wife was indeed speechless, but only for about four seconds, and then such a torrent of abuse poured on the poor Professor that he had no other alternative but to withdraw from the battle-field prematurely. Now, the conjurer saw his chance. He bought a number of eggs from the woman, opened some on the pretext of testing the quality and smuggled a gold coin into each broken egg. The woman said nothing until the third egg was "tested", then she loudly demanded back her golden eggs - and the conjurer had lost the bet as well. The Baron saw his chance and - talking soothingly to the woman - offered to purchase all the butter she had for sale. He piled her arms high with packets of butter, opened her mouth and spat a fair amount of chewing tobacco down

"The Crazy Baron leaps over the dinner table", oil painting by Fritz Grotemeyer

the poor creature's throat. This left her speechless for much longer than was necessary for the Baron to win the wager.

The Baron spent his whole life playing tricks on members of the nobility, commoners, clergymen and conceited persons whenever he was not busy quenching his enormous thirst in the company of Professor Landois in the pub owned by Louis Midy. Nobody was ever really safe from his sense of humour, but his favourite targets were those who had a very high opinion of themselves. He reacted to the arrogant remark of another aristocrat that members of the nobility should not mingle with the crowd by sitting high up on his coach box and being shaved in front of the astonished crowd. He explained his strange behaviour to the amused onlookers by telling them about the above-mentioned advice to members of the nobility.

Freiherr von Romberg died at home at Buldern Castle in November 1897. However, no story is quite as beautiful and convincing as a fabricated one. Advanced in years, but still an inveterate joker, he made a deal with the chaplain. In order to avoid the awkward situation of having to bury an unrepentant sinner, the chaplain gave his word to the "Crazy Bomberg" that before the actual funeral his hearse would be parked for a while in front of the pub as Romberg's very special way of saying farewell to alcohol. Provided the chaplain acted according to his wishes, Bomberg would accept the last rites. Finally, shortly before his death, Bomberg expressed his thanks for this "clerical willingness to compromise" by biting into the chaplain's hand instead of accepting the Host given to him as provisions for his last journey.

The "Lion of Münster"

Since the end of World War II, the courageous Bishop and later Cardinal Clemens August von Galen, a famous honorary citizen of Münster, has been honoured with the surname "Lion of Münster". He was one of the few to speak publicly against injustice being perpetrated under Nazi rule. In his sermons Galen attacked the Nazis publicly for the persecution and murder of members of the church and other citizens after several attempts to stop these crimes by handing in written protests had not been successful.

On March 16th, 1878, Clemens August Graf von Galen was born at Dinklage Castle in Dinklage, a town on the northern outskirts of the Münster diocese, which then belonged to the Grand Duchy of Oldenburg. His parents, Graf Ferdinand Herbert von Galen and his wife Elisabeth, née Reichsgräfin von Spee, brought their son up as a strict Catholic. He went to a Jesuit grammar-school and passed his school-leaving exams in 1896. First, he studied philosophy at the university of Fribourg (Switzerland), later he went to Innsbruck and Münster to study theology. In 1904, he was ordained a priest in Münster, where he held the post of chaplain at the cathedral for two years, before he went to Berlin as a chaplain. In 1929, von Galen was called back to Münster by his bishop, Johannes Poggenburg, to become the parish priest of St Lambert's Church. Finally, in September 1933, he became the 70th successor of St Luidger, when he was appointed Bishop of Münster by Pope Pius XI. At that time, his attitude towards the Nazis could be described as neutral or maybe even sympathizing. On October 19th, 1933, he swore an oath of allegiance to the Nazi government in the presence of Hermann Göring. Moreover, chroniclers tell us of a "pro-Nazi sermon preached in Recklinghausen in spring 1934" (cf. *Stattbuch für Münster, Münster* 1980). However, his attitude towards the Nazis changed drastically when the Gestapo started confiscating monasteries and nunneries. From 1941 onwards, von Galen attacked the expulsion and displacement of people vehemently in his sermons. Only from this time on did he really live up to his nickname "Lion of Münster", which is how he is known us today. On Sunday August 3rd, 1941, he preached a furious sermon against the practice of euthanasia: (excerpt)

"(...) Thus, it may well happen that the poor and helpless sick will be killed sooner or later. Why? Not because they committed a capital crime or because they attacked their warden or nurse so that they had to use force in an act of self-defence to protect their own lives. These are some cases, besides the killing of an armed enemy during the defence of one's country in a just war, where the use of force or even the killing of a person is justifiable and often required. No, not for these reasons are these unfortunate creatures killed. No, they have to die because some office or some report prepared by a commission considers them to be 'unworthy of life' as they belong to the 'unproductive national comrades'! (...) No, they

are human beings, our fellow-men, our brothers and sisters. Maybe they are poor people, maybe they are ill or unproductive people. But have they lost their right to live because of that? Do you, do I only have the right to live as long as we are productive, or as long as other people consider us to be productive? (...)"

Typically enough, the courageous bishop preached two of his three important sermons from the pulpit of St Lambert's Church. By choosing this historic church of the parish to which he belonged and which had always been closely connected to the daily life of its community, he wanted to make it perfectly clear that his words had a political meaning and were directed against the injustice committed by the ruling party.

"Then, all that is needed is some secret order that the tried and tested method applied to the mentally ill is to be used for other 'unproductive persons', too and that it is also (...) to be applied to soldiers badly wounded on active duty."

This sentence almost cost Galen his life. The Nazis were beside themselves with anger and they planned a treacherous murder in the night.
In no time at all, copies of this sermon were distributed all over Germany and among the army and naval forces on the front line. It caused great agitation. However, Hitler and Goebbels did not want to take the risk of making a martyr of a man as popular as Bishop Galen. Goebbels argued that, otherwise, Westphalia would no longer support the

Bishop Clemens August von Galen

Nazis in the war. Only after the "End-sieg" (final or ultimate victory) did they plan to "get even with" Galen. They even gave orders that euthanasia was to be stopped in Marienthal near Münster, a mental home under the supervision of the Bishop of Münster. So Galen won this trial of strength, and you have to assume that Münster's population would certainly have resisted the arrest of their bishop.

In March 1946, von Galen was appointed Cardinal by Pope Pius XII. But he was not to hold this office for long. On March 22nd, 1946, Cardinal von Galen died in Münster only six days after his 68th birthday after a short illness following complications in connection with appendicitis.

In the post-war years Galen was regarded as a hero. In the 1970s, however, this picture of Galen changed considerably when critics stated that the Cardinal had not shown true resistance to the Nazi regime but had only had the interests of the church in mind.

Though it is very difficult to decide which side is right, you can assume that a number of people could have been saved and that some personal tragedies would at least have been delayed, if more persons in public life had dared speak up against the Nazis.

First and foremost, it is not true that Galen only thought of his own church. On the contrary, his insistent sermons prove that he defended all those who were persecuted or oppressed without respect to their faith or race. Von Galen declared that he was "...prepared to put [his] freedom and even [his] own life at stake...". He also wanted to take the side of the Jews in his sermons, but Münster's Jewish community advised him not to do that so as not to make matters worse for them.

However, it is true that von Galen had a rather anti-modernistic and national-conservative point of view, and, although he rejected the neo-pagan heresy propagated by the Nazis, he nevertheless sympathized with their fight against liberalism and Marxism. Von Galen never questioned the legitimacy of the Nazis in general and their claim to power, and this is what invited criticism.

Today, his tomb in one of the chapels of the Cathedral and a memorial on the Cathedral Square commemorate this courageous bishop. Nevertheless, for quite a long time now, the beatification of Galen has not been pursued further in Rome.

T R A D I T I O N A L   D E T A I L S

Legends of the Münsterland

No description, however exact, neither a precise enumeration of activities nor correct quotations can give you more information about the people of a particular region than their legends and myths. They express the daily worries, the secret fears and wishes of people living there. Indeed, you can even distinguish between different regions if you compare the degree of variation in the traditional tales. This is also true of the Münsterland.

The progenitor of all Westphalians, a most stubborn and extremely down-to-earth individual, was, according to legend, created following a suggestion by Jesus Christ himself. Jesus was strolling through the then still unpopulated Westphalia. He was delighted by the landscape and asked the Lord why this beautiful part of the earth was uninhabited. The Lord thought about this and came to the conclusion that human beings should indeed be added to this area. Thus, he kicked at a stone which immediately turned into a human being. This man rubbed his eyes, turned to the Lord and angrily asked him: "Why did you kick me?". Then he saw Jesus and barked at him: "And what are you doing on my land?".

One of the best-known tales of the Münsterland is the story about the Grinkenschmied. This man must have been a direct descendant of the first Westphalian, as he was just as rough and rooted to the soil as his ancestor. However, he was also very good-natured and apparently possessed some mysterious talents. Anyone who was lucky enough to own a scythe forged by the Grinkenschmied never had to sharpen it because it never got blunt. But you had to be careful as a wound caused by careless handling of this tool would never close again.

Although he must have been as strong as an ox, the Grinkenschmied worked as a farm-labourer. Mind you, it is quite difficult to find out where exactly he worked, as the farm is usually located somewhere near the place where the narrator of the story lives.

Though the Grinkenschmied was usually a rather good-natured fellow, once he lost his patience he could no longer control himself. Anyone who had something to celebrate, be it a slaughtering day or a wedding, came to the legendary smith to borrow one of his incomparable skewers. In return for that, he was usually given a roast. Once, a farmer did not want to fulfil his part of the bargain. So he borrowed the skewer but brought it back without the usual roast for the smith. Thereupon, the Grinkenschmied, who knew his way around, went straight to the farmer's house, killed one of the horses in the stable and cut off one of its legs. According to the legend, no one ever tried to cheat the Grinkenschmied out of his traditional payment again.

Another tale is told - sometimes with slight variations - in other regions of Germany, too. Therefore it is not really a typical tale of the Münsterland. Anyway, it is the "Tale of the Cockerel": Münster was the declared target of an enemy attack and an ensuing siege. Of course, the main aim of a siege is to prevent anyone from breaking through the lines of the besiegers, either from the inside or from outside. Consequently, the town is blocked off from all supplies. On the other hand, a siege can be fairly boring for the attackers; all they have to do is wait patiently until the enemy are exhausted and have to give up.

Now this siege had lasted for quite a while already, and the attackers thought that soon the townspeople of Münster would have to capitulate. And indeed, hunger in the town was already great, so great that one miserly citizen who had not donated his cockerel for the common welfare, but had hidden it instead, thought that now the time had come to eat it. But the cockerel managed to escape and flew away onto the highest point it could find. Safely sitting on its high vantage-point, it could be seen by the attackers, too. They concluded that the townspeople could not be that hungry after all if they had not even killed all the poultry and thus ended the siege, feeling rather annoyed. In memory of this feathered hero, the mayor of the saved town ordered a silver tankard in the shape of a cockerel to be made, which has been carefully kept as part of the city treasure of Münster up to this day.

The next story is set in Münster and tells us about the constant temptations of the Devil. When the Church of Our Lady, today known as the Überwasserkirche, was built, the Devil became very angry when he thought of the magnificent building as another symbol of the glorification of God. So the Devil did not lose much time and tried to think of a way of preventing or at least disturbing the building of the new church. He transformed himself into a beautiful woman, braided his hair, put on very fine clothes and made his face up carefully to beguile everyone. Thus prepared, and equipped with a sack full of money and precious stones, the Devil set out to tempt the master builder. But the latter was not so easy to tempt and listened unmoved when the Devil in his beguiling disguise tried to win his favour. The master builder even refused the precious stones and the money offered to him, which really enraged the Devil. Furious, he stamped on the ground and disappeared, leaving behind a truly devilish smell. The imprint of the Devil's hoof on the stone on which he had stamped again and again in his fury could still be seen until fairly recently in front of the Überwasserkirche. Go and have a look, maybe you can still find the imprint of the horseshoe next to the church...

If you enjoyed these examples of legends from the Münsterland, and if you can read enough German, then you will find more entertainingly narrated tales in the following book:

Sauermann, Dietmar (Hrsg.):
Sagen aus Westfalen. 4. Auflage
Husum 1993, ISBN 3-88042-094-7

Münsterland Cuisine
A Choice of Recipes

Pfeffer-Potthast

All right, a city guide is not a cookery book. But a book which is meant to introduce you to a particular region, its inhabitants and their customs should also contain some information about food and drink. Though the rather simple but extremely substantial meals might not necessarily impress someone like Paul Bocuse, they are nevertheless very tasty and ideal for filling your stomach nicely. If you just happen to be without the necessary kitchen utensils as you are on holiday and far away from home - do not worry! After all, tasty Westphalian dishes are served in a number of special restaurants in Münster. Just check out "Westphalian" in the service section of this book.

Typical Münsterland dish, hot and substantial ...

Ingredients:

sirloin of beef

or a piece of rib roast

celeriac

old bread

1 bayleaf

onions

1 carrot

pepper

"Westphalian heaven" in the Mühlenhof Open-air Museum

141

Cut the boned beef or the rib roast into pieces of approx. 60 g, add the same amount of sliced onions, add water until beef and onions are just covered, then add celeriac, the carrot and bay-leaf before you bring the mixture to the boil. Skim carefully and season with salt and pepper. Take the vegeta-bles out when the meat is tender. Then grate old bread (remove the crust first!) into the gravy - but do not use too much bread. It will take a few minutes until the liquid starts to thicken. Pfef-ferpotthast does not look very appetiz-ing and loses flavour if it is too thick. Boil up again for a further five minutes and season with pepper again. Serve with a pickled gherkin and boiled potatoes.

Töttchen

Töttchen is so popular that you can buy it in tins. But anyone who wants to have a true Westphalian meal will not be satisfied with tinned food.

Ingredients:

1 tongue of a calf

500 g veal

(shoulder or breast)

2 onions

mixed herbs and vegetables for the broth

2 bayleaves

1 tsp of pepper

2 cloves

salt

for the gravy:

60 g butter

50 g flour

2 table-spoons of finely chopped onions

1 tbsp of mustard

1 pinch of white pepper and sugar

Cover the veal with water and bring to the boil, add the roughly chopped onions, spices and herbs. Cook for 85 minutes over a low heat, take the meat out and dice it. Then pour the broth through a sieve, melt the butter in a saucepan, blend with flour to get a roux. Then add onions and meat. Fill up the Töttchen with a little broth, cook it for further 7 minutes, then season with the spices and herbs.

Panhas

Ingredients:

250 g blood sausage

250 g onions

1 pinch of pimento (allspice)

1 pinch of white pepper & salt

250 g broken rice

250 g oat-meal

2-2.5 l sausage broth

Mince the blood sausage and the on-ions. Cook the rice and the spices in the sausage broth until the rice is done, add oat-meal and the sausage and onions. Stir over heat until you can easily remove the mixture from the bottom of the pan. Leave the mixture to cool, then cut into slices and fry. Serve for dinner.

Kutscherkuchen

(*coachman's cake* - for four people) Clever preparation turns simple ingredients into a delicious dessert.

Ingredients:

4 old rolls

milk

vanilla-sugar

rum

butter

flour

pumpkin jam

or plum jam

Grate off the crust of the rolls, then cut the rolls in half and remove a bit of the white inside. Sweeten the milk with the vanilla-sugar, add rum. Fill the rolls with jam and soak them in the milk. Then roll them in flour and whipped eggs which are also sweetened with vanilla-sugar. Now all you have to do is fry the coachman's cakes with butter until golden brown.

Struven

Ingredients:

750 g flour

4 eggs

60 g yeast

2/3 l milk

1/2 tea-spoon salt

melted butter

raisins, sugar

currants

This is a tasty dessert that can be prepared without great difficulties: prepare a yeast dough from the listed ingredients, let it rest for 90 minutes, and then form small pancakes and fry them in a pan.

With kind permission of the author, these recipes were taken from:

Rudolf Böckmann's collection of recipes *Das Westfälische Kochbuch.*

And now: enjoy your meal and have a good time cooking.

Asparagus season in the Münsterland

MÜNSTER AT A GLANCE

Sightseeing

(The circled numbers refer to the map)

Aasee: Artificial lake near the city centre. The boat "Professor Landois" - also called "Wasserbus" - sets off from the Goldene Brücke every hour on the hour (10 am - 6 pm; not during the winter months). Situated near the Aasee are the "**Mühlenhof**" **open-air museum (57), the Westphalian Museum of Natural History**,which also houses the **Planetarium (58)** and the

All-weather Zoo (59): More than 2800 animals of 330 species; a unique system of roofed paths connects the various animal houses. Visit the dolphinarium and the "Streichelzoo". Open from 9 am, ticket offices close in Jan. / Feb. / Nov. / Dec.: 4 pm, Mar. / Oct.: 5 pm, Apr. to Sept.: 6 pm).

Astronomical clock in the Cathedral (29): Procession of the Three Magi and glockenspiel, on weekdays at noon, on Sundays and religious holidays at 12.30 pm.

Biological Station "Rieselfelder": guided tours through the bird sanctuary available for groups by special appmt; tel.: 16 17 60.

Botanical Gardens (15) in the grounds of the Schloss cover 11.38 acres; 2000 m² in greenhouses. Open from 8 am - 4/5/7 pm (see *Museums*, p. 145).

Buddenturm (2): Once part of the fortifications erected before 1200. Still in remarkably good condition. After 1945, the neo-Gothic crenellated top was replaced by a tiled roof, which corresponded to the original construction of the tower.

Erbdrostenhof (36): Masterpiece of the baroque architect Johann Conrad Schlaun; built between 1753 and 1757.

Hall of Peace (33): Former Council Chamber; valuable Gothic carvings, which were evacuated during World War II and therefore escaped the bombing. In 1648, the hall witnessed the oath confirming the peace treaty between Spain and the Netherlands, which preceded the Treaty of Westphalia.

Krameramtshaus (32): Built in 1588, one of the oldest guild halls in Münster. Since 1995 House of the Netherlands, an academic centre of research and culture.

Prinzipalmarkt (bet. 11 and **31)**: Münster's "front parlour"; lined with stately arcaded gabled houses; centre of business life and shopping.

Promenade: Former rampart; today lined with linden trees; a green belt enclosing the old part of the town. The Zwinger **(54)** and the Buddenturm **(2)** are remains of the old fortifications.

City Hall (33): Arcaded building with magnificent, ornamented gable. Built in the middle of the 14th cent.; destroyed in the war; faithfully reconstructed in the 1950s.

Schloss (15): Former residence of the Prince-Bishop; 3-wing building built between 1767 and 1787 by Schlaun. Rich ornamental and figured decoration. Meticulous reconstruction of the façade after the war; functional interior. Today, main building of the university.

Municipal Library (5): opened in 1993; postmodern-avant-garde building, which arouses much interest.

Municipal Wine House (33): next to the City Hall; late Renaissance period; built in 1615 by Johann von Bocholt.

Watchman of St Lambert's (31): proclaims the time: 9 - 12 pm (every 30 mins; except Tue).

Zwinger (54): built in 1536 as part of the fortifications, later used as a prison; 6 ft thick walls.

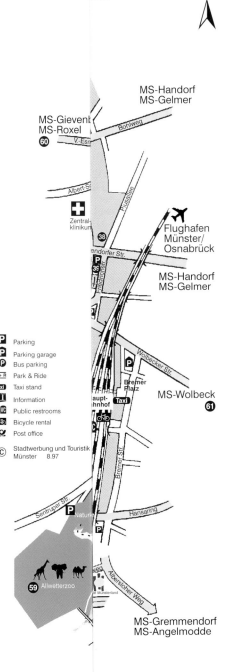

1 German-Dutch Corps
2 Buddenturm
3 Johanniskirche / Church of St John
4 Turkish Consulate General
5 Stadtbücherei / Municipal Library
6 Staatsarchiv / State Archives
7 Stadtarchiv / Municipal Archives
8 Martinikirche / Church of St Martin
9 Städtische Bühnen / Municipal Theatre
10 Apostelkirche / Church of the Apostles
11 Dutch Consulate General
12 Kiepenkerldenkmal
13 Observantenkirche / Franciscan Church
14 Überwasserkirche / Church of Our Lady
15 Schloß (Universität) / the castle (university)
16 College of Applied Sciences (dean's office and administration)
17 Westphalian School of Music
18 University Museum of Mineralogy
19 Land- u. Amtsgericht (law courts)
20 University Lecture Hall 1
21 University Bible Museum
22 University and Regional Library
23 Petrikirche / Church of St Peter
24 Aegidiimarkt, Adult Education Centre
25 University Museum of Geology and Paleontology
26 Fürstenberghaus on the Cathedral Square
27 Westphalian Museum of Art and Cultural History
28 Bischöfliches Palais und Generalvikariat / Bishop's Palace and office of the Vicar-General
29 St. Paulus-Dom / Cathedral of St Paul
30 Regional Government Offices
31 Lambertikirche / St Lambert's Church
32 Krameramtshaus / House of the Netherlands
33 Rathaus (City Hall)/ Friedenssaal (Hall of Peace)/ Stadtweinhaus (Municipal Wine House)
34 Dominikanerkirche / Dominican Church
35 Clemenskirche / Church of St Clemens
36 Erbdrostenhof
37 Stadtmuseum / City Museum
38 Landeshaus (main admin. office of the Regional Association of Westphalia-Lippe)
39 Erlöserkirche / Church of the Saviour
40 Servatiikirche / St Servatii
41 Synagogue
42 Raphaelsklinik (hospital)
43 St Ludgeri
44 St Aegidii
45 Administrative Court of Appeal of the Land North Rhine-Westphalia
46 Chamber of Handicrafts, French Consulate
47 Antoniuskirche / St Anthony
48 City Hall II
49 College of Music / Musikhochschule
50 Chamber of Agriculture of Westphalia-Lippe
51 Main Railway Station, Wolfgang Borchert Theatre
52 Halle Münsterland
53 New Apostolic Church
54 Zwinger / outer court
55 Centre of Natural Sciences of the University
56 University Medical Centre
57 Open-air Museum Mühlenhof
58 Westphalian Museum of Natural History and Planetarium
59 All-weather Zoo
60 Haus Rüschhaus
61 West Prussian State Museum
62 Stadthalle Hiltrup / Municipal Hall Hiltrup
63 Citizens' Centre Kinderhaus
64 Ice-skating arena
65 Museum of Lacquer Work
66 Thermal Baths

Parkhäuser / Parkplätze (car-parks)
- Aegidiimarkt, open Mon - Sat: 7 am - 2 am, closed on Sun.
- Bahnhofstrasse, daily: 6 am - 12 pm
- Bremer Platz, daily: 5.30 am - 12 pm in the parking garage, 24 h in the parking area on the ground floor
- Stubengasse, open Mon - Sat: 7 am - 12 pm, Sun: 9 am - 7 pm
- Theatre open Mon - Sat: 7 am - 12 pm

P Parking
P Parking garage
P Bus parking
P + R Park & Ride
Taxi Taxi stand
I Information
WC Public restrooms
Bicycle rental
Post office

© Stadtwerbung und Touristik Münster 8.97

Museums

Archäologisches Museum / University Archaeological Museum (26), Domplatz 20/22, tel.: 83-2 45 81.
Main focus on Graeco-Roman times.
Open: Tue, Thu, Fri: 1 - 3 pm, Wed: 4 - 6 pm, Sat: 11 am - 1 pm, Sun: 2 - 4 pm. Admission free.

Bibelmuseum/University Bible Museum, (21), Georgskommende 7, tel.: 83-2 25 80.
Illustration of Biblical history. Single sheets are printed with a reproduction of the famous Gutenberg press.
Open: Wed: 11 am - 1 pm, Thu: 5 - 7 pm, 1st Sat of the month: 10 am - 1 pm. Groups by appmt only. Admission free.

Botanischer Garten/Botanical Gardens (15), Schlossgarten 3, tel.: 83-2 48 19 / 83-2 38 27.
Open: Mar 15 - May 14: 8 am - 5 pm / May 15 - Sept 30: 8 am - 7 pm / Oct 1 - 31: 8 am - 5 pm / Nov 1 - Mar 14: 8 am - 4 pm. Admission free.

Domkammer/Cathedral Chamber (29), Horsteberg, tel.: 424 71.
Objects from 10 centuries illustrate the art and religious culture of the cathedral .
Open: Tue - Sun: 11am - 4 pm.

Droste-Museum Haus Rüschhaus (60), MS-Nienberge, tel.: 0 25 33 / 13 17.
Built by J. C. Schlaun in the baroque style (1745). Here, Annette von Droste zu Hülshoff wrote unforgettable poetry. Paintings, manuscripts and valuable pers. possessions.
Open/guided tours: Mar 1 - Apr 30 / Nov 1 - Dec 23: Tue - Sun: 11 + 12 am / 2 + 3 pm; May 1 - Oct 31: Tue - Sun: 10, 11, 12 am / 2.30 - 4.30 pm half-hourly.

Eisenbahnmuseum/Railway Museum of the Carnival Assn 'Pängelanton', Albersloher Weg, MS-Gremmendorf. Steam engines.
Open: Sun: 11 am - 12.30 pm, groups by appmt, tel.: 61 73 13, Admission free.

Eisenbahnmuseum Münster / Railway Museum ('Friends of the Railways'), former engine shed, Lippstädter Str. 80, tel.: 66 23 36 or 025 06 / 79 11.

Friedenssaal im Rathaus/Hall of Peace (33), tel.: 4 92-27 24.
Open: Mon - Fri: 9 am - 5 pm, Sat: 9 am - 4 pm, Sun / publ. holidays: 10 am - 1 pm.

Geologisch-Paläontologisches Museum/ University Museum of Geology & Palaeontology (25), Pferdegasse 3, tel.: 83-2 39 42.
Finds from millions of years on display. The world's largest skeleton of a mammoth.
Open: Mon - Fri: 9 am - 5 pm; Sun: 10.30 am - 12.30 pm. Admission free.

Hiltruper Museum (former steam-powered Wentrup mill), Osttor 2, tel.: 02501/10 63.
Open: Sun: 10.30 - 12 am, groups by appmt. Admission free.

Karnevalsmuseum / Carnival Mus., Paohlbürgerhof, Heumannsweg 127, tel.: 31 59 27.
Open: by appointment.

Lepramuseum / Leprosy Museum, MS-Kinderhaus, Kinderhaus 15, tel.: 28 51-0.
Paintings, maps and models document the history of leprosy. *Open*: by appointment.

Mineralogisches Museum / University Museum of Mineralogy (18), Hüfferstr. 1, tel.: 83-3 34 51. Extensive collections: crystals, minerals, stones, precious stones.
Open: Wed: 3 - 6 pm, Sun: 10.30 am - 12.30 pm. Groups by appointment. Admission free.

Mühlenhof-Freilichtmuseum/open-air museum (57), Theo-Breider-Weg 1, tel.: 98 12 00.
History live: e.g. special mills (Bockwindmühle, Rossmühle), baking-house, grain store, miller's house, Gräftenhof and village pub.
Open: Mar 16 - Oct 15: daily from 10 am - 6 pm (ticket off. close at 5 pm); Oct 16 - Mar 15: Sun: 11 am - 4.30 pm, Tue - Sat: 1 pm - 4.30 pm (ticket off. close at 5 pm). Tours for groups outside the regular open. hrs by appmt; excellent guided tours on offer: vigorous Kiepenkerle take you on an entertaining tour through the grounds of the museum. Café (open daily during the summer; rest of the year at the week-ends only).

Museum für Lackkunst /Mus. of Lacquer Work (65), Windthorststr. 26, tel.: 418 51-0.
The world's only collection of this kind pre-

sents the hist. of lacquer work over the last 2000 years; exhibits from Eastern and Southeast Asia, Europe and the Islamic world. Special exhibitions round off the programme. *Open*: Tue: 12 am - 8 pm, admission free; Wed - Sun & pub. hols: 12 am - 6 pm. Free guided tour on Sundays at 3 pm.

Orgelmuseum / Organ Museum, Sessendrupweg, MS-Nienberge, tel.: 0 25 33 / 22 10. Organ from around 1870, single organ elements, models, enlarged photos. Open by appointment. Admission free.

Stadtmuseum / City Museum (37), Salzhof / Salzstrasse 28, tel.: 4 92-45 03.
Wide variety of exhibits related to the hist. of Münster from the beginning up to the present. *Open*: Tue - Sun: 10 am - 6 pm. Guided tours on Sun at 4 pm. Groups also on weekdays (exc. Mon) by appointment. Admission free.

Westf. Landesmuseum f. Kunst u. Kulturgeschichte / Westph. Museum of Art & Cult. History (27), Domplatz 10, tel.: 59 07 - 01.
Paintings from the early Middle Ages, sculptures. Glass paintings, Westphalian panel painting from the late Gothic period. Arts, craftwork and regional history up to the present. Modern period: Impressionism, Expressionism, Bauhaus, Informal art, Constructivism, Op art, Nouveau Réalisme.
Open: Tue - Sun: 10 am - 6 pm. Café, shop.

Westfäl. Museum für Archäologie / Westphalian Museum of Archaeology (27), Rothenburg 30, tel.: 59 07 02.
Prehistory and early history of Westphalia, antiquities from the Bronze and pre-Roman Iron Age as well as Westphalian finds up to the early Middle Ages.
Open: Tue - Sun: 10 am-6 pm.

Westfäl. Museum für Naturkunde / Westphal. Museum of Natural History and **Planetarium (58)**, Sentruper Str. 285, tel.: 591 05. Programme Planetarium: tel.: 591-60 00.
Special exhibitions: "Indians" and "dinosaurs", astronomy, mineralogy, palaeontology, indigenous mammals (dioramas), evolution of man. *Open* Museum: Tue - Sun: 9 am - 6 pm. Guided tours (charged extra) by appmt, tel.: 5 91 60 97; Appointments for museum edu-

cationalist: tel.: 5 91 60 50. Admission free on Fridays. Presentations in the **Planetarium** (different daily and monthly programmes): Tue - Fri: 10 + 11 am/ 3 pm, Sat: 3/ 4 pm, Sun + pub. hols: 2/ 3/ 4/ 5 pm; other events: tel.: 5 91 - 60 00 (tape). Groups, please contact tel.: 5 91-60 99, Mon - Thur: 10 - 12 am/ 2 - 3 pm; Fri: 10 - 12 am.

Westpreussisches Landesmuseum / West Prussian State Museum (Drostenhof), MS-Wolbeck, Am Steintor 5, Tel. 0 25 06/ 25 50. Important West-Prussia Collection with special sections.
Open: Tue-Sun: 10 am - 6 pm.

Surrounding area:

Baumberger Sandstein-Museum / Sandstone Museum, Gennerich 9, 48329 Havixbeck, tel.: 0 25 07/3 31 75. Permanent exhibition on the 1000 years of mining history and the artistic working of the sandstone, and a professional stone-cutter at work.
Open: Tue - Sun, Mar - Oct: 11 am - 6 pm, Nov - Feb: 1 - 6 pm. Closed from Jan 5 - 19. Admission free. Café.

Droste-Museum Burg Hülshoff, 48329 Havixbeck, tel.: 0 25 34 / 10 52 or 6 57 21.
Here, the poetess Annette von Droste zu Hülshoff was born in 1797. Equipped with special felt overshoes and listening to the taped commentaries, visitors shuffle through the historical yet very comfortable rooms filled with Droste memorabilia. Large gardens. Restaurant in the cellars of the moated castle.
Open: Mar 13 - Dec 20 daily 9.30 am - 6 pm (park and museum). Groups can visit the museum also during the winter months (by appmt).

Museum der historischen Waschtechnik/ Museum of the History of Washing Techniques, 48346 Ostbevern, Schmedehausener Str. 6, tel.: 0 25 32 / 82 16.
Open: Sun: 11 am - 6 pm (Apr 1 - Nov 15) Groups any time by appointment.

Schiffs-Museum / Ship Museum, 48308 Senden, Kanalstr., tel.: 0 25 97 / 83 20.
Open: Tue - Fri: 10 am - 1 pm and 2.30 - 6 pm, Sat: 10 am - 1 pm and 2 - 6 pm, Sun: 10 am - 6 pm.

Churches in Münster

"It either rains or the church bells ring - and, when these two things coincide, it is bound to be Sunday." Though this popular saying does not sound terribly friendly, it nevertheless takes into account that there are really quite a number of churches in Münster. Wonderful churches in fact that are well worth visiting. But, although each church has something different that makes it special, you should nevertheless refrain from trying to visit as many of them as possible in one afternoon just because we tried to list the most interesting and beautiful ones. We have given only the German names to make it easier for you if you have to ask someone the way.
("Stufenhallenkirche" = church with a nave slightly higher than the side-aisles
"Hallenkirche" = church with nave and side-aisles of equal height)

St. Aegidii (44): Aegidiikirchplatz. Former Capucin monastery, consists of only the nave, built bet. 1724 and 1728, early work of Schlaun. ☞ Sandstone façade, wooden pulpit decorated with carvings, paintings by the Nazarenes in the nave.

Apostelkirche (10): An der Apostelkirche. Former church of the Minorite monastery, built *ca* 1200. Oldest Gothic "Hallenkirche" in Münster, extensions dating from the 16th and 17th cent.
☞ paintings in the vaults dating from the 15th to 17th cent.

Clemenskirche (35): Klemensstr. Most important baroque church in northwest Germany, cylindrical build. with a dome-shaped roof, façade Westph. baroque, interior with rococo elements, built bet. 1745 and 1753 by Schlaun, originally part of a complex consisting of the St Clemens monastery and hospital of the order of the Brethren of Charity, today solitary building.
☞ fresco in the cupola depicting the ascension of St Clemens, altarpieces.

Dominikanerkirche (34): Salzstr. Built bet. 1705 and 1725 in the Roman baroque style by Lambert Friedrich von Corfey, a mentor

Tomb of Bishop Erpho in St Mauritz

of Johann Conrad Schlaun; today Rom. Cath. university church; on the left-hand side detached ruin of the façade of the former monastery.
☞ baroque sandstone façade with Roman elements, richly decorated baroque altar by Heinrich Gröne.

Erlöserkirche (39): Friedrichstr. Protest. church built in 1900, destroyed in World War II; new church built in 1950 as part of the "Otto Bartning (arch.) Emergency Churches Programme"; financed by the American section of the Intern. Union of Lutheran Churches.
☞ modern wooden interior.

Johanniskapelle (3): bet. Breul and Bergstrasse. Originally church of the order of St John, building began in 1311; in 1620 the façade was adapted to fit the late Renaissance style.

Kirche der Lotharinger Chorfrauen (7): Hörster Str. / Lotharinger Str. Built bet. 1764 and 1772 by Schlaun; today, Municipal Archives.

St. Lamberti (31): Prinzipalmarkt. "Hallen-kirche" from the Westphalian late Gothic period, built bet. *ca* 1375 and 1450.

☞ Attached to the base of its neo-Gothic spire (built in 1898 on the model of Freiburg Minster) are the cages in which the corpses of the Anabaptists' leaders were put on public display in 1536. Still today there is a watchman in the tower; large relief of the Tree of Jesse in the pointed arch above the south portal, figures of the Apostles in the choir (*ca* 1600) and figures of the Church Fathers in the side choir, statue of the Virgin Mary at the southern column of the choir, modern glass paintings in the choir, winged altar-piece, *ca* 16th cent.

St. Ludgeri (43): Marienplatz. Presumably the oldest "Stufenhallenkirche" in the Münsterland, built around 1200, new choir after a fire in the 14th cent.; Romanesque crossing-tower, Gothic "crown" added later.

☞ baptismal font from the beg. of the 16th cent., madonna (15th cent.), baroque organ from 1750, choir-stall carvings from the 16th cent., panel paintings by Nikolaus tom Ring the Younger from 1598, wooden crucifix created by Heinrich Bäumer (1929).

St. Martini (8): Martinistr. Gothic "Hallen-kirche", middle of the 14th cent., Romanesque tower with baroque tower roof by Schlaun (1760).

☞ Star-vaulting from the 14th cent., silver candelabra from the 18th century.

St. Mauritz: Stiftsstrasse / Hohenzollern-ring. Former collegiate church on the eastern fringe of the city centre, several extensions and alterations, early Romanesque basements of the main tower and the choir towers are remains of the first church build. (oldest ecclesiastical monuments in Münster), Gothic choir, baroque western tower roof, late Romanesque nave is an imitation from the 19th cent.

☞ Tomb of Bishop Erpho, eastern towers with sandstone relief (1090), panel painting (Hermann tom Ring), Cross of Erpho.

Observantenkirche (13): Schlaunstrasse. Built around the end of the 17th cent. for the Franciscan observants, typical "Jesuite sty-le", i.e. a combination of Gothic and baroque elements; now Protestant university church.

St. Paulus-Dom (29): Domplatz. Last of three cathedral buildings, built 1225-1265, basilica with eastern and western transept, late Romanesque cathedral with late Gothic alterations and extensions from the 16th and 17th cent.; modern western front following the destruction of the old façade in World War II.

☞ "Paradies" (portico) with remarkable pieces of sculpture: Statues of the Apostles (13th cent.); bronze baptismal font (14th cent.), astronomical clock from 1542 with perpetual calendar, larger than life statue of St Christopher from 1627, Chapel of St Liudger with the tomb of Cardinal von Galen, tomb of the Prince-Bishop Christoph Bernhard von Galen, retables (16th cent.), treasury with golden head-shaped reliquary of St Paul (12th cent.) next to the cloister.

Petrikirche (23): between Pferdegasse and Krummer Timpen. Gothic basilica with Renaissance elements, built bet. 1591 and 1598, originally a Jesuit church, it later became the church of the Gymnasium Paulinum, new interior created by contemporary artists.

St. Servatii (40): Klemensstrasse. Late Romanesque "Hallenkirche" with pointed arches in the vault marking the transition to the early Gothic period, built around 1230; late Gothic choir added ca 1500.

☞ left side-aisle with late Gothic winged altar from 1480; this church was almost completely destroyed in World War II; meticulously reconstructed after the war.

Überwasserkirche (14): also called Lieb-frauenkirche, Katthagenstrasse / Überwasserkirchplatz, Gothic "Hallenkirche", built between 1340 and 1370.

☞ richly ornamented portal, some of the original portal sculptures are now to be seen in the Westph. Mus. of Art & Cult. Hist., interior of the church destroyed in the war, therefore modern elements such as the bronze doors of the south portal (1971) and glass paintings (1972); missing Gothic spire was dragged down by the Anabaptists, who used the tower as a platform for their cannons.

Sculpture - A Selection

The following list of pieces of sculpture and memorials in Münster is a rather subjective selection of interesting outdoor objects. Some of them were part of the 1977, 1978 and 1997 open-air sculpture exhibitions. We decided to dispense with long explanations as no description can really replace the direct confrontation with a work of art.

near the Aasee:

Ilya Kabakov: *"Blickst Du hinauf und liest die Worte..." / "Looking up. Reading the words..."* (1997) Out of the city centre on the right-hand shore of the Aasee just before you reach the big Aasee bridge.

Mario Merz: *Die optische Ebene / The visual aspect* (1987) in the cage in the Old Zoo in front of the WestLB building.

Henry Moore: *Three Piece Sculpture: Vertebrae / Dreiteilige Skulptur: Wirbel* (1968/69) Himmelreichallee, grounds of the Old Zoo / park around the WestLB building

Claes Oldenburg: *Giant Pool Balls* (1977) On the lawn next to the Aasee; towards the city centre.

Jorge Pardo: *Pier / Installation* (1997) Northern shore of the Aasee; near Tormin bridge

near the Promenade:

Karl Hans Bernewitz: *Magd mit Ochs und Bauer mit Pferd / Maid and Ox, Farmer and Horse* (1912) in front of the Stadthaus II at the Ludgeriplatz roundabout

Anni Buschkötter: *Unteilbares Deutschland/Indivisible Germany* (1960) small park next to the Promenade at the corner Salzstrasse / Von-Vincke-Strasse

Bernhard Frydag: *Kriegerdenkmal für die Einigungskriege/War Memorial to the French-German War of 1871*(1909) small park on the Promenade north of the Mauritztor

Unknown Gardener: *artistically trimmed hedge with animal motifs* (carefully kept in form during the summer) Westerholtsche Wiese, near Promenade; left-hand side of the Schloss

George Rickey: *Rotierende Quadrate/Rotating Squares* (1973) Engelenschanze

Anton Rüller / Heinrich Fleige: *Annette von Droste Hülshoff* (1896) Kreuzschanze, on the Promenade, on a level with the Buddenturm

Herman de Vries: *Sanctuarium* (1997) In the park north of the Schlossgraben (moat)

in the city centre: (inside Promenade ring)

Lothar Baumgarten: *Irrlichter/Will-o'-the-Wisps* (1987) In the cages of St Lambert - they glow in the evening

Eduardo Chillida: *Toleranz durch Dialog/ Tolerance through Dialogue* (1993) inner court of the City Hall

Heinrich Fleige / Lenz: *Franz Freiherr von Fürstenberg* (1875) on the lawn in front of the Fürstenberghaus next to the Cathedral Square

(concept) **Hubert Gerhard:** *Mariensäule/ St Mary's Column* (1899) Marienplatz, at the end of Ludgeristrasse (pedestrian precinct)

Heinrich Lienkamp: *Madonna an der Aa/ Madonna on the River Aa* (1965) on the bank of the Aa, close to the Überwasserkirche and the nearby small bridge over the Aa (Spiegelturm)

Albert Mazzotti sen. / Ostlinning: *Kiepenkerl* (1953) Spiekerhof / Bogenstrasse

Ulrich Rückriem: *Dolomit zugeschnitten/ Dolomit Cut to Size* (1976) Jesuitengang, opposite the Petrikirche, half-way bet. Westph. Mus. of Art&Cult. Hist. and Juridicum

Thomas Schütte: *Kirschensäule/Cherry Column* (1987) on the Harsewinkelplatz, only a few steps away from the Ludgeristrasse (pedestrian precinct)

Tom Otterness: *Überfrau / Superwoman* (1993) Alter Steinweg, bet. the wings of the Municipal Library

149

Moated Castles

The Münsterland without its numerous moated castles is as difficult to imagine as Münster without its famous historical City Hall. Neither of them should be missed if you visit this region. Some castles and aristocratic mansions have already been presented in the chapter "Discover Münster's Surroundings". As there is a vast number of moated castles ("Wasserschloss" or "Wasserburg") and mansions as well as "Gräftenhöfe" (farmhouses on moated farmsteads) scattered all over the region, not all of them could be mentioned. Therefore, we have prepared another small selection for you. In addition, you can ask the tourist information office for further details. They provide brochures and guided tours to various castles in and around Münster and the Münsterland (such as the "100-castles route"). If you should wish to visit all the castles by bicycle, you have to cover a distance of a mere 2000 km. Good luck!

Ahaus:

- *Wasserschloss Ahaus*, exterior accessible, guided tours (of the ext.) by appmt: Tel. 0 25 61 / 7 22 - 88 / 7 22 - 84.

Ascheberg-Herbern:

- *Schloss Westerwinkel*, tel.: 0 25 99/ 9 88 78 open (interior): May - Oct: Fri - Sun and on public holidays: 2 - 5 pm, park.

Bad Bentheim:

- *Burg Bentheim*, tel.: 0 59 22 / 50 98 / 73 13, open (interior): Mar 1 - Oct 31 daily from 10 am - 6 pm; Nov, Jan and Febr: Sat, Sun and public holidays from 10 am till dusk.

Borken:

- *Burg Gemen*, tel.: 0 28 61/ 92 20-0, guided tours of the exterior and interior only by appmt, tel.: 0 28 61/ 9 39-2 52 (see photo on the right-hand side)

Drensteinfurt:

- *Haus Steinfurt*, tel.: 0 25 08/ 9 95-1 64(-163), Guided tours (of the ext.) by appmt.

Ennigerloh-Ostenfelde:

- *Schloss Vornholz*, tel. 0 25 24/ 83 00, tours of the interior only for groups by appmt, exterior accessible any time.

Havixbeck:

- *Burg Hülshoff*, tel.: 0 25 34/ 10 52/ 6 57 21 open: Mar 13 - Dec 20 daily from 9.30 am - 6 pm, Droste-Museum (guided tours / tape recordings), large gardens, restaurant, game enclosure.

- *Haus Stapel*, tel. 0 25 07 / 75 10, not open to the public.

Lüdinghausen:

- *Burg Vischering*, tel.: 0 25 91 / 36 72/ 36 21, open (interior) Tue - Sun: 10 am - 12.30 pm/ 1.30 - 5.30 pm, Nov- Mar: only till 4.30 pm, exterior any time, restaurant in the vaults.

Münster: (excluding the city centre: Schloss and Erbdrostenhof - see index)

- *Haus Rüschhaus* (Nienberge), Droste-Museum, guided tours of the rooms: Mar 1- Apr 30 and Nov 1 - Dec 23: Tue - Sun: 11+ 12 am, 2 + 3 pm, May 1 - Oct 31: Tue - Sun: 10, 11 and 12 am and from 2.30 to 4.30 pm half-hourly, grounds open to visitors, tel.: 0 25 33 / 13 17.

- *Schloss Wilkinghege*, grounds open to visitors any time, restaurant, café, hotel.

- *Wallburg Haskenau*, motte-castle in the woods near Gelmer, easy to get at.

- *Drostenhof Wolbeck* (Wolbeck), Westpreußisches Landesmuseum, Am Steintor 5, tel.: 0 25 06/ 25 50, open: Tue - Sun: 10am - 6 pm, grounds open to visitors any time.

- *Dyckburg* (Handorf), tel. 02 51 / 3 23 50, ext. accessible, church not during service.

Wasserburg Gemen

Nordkirchen:

- *Schloss Nordkirchen*, tel. 0 25 96 / 91 71 37 (tourist inf.) / 93 34 02. Open (interior): Sun: 2 - 6 pm; by appmt daily from 9 am - 6 pm, grounds open to the public any time, restaurant.

Ochtrup-Welbergen:

- *Haus Welbergen*, tel.: 02 51/ 48 48 80, tours of the interior only for groups, by appmt; exterior accessible any time.

Raesfeld:

- *Schloss Raesfeld*, tel.: 0 28 65 /95 51 27, Museum and chapel open on Sat and Sun from 2.30 to 6 pm, exterior accessible any time, restaurant.

Sassenberg-Füchtorf:

- *Schloss Harkotten-Korff*, tel.: 0 54 26/ 22 16 grounds open to the public, visit of the chapel by appmt.

Selm-Cappenberg:

- *Schloss Cappenberg*, tel.: 0 23 06 / 7 11 70, Open during exhibitions only, branch of the Westphalian Museum of Art and Cultural History in Münster.

Senden:

- *Schloss Senden*, tel.: 0 25 97/ 69 92 08, exterior accessible any time; restaurant.

- *Haus Alvinghoff* (Bösensell), tel.: 0 25 36/ 2 13, exterior accessible by appmt only.

- *Haus Ruhr* (Bösensell), tel.: 0 25 36/ 2 51, exterior accessible by appmt only.

Steinfurt-Burgsteinfurt:

- *Schloss Steinfurt*, only groups, guided tours obligatory: tel.: 0 25 51 / 13 83, exterior accessible.

Velen:

- *Schloss Velen*, tel.: 0 28 63 / 9 26-2 19 / 20 30, exterior accessible any time.

Calendar of Events

January:
- 4-day Riding and Show Jumping Competition in Münster
- International Münster Jazz Festival (every other year,1999, 2001 ...)

February:
- Carnival parade on the Monday preceding Ash Wednesday
- Antique Fair (Halle Münsterland)

March:
- "Send" - large fair on the Hindenburgplatz in Münster (5 days)

April:
- Gronau Jazz Festival
- traditional bonfires lit on Easter Saturday in the Münsterland

May:
- "Wild Horse Round-Up" in the Merfelder Bruch near Dülmen (last weekend in May)
- Big flea market on the Hindenburgplatz
- Münster Motorcycle Days
- May or June, every 3 years (1998, 2001 usw.) festive procession of the bakers' guild in Münster (Good Monday)
- "Stadtfest" Münster - arts and crafts stalls, musical events on several open-air stages, food and drink stalls and much more to enjoy in the city centre (May or June)
- Wine Festival in the Schlossgarten organized by the Münster wine dealers

June:
- "Send" on the Hindenburgplatz (5 days)
- University Summer ball in the Schloss
- Baroque Festival in Münster and the Münsterland
- Festival of Painting (Aegidiimarkt)

July:
- big flea market on the Hindenburgplatz
- Great Procession (city centre / cathedral)

August:
- "Turnier der Sieger". Important riding and show jumping event in Münster

"Turnier der Sieger"

- Kite Flying Festival by the Aasee
- Big flea market on the Hindenburgplatz
- Palatinate Wine Festival (at the Stadthaus I)

September:
- St Lambert's Day celebrations in Münster: lantern processions for the children
- "Hengstparade" in Warendorf (Stallion Show, presentation of horsemanship and dressage)
- Big flea market on the Hindenburgplatz
- "Mariä-Geburts-Markt" in Telgte, biggest horse market in the region, also a fair
- Arts and Crafts Fair in the inner court of the City Hall / Münster
- Pottery Fair (at the Aegidiimarkt)
- "Stadtschützenfest" - competition feat. the rifle clubs of Münster (Hindenburgplatz)

October:
- Warendorf Stallion Show
- "Send" (5 days) on the Hindenburgplatz

November:
- "Europe's Largest Ninepin Bowling Party" in the Halle Münsterland in Münster
- Start of the Christmas markets

December:
- Christmas markets in Münster (at St Lambert's Church, in the Kiepenkerl Quarter, inner court of the City Hall, Aegidiimarkt)
- Holiday on Ice (Halle Münsterland)

Historical Outline

from 6th cent. B.C. proofs of settlements on what was later to become the Cathedral Hill

2nd cent. A.D. Frankish settlement on the Horsteberg

7th cent. A.D. Saxon settlement on the Horsteberg named "Mimigernaford"

792 Charlemagne sends the Frisian missionary Liudger out to convert the inhabitants of Westphalia (West Saxons)

from 793 building of a fortified monastery ("Monasterium") on the Horsteberg under the direction of the missionary Liudger

805 the monk Liudger is consecrated first bishop of Münster

10th cent. protected cathedral stronghold attracts traders; first merchant settlement

1090 Bishop Erpho consecrates the 2nd cathedral building

1121 settlement destroyed by the Duke Lothar von Supplinburg

1150 ramparts surrounding the whole settlement replace the fortifications around the cathedral stronghold; gradually, the settlement develops into a town with specific rights and a growing independence from its bishop

around 1200 first city wall is built in the area of the ramparts

from 12th cent. flourishing economy, far-reaching trade relations

1246 Treaty of Ladbergen signed by Münster, Osnabrück, Minden, Herford and Coesfeld for the mutual protection of their travelling merchants against robbery

from 13th cent. Münster is admitted to the Hanseatic League, 1253 town alliance with Dortmund, Lippstadt and Soest

1264 consecration of the 3rd cathedral building (Cathedral of St Paul)

1350 the Black Death strikes Münster, persecution of supposedly responsible Jews

1450-1457 "Münsterische Stiftsfehde" (diocese feud). Open conflict bet. clergy and the townspeople. The guilds finally succeed in sending representatives into the council, the town strengthens its rights in relation to the prince-bishop

since 1500 growing displeasure at the church property's exemption from taxes, beginning of the reformation in 1517, Luther's teachings are preached from the pulpits in Münster, too

1534 terror of the Anabaptists' reign; Münster is besieged by the troops of the Prince-Bishop Franz von Waldeck

June 1535 von Waldeck recaptures Münster thanks to an act of betrayal by one of the besieged

January 1536 public execution of the Anabaptists' leaders Bernd Krechting, Bernd Knipperdollinck and their "King" Jan van Leiden

1541-1553 restoration of the municipal rights and liberties

1618-1648 Thirty Years' War

1643-1648 Münster receives neutral status during the time of the peace congress

1648 Treaty of Westphalia, ratification of the peace treaty bet. Spain and the Netherlands, treaties bet. the Emperor and France as well as Sweden

1650-1678 Christoph Bernhard von Galen rules as Prince-Bishop of Münster

1661 after a long siege, Münster finally surrenders to the prince-bishop; reduction of municipal rights; a citadel is built

1756-1763 Seven Years' War, Münster under changing rule; sieges and bombardment of the city

1764 Franz von Fürstenberg, the electoral minister, orders the dismantling of the fortifications, conversion into a promenade; expansion of the city; the Schloss is built

1773 foundation of the university

1802 Prussians seize power under the leadership of General Blücher in the episcopal principality of Münster, 1803 secularization

1816 After a few years under French rule, Münster becomes the capital of the Prussian province of Westphalia.

1821 the diocese is re-established

1848 First railway link between Münster and Hamm

1899 official opening of the Dortmund-Ems Canal by Emperor Wilhelm II; a connection to the Ruhr area and to the North Sea

1914-18 World War One, Münster's population reaches the 100,000 mark, the war causes suffering here and everywhere else

1927 construction of the Aasee starts

1930 Dr Heinrich Brüning, born in Münster, becomes the Chancellor of the Reich

1941-45 102 allied air raids destroy 51% of the town, more than 90% of the old part of Münster lies in ruins

1941 Bishop Clemens August Graf von Galen preaches against euthanasia, terror and despotism of the Nazi regime; in 1946, von Galen is appointed cardinal by the pope.

1945 After the end of World War II, the city is occupied by the Allied Forces and be-

comes part of the British occupied zone; a newly appointed Provincial Government for Westphalia has its seat in Münster

in the 50s post-war reconstruction, partly with the help of old building plans and photos (old part of the town, esp. the hist. City Hall), partly modern buildings (Municipal Theatre, admin. buildings; important institutions such as the Const. Court of Law of North-Rhine Westphalia are established.

1954 last tram removed from the streets

1966 population of Münster reaches the 200,000 mark; university gains more and more importance

1975 Communal restructuring of NRW; the neighbouring villages of Albachten, Amelsbüren, Angelmodde, Handorf, Hiltrup, St. Mauritz, Nienberge, Roxel and Wolbeck incorporated into Münster

1981 270,000 inhabitants

1990 meeting of the German and Soviet foreign ministers in Münster's City Hall (Genscher / Schewardnadse)

1992 European economic summit; the former Soviet president Gorbatschow visits the city

1993 1200-year city jubilee ("Tolerance" as the leading idea); opening of the new Municipal Library and technology centre

1994 for the first time since 1945 the Christian Dem. Party forms the opposition in Münster: a coalition of Social Dem. and the Green Party rules in the City Hall. Marion Tüns is the first female mayor in the history of Münster

1997 third intern. renowned sculpture exhibition "Skulptur. Projekte in Münster 97"

1998 350-year celebrations commemorating the "Treaty of Westphalia" of 1648

S E R V I C E

Culinary Münster

The next chapter will help you to find your way through "culinary Münster". No matter whether you are a "traditionalist" or more of an "experimentalist" among the gourmets, you will find something that suits your taste. A wide range of restaurants in Münster serves almost everything from Westphalian to typical Russian meals.

You do not have to suffer from thirst either: numerous cafés, restaurants and pubs cater for the many visitors. We have prepared a selection for you. Now then, "Guten Appetit" and "Zum Wohl" in Münster.

First-class restaurants

Krautkrämers Restaurant in the **Waldhotel Krautkrämer.** Am Hiltruper See, Mon - Sun: 12 am - 2.30 pm / 6.30 - 10 pm, tel.: 0 25 01 / 80 50

Schloss Wilkinghege. Steinfurter Str. 374, Mon - Sun: 12 am - 2 pm / 6 - 10 pm, tel.: 21 30 45/46

Villa Medici. Ostmarkstr. 15, Tue - Sat: 6 - 10.30 pm / at noon by appmt (closed Sun, Mon), tel.: 3 42 18

Quality restaurants

Altes Brauhaus Kiepenkerl. Spiekerhof 45, Wed - Mon: 11 am - 12 pm, (closed Tue) tel.: 4 03 34

Bakenhof. Roxelerstr. 376, Wed - Sun: 12 am - 2 pm, Thur: 6 - 10.30 pm, Wed + Fri - Sun: 6 - 10 pm (closed Mon, Tue), tel.: 86 15 06

Das Torhaus. Mauritzstr. 27, Wed - Sun: 6 pm - 1 am (closed Mon, Tue), tel.: 4 53 73

ET up'n Bült. Bült 23, Mon - Sat: 5 pm - 1am, Sun + pub. hols: 6 pm - 1 am, tel.: 4 32 35

Feldmann. In the Hotel Feldmann, Klemensstr. 23-24, Mon - Sat: 12 am - 2 pm / 5.30 - 10 pm, tel.: 4 14 49-0

Giverny. Königspassage / Hötteweg 9, Tue - Sun: 11 am - 3 pm / 6 - 12 pm (closed Mon), tel.: 51 14 35

Hof zur Linde. Handorfer Werseufer 1, Mon - Sun: 12 am - 10 pm, tel.: 32 75-0

Il Cucchiaio d'argento. Warendorfer Str. 177, Sun - Fri: 12 am - 2 pm / 6 - 11 pm, Sat: 6 - 11pm, tel.: 39 20 45

Kleines Restaurant im Oer'schen Hof. Königsstr. 42, Tue - Sat: 12 am - 2 pm / 7 - 9.30 pm (closed Sun, Mon), tel.: 4 20 61

Lotusgarten. Marktallee 22 (Hiltrup), Mon - Sun: 12 am - 2.30 pm / 5.30 - 11.30 pm, tel.: 0 25 01 / 74 04

Landhaus-Restaurant. In the Parkhotel **Schloss Hohenfeld** (Roxel). Dingbängerweg 400, Mon - Sun: 12 am - 2 pm / 6 - 9.30 pm, tel.: 0 25 34 / 8 08-100

Pleister-Mühle. Pleistermühlenweg 196, Thur - Tue: 11 am - 12 pm, tel.: 31 10 72

Prinzipal. (**Dorint**-Hotel) Engelstr. 39, Mon - Sun: 12 am - 2.30 pm / 6.30 - 10 pm, tel.: 4 17 16 40. Tacko-Bar: Mon - Sun: 7 - 1 am, tel.: 4 17 13 00 (Café-Bistroll: Mon - Sun: 11 am - 11pm)

Rössli. (**Mövenpick**) Kardinal-v.-Galen-Ring 65, Mon - Sun: 12 am - 3 pm / 5 - 12 pm, Sat: only 6 - 12 pm, tel.: 89 02-6 27

Steinburg am Aasee. Mecklenbecker Str. 80, Mon - Sun: 12 am - 2 pm / 6 - 9.30 pm, tel.: 7 71 79

Tannenhof. Prozessionsweg 402, Tue - Sun: 12 am - 2 pm / 6 - 11.30 pm, tel.: 3 13 73

Tokyo Acacia. Friedrich-Ebert-Platz 2, Tue - Sat: 6 - 10 pm (closed Mon, Sun), tel.: 52 79 95

Wein- und Austernkeller in the **Butter-handlung "Holstein".** Bogenstr. 9, Tue, Wed: 10 am - 7 pm / Thur, Fri: 10 am - 7.30 pm / Sat: 9 - 3 / 4 / 6 pm, tel.: 4 49 44

Plain cooking

Elisabeth zur Aa. Bergstr. 67, Mon - Sun: 11.30 am - 12 pm, tel.: 5 89 51

Gast bei FF. Rothenburg 5, Mon - Fri: 11 am - 11 pm / Sat: 11 am - 3 / 7 pm, tel.: 4 35 58

Münnich. Heeremansweg 11, Mon - Sun: 10 am - 12 pm, tel.: 61 87-4 91

Nemann's Gasthaus. Metzer Str. 58, Mon - Sat: 10 am - 12 pm, Sun: 10 am - 3 pm / 5 -12 pm, tel.: 77 67 39

Pulcinella. Kreuzstr. 28/29, Mon - Sun: 6 - 12 pm, kitchen open till 11.30 pm, tel.: 4 66 40

Restaurant in the **Kolping-Tagungshotel.** Aegidiistr. 21, Mon - Sun: 6.30 am - 10 pm, tel.: 48 12-0

Stuhlmacher. Prinzipalmarkt 6, Mon - Thur: 10 am - 12 pm, Fri, Sat 10 - 1 am, Sun: 11 am - 12 pm, tel.: 4 48 77

Wielers Kleiner Kiepenkerl. Spiekerhof 47, Tue - Sun: 10.30 am - 12 pm (closed Mo), tel: 434 16

Wienburg. Kanalstr. 237, Tue - Sun: 10 am - 12 pm (closed Mon), tel.: 29 33 54 / 27 32 34

Zum alten Pulverturm. Breul 9, Mon - Sun: 5 - 12 pm (winter), Mon - Fri: 4 - 12 pm, Sat, Sun: 12 am - 12 pm (summer), if it's "beer garden weather": Mon - Sun: 12 am - 12 pm, tel.: 45830

Specialties:
From American to Westphalian

American

Alabama. Aegidiistr. 46, Sun - Thur: 5 pm -1 am, Fri - Sat: 5 pm - 3 am, tel.: 4 44 37

John Doe's Diner. Spiekerhof 44, Mon - Fri: 5.30 pm - 1 am, Sat: 10.30 - 1am, Sun: 10.30 am - 12 pm, tel.: 51 84 06

Pizza-Hut. Berliner Platz 22, Mon - Thur: 11.30 am - 11pm, Fri, Sat: 11 - 1am, Sun, public hols: 12 am - 11 pm, tel.: 55007

Roadhouse. Rudolf-Diesel-Str. 5-7, Mon - Fri: 8.30 am - 12 pm, Sat, Sun: 10 am - 12 pm, tel.: 1427 22

Chicken

Nordstern. Hoyastr. 3, Mon - Fri: 4 pm - 3 am, Sat, Sun: 11 - 3 am, tel.: 2 21 41 / 2 06 23, chicken till 2.30 am

Wienerwald. Berliner Platz 39, Mon - Sun: 11 - 2 am, tel.: 4 65 75

Chinese

Alt Mandarin. Alter Steinweg 31, Mon -Sun: 12 am - 3 pm / 5.30 - 12 pm, Sat / Sun:12 am - 12 pm, tel.: 4 66 64. Near the Erbdrostenhof.

Hai Cheng. Warendorfer Str. 11, Mon - Sat: 12 am - 3 pm / 5.30 - 12 pm, Sun: 12 am - 12 pm, tel.: 5 44 99

Hong Bin. Kanalstr. 49, Mon - Sat: 12 am - 3 pm / 5.30 - 12 pm, Sun: 12 am - 12 pm, tel.: 2 55 13

Jong Hwa. Bült 2, Thur - Tue: 12 am - 3 pm / 5.30 - 11.30 pm (closed Wed), tel.: 4 62 17

Shanghai. Verspohl 22, Mon - Sun: 11.30 am - 11.30 pm, tel.: 5 64 77. At the end of the Ludgeristrasse (pedestrian precinct).

Crêpes / Baguettes

Château. Kellermannstr. 23, Mon - Sun: 11 am - 11 pm, tel.: 2 21 57

Filou. Warendorfer Str. 57, Mon - Fri: 11.30 am - 2.30 pm / 6 - 12 pm, Sun: 6 - 12 pm (closed Sat), tel.: 3 53 49

French

Das Torhaus. Mauritzstr. 27, Wed - Sun: 6 am - 1 am (closed Mon, Tue), tel.: 4 53 73

Giverny. Königspassage/Hötteweg 9, Tue - Sun: 11 am - 3 pm / 6 - 12 pm (closed Mon), tel.: 51 14 35

Kleines Restaurant im Oer'schen Hof. Königsstr. 42, Tue - Sat: 12 am - 2 pm / 7 - 9.30 pm (closed Sun, Mon), tel.: 4 20 61

Le Midi. Bohlweg 37, Mon - Sun: 6 pm - 1 am, tel.: 44539

Greek

Ambeli. Bohlweg 20, Mon - Sun: 5.30 - 12 pm, tel.: 5 58 45

Odysseus. Engelstr. 60, Mon - Sun: 12 am - 3 pm / 5.30 pm - 1 am, tel.: 53 27 75

Santorin. Schillerstr. 30, Mon - Sun: 6 pm - 1am, tel.: 6 59 39

Tonne des Diogenes. Bergstr. 19, Mon - Fri: 4 - 12 pm, Sat, Sun: 12 am - 12 pm, tel.: 4 74 11

Zorbas. Universitätsstr. 29, Mon - Sun: 12 am - 3 pm / 5.30 - 12 pm / Sat, Sun: 12 am - 12 pm, tel.: 4 59 91

Indian

Delhi. Hamburger Str. 2, Tue - Sun: 6 - 12 pm, tel.: 6 03 00

Taj-Mahal. Bahnhofstr. 64, Mon - Sat: 6 - 12 pm / Sun: 12 am - 3 pm / 6 - 12 pm, tel.: 51 99 85

Indonesian

Bali. Neubrückenstr. 28, Mon - Sun: 12 am - 3 pm / 5.30 - 11.30 pm, tel.: 5 15 51

Italian

"Italian restaurants are really two a penny", the lovers of Mediterranean food might enthuse if they think of the many pizza places, trattorias and ristorantes in Münster. After all, quality prevails.

Al Gambero. Inselbogen 19, Mon - Sun:12 am - 2.15 pm / 6 - 11.30 pm, tel.: 79 27 57

Bella Italia. Oststr. 16 (Hiltrup), Mon - Sun: 12 am - 2.30 pm / 5.30 - 11.30 pm, tel.: 0 25 01 / 1 69 14

Castellino. Warendorfer Str. 44, Mon,Wed - Sat: 11.30 am - 3 pm / 6 -12 pm, tel.: 3 39 95

Dell'Isola. Aegidiistr. 59, Mon - Sat: 11.30 am - 2.45 pm / 6 - 11.30 pm, Sun: 12 am - 2.30 pm / 5.30 - 11pm, tel.: 4 22 35

Il Cucchiaio d'argento. Warendorfer Str. 177, Sun - Fri: 12 am - 2 pm / 6 - 11 pm, Sat: 6 - 11 pm, tel.: 39 20 45, beer garden

Il Gondoliere. Von-Esmarch-Str. 28, Tue - Sun: 11.45 am - 2.45 pm / 5.45 - 11.30 pm, tel.: 828 77

La Cantina. Tibusstr. 7-11 (wine-cellar), Mon - Sun: 6 pm - 1 am, tel.: 5 89 63

La Gondola D'Oro. Hüffer Str. 34, Mon - Sun: 12 am - 2.30 pm / 6 - 11.30 pm, tel.: 80199

Laguna Blu. Grevener Str. 89, 12 am - 2.30 pm / 6 - 12 pm, tel.: 27 45 21

L'Antica. Mauritzstr. 22, Mon - Sat: 6 pm - 1 am (closed Sun), tel.: 4 55 45

La Vela. Mecklenbeckerstr. 112, Mon - Sun: 11.30 am - 3 pm / 5.30 - 11 pm, tel.: 79 67 65

L'Ostaria Pasta e Basta. Neubrückenstr. 35-37, Mon - Sat: 12 am - 2.30 pm / Mon - Sun: 6 - 12 pm, tel.: 4 42 94

Pane e vino. Neubrückenstr. 35-37, Mon - Thur: 5.30 pm - 1 am, Fri: 5 pm - 3 am, Sat: 12.30 pm - 3 am, Sun: 5.30 pm - 1am, tel.: 5 46 45

Philitia. Mangiare all' italiana. Frauenstr. 32, Mon - Sat: 12 am - 2.30 pm / 6 - 11 pm, Sun: 5.30 - 11 pm, tel.: 5 55 77

Piccolo. Frauenstr. 26, Mon - Sun: 11.30 am - 3 pm / 5.30 - 0.30 am, tel.: 5 89 40

Portofino. (Gremmend.) Paul-Engelhard-Weg 1-3, Tue - Sat: 12 am - 12 pm, Sun: 12 am - 11 pm, tel.: 61 95 08

San Marco. Königsstrasse. 37, Mon - Sun: 11.30 am - 3 pm / 5.30 - 12 pm, tel.: 4 46 17

Trattoria Salvatore. Eisenbahnstr. 15,Tue - Sun: 12 am - 2.30 pm / 6 - 12 pm, tel.: 5 17 22

Villa Medici. Ostmarkstr. 15, Tue - Sat: 6 - 11.30 pm / at noon by appmt (closed Sun, Mon), tel.: 3 42 18

Japanese

Sushi-Bar in the **Otmar.** Ludgeristr. 100, Mon - Fri: 11 am - 8 pm, Sa: 11 am - 4 pm

Tokyo Acacia. Friedrich-Ebert-Platz 2, Tue - Sat: 6 - 10 pm (closed Mon, Sun), tel.: 52 79 95

159

Latin-American

America Latina. Neubrückenstr. 50, Mon - Fri: 7 - 1 am / Sat, Sun: 12 - 1 am, tel.: 5 56 66

Café Brasil. Hafenstr. 21, Mon - Sun: 6 pm - 1 am, tel.: 53 22 56

Havana 1. Münzstr. 49 / corner Jüdefelderstr. (in the "Kuhviertel"), Mon - Sat: 6 pm-1 am, Sun & pub. hols: 4 pm - 1 am, tel.: 51 88 92

Ipanema. Mauritzstr. 24, Mon - Sun: 12 - 3 am, tel.: 40 40 9

Sabroso. Mauritzstr. 19, Mon - Sun: 6 pm - 3 am (kitchen till 2 am), tel.: 5 59 40

Salsa Verde. Neubrückenstr. 73, Mon - Sun: 11 - 1am, tel.: 4 36 82

Lebanese

Phoenicia. Steinfurter Str. 37, Mon - Sun: 12 am - 12 pm, tel.: 27 87 94. Belly dancing on Tue and Sat

Mexican

Coco Loco. Hindenburgplatz 20, Mon - Fri: 9 - 1 am / Sat, Sun: 5 pm - 1 am, tel.: 4 54 53

Dos Passos. Weseler Str. 32, Mon - Sun: 6 - 12 pm, tel.: 52 26 84

Enchilada im "Lortzingsaal". Arztkarrengasse 12, Mon - Sun: 6 pm - 1 am, tel.: 4 55 66

Persian

Karun. Moltkestr. 13-15, Mon - Sat: 6 pm - 1 am, Sun, pub. hols: 12 - 1 am, tel.: 52 28 81

Russian

Bolschoy. Restaurant, tea-house and café. Steinfurter Str. 130, Mon - Sun: 6 pm - 1 am, tel.: 29 33 61

Spanish

Almeria. Von-Kluck-Str. 15, Mon - Sun: 5 pm - 1 am, tel.: 52 35 62

Cadacqués. Ludgeristr. 62, Mon - Thur: 10.30 - 1 am / Fri, Sat: 10.30 - 3 am, Sun and pub. hols: 3 pm - 1 am, tel.: 4 30 28

El Gran Duque. Hammer Str. 66, Mon - Fri: 12 am - 3 pm / 6 - 11.45 pm, Sat, Sun: 11.30 am - 11.45 pm, tel.: 52 72 22

Steaks

Churrasco. Steakhouse, Neubrückenstrasse 69, Mon - Sun: 11am - 12 pm, tel.: 4 24 12

Tascaria Maredo. Alter Fischmarkt 26, Mon - Sun: 11am - 12 pm, tel.: 5 16 26

Turkish

Anadolu. Café-restaurant. Von-Esmarch-Str. 18, Mon - Sat: 9 am - 11 pm, Sun: 10 am - 11 pm, tel.: 8 24 47

Bogazici. Hammer Str. 61, Mon - Sat: 5.30 pm - 1am, Sun: 12 am - 3 pm / 5.30 pm - 1 am, tel.: 52 73 64

Deniz. Friedrich-Ebert-Str. 8, Tue - Sun: 11am - 2.30 pm / 5.30 - 11 pm, tel.: 53 16 46

Euphrat. Kanalstr. 15, Mon - Sun: 11.30 am -2.30 pm / 6 - 12 pm, tel.: 27 17 24

Vegetarian / Whole-Food

Bio Corner. Bahnhofstr. 19-21 (cent. station), Mon - Sun: 9 am - 8.30 pm, tel.: 4 17 06 26

Bio Corner 2. In the **Otmar**, Ludgeristr. 100, Mon - Sat: 10 am - 8.30 pm, tel.: 5 10 53 96

EssPlanet. Salzstrasse 26 / Salzhof, Mon - Sun: 10 am - 8 pm, tel.: 5 10 53 33

Prütt-Café. Bremer Str. 32, Tue - Sun: 10 - 1 am / Mon: 6 pm - 1 am, tel.: 66 55 88

Rico. Rosenplatz 7, Mon -Fri: 11.30 am - 6.30 pm, Sat: 11.30 am - 5.30 pm, tel.: 45979

Westphalian / German

Alter Steinweg. Alter Steinweg 25, Mon - Sat: from 12 am, tel.: 4 73 56

Altes Gasthaus Leve. Alter Steinweg 37, Tue - Sun: 10 am - 12 pm, tel.: 4 55 95

Börneken. At the Parkhotel Schloss Hohenfeld (Roxel). Dingbänger Weg 400, Mon - Sun: 5 pm - 1 am, tel.: 0 25 34 / 80 8-1 02

Bullenkopp. Alter Fischmarkt 24, Mon - Fri: 4 pm - 3 am, Sat: 11 - 3 am (closed Sun), kitchen open till 2.30 am, tel.: 4 49 42

Drübbelken. Formerly "Westfälischer Friede". Buddenstr. 14-15, Mon - Sun: 11 - 1 am, tel.: 42115

Nemann's Gasthaus. Metzer Str. 58, Mon - Sat: 10 am - 12 pm, Sun: 10 am - 3 pm / 5 - 12 pm, tel.: 77 67 39

Pinkus Müller. Kreuzstr. 4-10, Mon - Fri: 11.30 am - 2 pm / 5 - 12 pm, Sat: 11.30 am - 12 pm, (closed Sun, public hols), tel.: 4 51 51

Stuhlmacher. Prinzipalmarkt 6, Mon - Thur: 10 am - 12 pm, Fri, Sat 10 - 1 am, Sun: 11 am - 12 pm, tel.: 4 48 77

Yugoslavian / Balkan

Balkan Hütte. Ludgeriplatz 7, Mon - Sun: 11.30 am - 2.30 pm / 6 pm - 0.30 am, tel.: 5238 80

Pubs

A lot of pubs in Münster are truly "students' pubs". Small wonder in a city with roughly 54,000 students. But do not let that keep you from visiting the pubs even if you are not a student. People are fairly tolerant, and, besides, you will very likely meet quite a few guests who, though over 35 years old, simply could not part with their student's card even though they are often well and truly members of the "bourgeois establishment".

Alabama. Aegidiistr. 46, Sun - Thur: 5 pm - 1 am, Fri - Sat: 5 pm - 3 am, tel.: 4 44 37. American pubs are "in". Those who get hungry after trying the US beer can order "All you can eat".

Alex Brasserie. Salzstr. 35, Mon - Thur: 9 - 1 am / Fri - Sat: 9 - 3 am / Sun: 9 - 1 am, tel.: 40156. All those for whom Paris is too far away can be seen in this bistro-pub next to the Promenade.

Al Forno. Neubrückenstr. 35-37, Mon - Fri: 9 - 1 am, Sat: 11 - 1 am, Sun: 4 pm - 1 am, tel.: 4 57 87. Friendly bistro-pub serving Italian food.

Alter Steinweg. Alter Steinweg 25, Mon - Sat: from 12 am, tel.: 4 73 56. Guests take their time over a draught beer and enjoy the relaxed atmosphere of the old building.

America Latina. Neubrückenstr. 50, Mon - Fri: 7 - 1 am / Sat, Sun: 12 - 1 am, tel.: 5 56 66. Pubs come and go - the AL will remain. Usually a mixed crowd in an informal atmosphere.

Arthur. Kanonierstr. 3, Mon - Sun: 6.30 pm -1 am, tel.: 27 83 39. Only a stone's throw away from the cinema "Schlosstheater" - ideal for discussing the film afterwards.

Atelier. Das Nachtlokal. Bült 2, Mon - Fri: 6 pm - 6 am, Sat, Sun: 8 pm - 6 am, tel.: 5 74 55. Diagonally opposite the Municipal Theatre - a late-night pub not only for theatre-goers.

Biergalerie. Kreuzstr. 4-10, Mon - Fri: 5 - 12 pm, Sat: 11.30 am - 12 pm, tel.: 4 29 13. Sale of the various brands of "Pinkus" beer.

Blechtrommel. Hansaring 26, Mon - Sun: 6 pm - 1 am, tel.: 6 51 19. Pub on the corner with tasty food - sometimes live music.

Buddenturm. Buddenstr. 1-2, Sun - Thur: 7 pm - 1 am, Fri: 7 pm - 3 am, Sat: 3 pm - 3 am, tel.: 5 60 24. Students' pub opposite the medieval tower of the same name.

Bullenkopp. Alter Fischmarkt 24, Mon - Fri: 4 pm - 3 am, Sat: 11 - 3 am (closed Sun), kitchen open till 2.30 am, tel.: 4 49 42. In the old days, one used to drink the beer from the handy 6-litre tankard, the so-called "Bullen-kopp" (bull's head).

Cadacqués. Ludgeristr. 62, Mon - Thur: 10.30 - 1 am / Fri, Sat: 10.30 - 3 am, Sun and public hols: 3 pm - 1 am, tel.: 4 30 28. Dali would have felt reminded of his Catalonian home: Tapas and Paellas as delicious as in the south.

Café Brasil. Hafenstr. 21, Mon - Sun: 6 pm -1 am, tel.: 53 22 56. This is the meeting-place for South America fans.

Café del Arte. Königsstr. 45, Mon - Sat: from 9 am (disco: Wed, Fri, Sat: 10 pm - 5 am) Sun: 10 - 1 am, tel.: 51 10 29. A highly popular place - this multi-functional café offers breakfast in the morning, then turns into a café and restaurant during the day. In the evening, the combination of disco and pub attracts many visitors.

Café Fundus. Berliner Platz 23, Mon - Thur: 8 - 1 am, Fri: 8 - 3 am, Sat: 10 - 3 am, Sun: 10 - 1 am, tel.: 4 63 59. The light rooms attract many visitors, among them often theatre-goers (as the Wolfgang-Borchert theatre is right next door). Live music in the **Cascade** (also next door).

Café Kolk. Kerssenbrockstr. 30, Mon - Fri: 11 - 1 am / Sat: 2 pm - 1 am / Sun: 10 - 1 am, tel.: 27 96 01. A café in the "Kreuzviertel" that has a certain atmosphere.

Cavete. Kreuzstr. 37/38, Mon - Sun: 7 pm - 1 am, kitchen open till 0.30 am, tel.: 4 57 00. Oldest students' pub in Münster. Simply a "must" for every student.

Coco Loco. Hindenburgplatz 20, Mon - Fri: 9 - 1 am / Sat, Sun: 5 pm - 1 am, tel.: 4 54 53. Here, students build up their strength before, after, and during the lectures. If the weather is fine, you can sit outside during the summer.

Cuba-Kneipe. Achtermannstr. 10-12, Mon - Fri: 5 pm - 1 am / Sat, Sun: 6 pm - 1 am (parties: 1st, 3rd and 4th Sat of the month: 9 pm - 3 am), tel.: 5 82 17. Spacious students' pub with 9 brands of beer on draught.

Das Blaue Haus. Kreuzstr. 16/17, Mon - Sun: 7 pm - 1 am, kitchen open till 0.30 am, tel.: 4 21 51. Bright blue façade - hence the name of the pub.

Der Bunte Vogel. Alter Steinweg 41, Mon - Thur: 11 - 1 am, Fri, Sat: 11 - 2 am, Sun: 12 - 1 am, tel.: 5 65 24. Hustle and bustle on two floors. Some claim that future medics spend most of their spare time in this pub, others say it's mostly law students ... Anyway, at the week-ends, most of Münster's students stop by at least once.

Destille. Kuhstr. 10, Mon - Sun: 8 pm - 1 am, tel.: 4 37 26. Rather small but very nice. For 20 years stars not only from the local jazz and blues scene have been appearing live on stage. Here, there is even a chance of a chat with the musicians.

Dialog. Aegidiistr. 21 (in the "Kolping-Tagungshotel"), Mon - Sat: 11 - 1 am, tel.: 48 12-145. Nomen est omen. But you're allowed to have a drink as well. Beer garden.

Diesel. Harsewinkelplatz, Sun - Wed: 11 - 1 am, Thur, Fri: 11 - 3 am, Sat: 10 - 3 am, tel.: 5 79 67. No, there are no huge lorries in sight - it's a central café-cum-pub in the pedestrian precinct.

Einspruch. Hindenburgplatz 2, Mon - Fri: 9 - 1 am, Sat: 2 pm - 1 am, Sun: 12 am - 11 am, tel.: 4 52 23. Lost your case in the court opposite? Never mind, you can come here to drown your sorrows.

Frauenstr. 24. Frauenstr. 24, Mon - Fri: 9.30 - 1 am / Sat, Sun: 12 - 1 am, tel.: 5 12 06. Typical students' pub in a house formerly occupied by squatters - a wall-painting tells you all about it.

Gambrinus. Königsstr. 34, Mon - Fri: 10 - 1 am / Sat: 12 - 1 am, Sun: 10 am - 3 pm / 6 pm - 1 am, tel.: 5 87 38. Enjoy beer and schnitzel at pre-war prices.

Grand Café. Hörsterstr. 51, Tue - Thur: 5 pm - 1 am, Fri, Sat: 5 pm - 3 am (Fri, Sat: disco 11 pm - 3 am), Sun: 6 pm - 1 am, tel.: 5 75 17. See and be seen. Often absolutely crammed with good-looking people - the rest pretend to be rich.

Havana1. Münzstr. 49 / corner Jüdefelder-str. (in the "Kuhviertel"), Mon - Sat: 6 pm - 1 am, Sun and pub. hols: 4 pm - 1 am, tel.: 51 88 92. Friendly atmosphere - nice pub at the beginning of the "pub mile" on the Jüdefel-derstr. You have to try "Rollo" with ham, pineapple chunks and vanilla sauce (!).

Ipanema. Mauritzstr. 24, Mon - Sun: 12 - 3 am, tel.: 40 40 9. Pub-cum-restaurant near the city centre with Latin-American touch. Look out for the special "filling-pump" at the bar...

Johann Conrad. Sonnenstr. 82, Mon - Sat: 10 - 1 am, Sun: 1 pm - 1 am, tel.: 4 35 14. Pub next to the Promenade. If just having a drink is too boring, you can always try one of the more than 70 parlour games stored there.

John Doe's Diner. Spiekerhof 44, Mon - Fri: 5.30 pm - 1 am, Sat: 10.30 - 1 am, Sun: 10.30 am - 12 pm, tel.: 51 84 06. Save yourself the money for the ticket to N.Y. - if you just want to enjoy a meal (generously portioned) and a drink in the classic American style.

Kalkmarkt. Münzstr. / corner Hindenburg-platz, Mon - Sun: 6 pm - 1 am, tel.: 5 44 49. Simple pub on the corner - but the meals are absolutely delicious.

Kaufleuten. In the Deilmannhof. Rothenburg 14-16, Mon - Sun: 9 am - 12 pm (bar open till 3 am), tel.: 4 49 91. Don't be confused by the name - not only businessmen (Kaufleute) like to spend their spare time here.

Kreuzeck. Maximilianstr. 47a, Mon - Fri: 6 pm - 1 am, Sat: 7 pm - 1 am, tel.: 27 74 23. Pub in the popular "Kreuzviertel".

Kristall. Kanalstr. 133, Mon - Sat: 6 pm - 1 am, Sun: 2.30 pm - 1 am, tel.: 29 66 37. Lots of antique furniture and a pretty conservatory invite you to stay a little longer (beer garden).

Krone. Hammer Str. 67, Mon - Fri: 11.30 - 1 am, Sat, Sun: 2 pm - 1 am, tel.: 7 38 68. Pub in warm shades of yellow - frequented by students and people living in the quarter alike.

Krusebaimken. Am Stadtgraben 52, Mon - Sun: 4 pm - 1 am, tel.: 4 63 87. Students love the big beer garden.

Le Midi. Bohlweg 37, Mon - Sun: 6 pm - 1 am, tel.: 44539. Here, carefully chosen bits and pieces of furniture bear witness to the landlord's many trips to France. A successful attempt to import a bit of authentic atmosphere from the south of France to Münster.

Limericks. Irish Pub. Am Stadtgraben 3, Sun - Thur: 6 pm - 1 am / Fri, Sat: 6 pm - 3 am, tel.: 51 89 89. Original Irish pub offering Guinness, original Kilkenny and darts.

Metro. Mauritzstr. 25, Sun - Tue: 6.30 pm - 1 am / Wed - Fri: 6.30 pm - 3 am / Sat: 2 pm - 3 am, tel.: 4 52 80. Comfortable pub-cum-restaurant with a selection of tasty potato dishes - next to the Promenade. On Saturdays top match (soccer) of the week.

Mocambo. Mauritzstr. 34, Mon - Sun: 10 pm -5 am, tel.: 51533. The bar takes up almost one whole side of the pub - a meeting-place for night owls looking for an early-hour alternative to the disco.

Nachtcafé. Bahnhofstr. 44, Mon , Tue, Thur: 7 pm - 3 am, Wed, Sat: 7 pm - 5 am, tel.: 4 24 90. The name fits - so many visitors that you all too easily forget it's already long after midnight. Half of Münster's student population is there to have a chat and "tuck in" in the front room and to dance the night away in the back room.

Nordstern. Hoyastr. 3, Mon - Fri: 4 pm - 3 am / Sat, Sun: 11 - 3 am, tel.: 2 21 41 / 2 06 23. Here, you get the best chicken in the whole of Münster - and you can order it until 2.30 am.

Odeon. Frauenstr. 51-52, Thur, Fri, Sat: 9 pm - 3 am, tel.: 4 34 47. At disco time for the more hardened guests - in the pub in the front rooms it's a bit quieter, though - and you can even take off your leather jacket.

Pinkus Müller. Kreuzstr. 4-10, Mon - Fri: 11.30 am - 2 pm / 5 - 12 pm, Sat: 11.30 am - 12 am, (closed Sun, public hols), tel.: 4 51 51. *The* traditional Westphalian pub, well-known far beyond Münster not least because of the "Altbier" that is brewed here.

Rick's Café. Aegidiistr. 56, Mon - Sun: 10 - 1 am, tel.: 4 29 84. The beginning of a wonderful friendship.

Sabroso. Mauritzstr. 19, Mon - Sun: 6 pm - 3 am (kitchen open till 2 am), tel.: 5 59 40. Many guests come even from the other side of the city to savour their Caipirinha; Mexican food (till 2 am).

Salsa Verde. Neubrückenstr. 73, Mon - Sun: 11 - 1 am, tel.: 4 36 82. Attractive restaurant-cum-pub right in the city centre.

Schluckspecht. Jüdefelder Str. 54, Mon - Sun: 8 pm - 1 am, tel.: 4 30 06. Here, the clocks stopped in the 70s - but that makes a nice change for a while.

Schoppenstecher. Hörsterstraße 18, Tue-Sun: 6 pm - 1 am, tel.: 4 71 14. There are only a few wine-bars in Münster. This is one of the oldest in Münster with an atmosphere that simply invites a chat.

Scott's View. Sonnenstr. 42, Mon -Sun: 6 pm - 1 am, tel.: 4 42 66. Greetings from Scotland - more than 30 brands of malt and a selection of traditional dishes to serve as a foundation before you taste them.

Töddenhoek. Rothenburg 41, Mon - Sat: 10.30 - 1 am, Tel 4 31 56. It still exists - the Westphalian pub where you can see the native "Münsteraner" *and* a number of students.

Treibhaus. Steinfurter Str. 66, Mon - Sun: 6 pm - 1 am, tel.: 29 80 40. The name (hothouse) is a bit misleading - it's not a hot disco but a friendly pub.

Tribunal. Kampstr. 26, Mon - Sun: 18-1 m, tel.: 27 47 00. Popular meeting-place for the people of this quarter - nice beer terrace in the shade of the Kreuzkirche.

Türmchen. Prinz-Eugen-Str. 60-62, Thur - Tue: 5 pm - 1 am, tel.: 7 26 12. Not only students enjoy a cool "Pott's" with their meal - during the summer in the beer garden, during the winter in front of the fireplace.

Vis-à-Vis. Hörsterstr. 10, Mon - Sun: 11 - 1 am, tel.: 51 11 99. Indeed, from here you can reach the two other well-known pubs and discos almost without getting wet when it rains.

Wasch-Bar. Alter Steinweg 32, Mon - Thur, Sun: 6 pm - 1 am / Fri, Sat: 6 pm - 3 am, tel.: 5 50 30. Please, don't take off your trousers just because the whole place is full of old washing-machines! Clean drinking!

Wolters. Hammer Str. 37, Mon - Sat: 5 pm - 1 am / Sun: 10 - 1 am, tel.: 52 44 08. Big breakfast buffet.

Ziege. Kreuzstr. 33/34, Mon - Sun: 8 pm - 1 am, tel.: 51 90 37. Not much bigger than a wardrobe: intimate drinking.

Zinc. Mauritzstr. 30, Mon - Sun: 7 pm - 3 am, tel.: 5 68 81. Uncompromising drinking at the specialist shop. Thur: 10 pm - 2 am finest vinyl on the turntable with DJ "My-t-Condor".

Late-night Cafés

In Münster, too, there is a growing trend towards longer opening hours. There are more
and more late-night cafés and bars. Not surprisingly, in times of high unemployment
figures, and - at the same time - fewer working
hours for those who have a job. Happy are
those who can turn night into day...

Alabama. Aegidiistr. 46, Sun-Thur: 5 pm -
1 am, Fri - Sat: 5 pm - 3 am, tel.: 4 44 37.
Here, you can have an original American
beer even after the usual closing time.

Atelier. Das Nachtlokal. Bült 2, Mon - Fri:
6 pm - 6 am, Sat, Sun: 8 pm - 6 am, tel.: 5 74
55. This late-night café has closed the last
gap in the pub mile around the theatre.

Kaufleuten. In the Deilmannhof. Rothenburg 14-16, Mon - Sun: 9 am - 12 pm (bar
open till 3 am), tel.: 4 49 91. The bar in the
cellar of this multi-functional place has an
interesting interior design characterized by
purist understatement.

Mocambo. Mauritzstr. 34, Mon - Sun: 10
pm - 5 am, tel.: 51533. On the walls record
sleeves from the 70s - to match that, the
premises are sparsely furnished and lit - it's
just like the old days again...

Nachtcafé. Bahnhofstr. 44, Mon , Tue, Thur: 7
pm - 3 am, Wed, Sat: 7 pm - 5 am, tel.: 42490. Tired
of discos but looking forward to a little chat in
the middle of the night? If you feel like dancing
again, you can hit the dance floor next door.

Theatercafé. (Municipal Theatre) Neubrük-
kenstr. 63, Mon -Thur: 5 pm - 3 am, Fri, Sat:
5 pm - 5 am, Sun: 10 - 3 am, tel.: 51 13 29.
Informal atmosphere. Popular place to start
or finish a nice pub crawl.

Zinc. Mauritzstr. 30, Mon - Sun: 7 pm - 3 am,
tel.: 56881. Impressive zinc bar with a vast
assortment of whisky brands. You need time to
try them all - that's why they dispensed with the
normal closing time here.

Cafés / Bistros

Aaseeterrassen. Annette-Allee 3, Sat - Thur:
10 am - 7 pm, tel.: 8 18 10. Nice view of the
Aasee and the little landing-place. Sun terrace, boats for hire.

Al Forno. Neubrückenstr. 35-37, Mon - Fri:
9 - 1 am, Sat: 11 - 1 am, Sun: 4 pm - 1 am, tel.:
4 57 87. Bistro-cum-pub near the theatre.

Café Extrablatt I & II. Salzstr.7, Mon - Sun:
8 - 1 am, tel.: 4 44 45/**II.** /Königsstr. 31, Mon -
Sat: 9 - 1 am, Sun:10 - 1 am, tel.: 4 33 06. Two
nicely furnished cafés in the city centre.

Drubbel. Café-Bar. Drubbel 19, Mon - Fri:
9 - 1 am, Sat: 8 - 1 am, Sun: 10 - 1 am, tel.:
5 70 40. Little café with a central location.
From the terrace you have a good view of St
Lambert's Church and the Prinzipalmarkt.

Firenze. Königsstr. 12 (Königspassage)/Bo-
genstr. 15, Mon - Sun: 10-24 m, tel.: 51 84
84/ 5 56 70. Ice-cream parlour (open all year
round) serving the biggest sundaes around.
On both terraces you can have a cappuccino
and watch the passers-by at your leisure.

Café Fundus. Berliner Platz 23, Mon -
Thur: 8 - 1 am, Fri: 8 - 3 am, Sat: 10 - 3 am,
Sun: 10 - 1 am, tel.: 4 63 59. Friendly café at
the central station. The staff are instructed to
prevent all trains from leaving until the
guests have drunk their coffee.

Grotemeyers CoLibri. In the Municipal
Library. Alter Steinweg 11, Mon - Fri: 9 am
- 7 pm, Sat: 9 am - 6 pm, tel.: 4 01 43. A café-
cum-bistro that invites communication and
which is situated in the post-modern Municipal Library. The CoLibri has soon become
very popular as it offers a selection of light
meals and snacks, and drinks are even served in the reading-room of the library next
door, where you find the international papers.

Jörgs Art Cocktail Café. Königspassage,
Mon - Sat: from11 am (closed Sun + pub.
hols), tel.: 4 35 13. Multi-functional (late-

night)café: ideal for "après-shopping" or a stop before or after an evening at the theatre.

John Doe's Diner. Spiekerhof 44, Mon - Fri: 5.30 pm - 1 am, Sat: 10.30 - 1 am, Sun: 10.30 am - 12 pm, tel.: 51 84 06. American style - nobody has ever met John Doe, but anyway, if something goes wrong - he is to blame!

Kaufleuten. In the Deilmannhof. Rothenburg 14-16, Mon - Sun: 9 am - 12 pm (bar open till 3 am), tel.: 4 49 91. The furniture of the defunct traditional Café Schucan - formerly on the Prinzipalmarkt - has been integrated into this new café.

Café Malik. Frauenstr. 14, Mon - Sun: 9 - 1 am, tel.: 4 42 10. On the way to university many a student of the humanities has been seen going in here.

Marktcafé. Mon , Tue, Thur, Fri: 8 - 1 am, Wed, Sat: 7 - 1 am, Sun: 10 - 1 am, tel.: 5 75 85. It might take some time before you can spot your date: though an unusually large café, the place has a nice, friendly atmosphere; located on the Domplatz (Cathedral Square).

Palmen-Café. Aegidiimarkt 1, Mon - Fri: 9 am - 7.30 pm, Sat: 9 am - 6.30 pm, Sun and public hols: 11 am - 6.30 pm, tel.: 4 78 58. Café overlooking the Aegidiimarkt and the Rothenburg - if there isn't a palm blocking your view.

Pasadena. Hörster Str. 10, Mon - Thur: 5 pm - 2 am / Fri: 5 pm - 3 am / Sat: 12 - 3 am / Sun and public hols: 7 pm - 2 am, tel.: 51 17 28. Friendly little bistro: come and have a chat and try the drinks and snacks. Terrace.

Pronto Pronto. Ludgeristr. 115, Mon - Fri: 9 am - 20 am, Sat: 9 am - 5 pm, Sun: 12 am - 6 pm, tel.: 45033. You can't get more central than this. Small, but very nice cappuccino-bar in the pedestrian precinct.

Rick's Café. Ägidiistr. 56, Mon -Sun: 10-1 m, tel.: 4 29 84. Coffee and beer Casablanca style - not only for the usual suspects.

Traditional Cafés

Café Grotemeyer. Salzstr. 24, Mon - Fri: 9 am - 8 pm / Sat: 9 am - 6 pm / Sun: 10 am - 6 pm, tel.: 4 24 77. Café rich in tradition with an excellent choice of delicious sweets and chocolates on offer and a very popular terrace vis-à-vis the Erbdrostenhof.

Café Kleimann. Prinzipalmarkt 48, Mon - Fri: 7.30 am - 6.45 pm / Sat: 7 am - 5.30 pm (closed Sun), tel.: 4 30 64. Look at the mouthwatering creations from their own confectionery - and forget about calorie counting. Small terrace opposite St Lambert's Church.

Café Kerkhoff. Melchersstr. 76, Tue - Fri: 6.30 am - 6.30 pm, Sat: 6.30 am - 6 pm, Sun: 10 am- 6 pm, tel.: 29 34 85. Here, you can savour your cup of coffee in authentic 1950-surroundings. Home-made chocolate and truffles.

Café Krimphove. Ludgeristrasse 85, Mon: 8 am - 6.30 pm, Tue - Sat: 8 am - 9 pm, tel.: 4 32 82. Almost one hundred years of tradition.

Steinburg am Aasee. Mecklenbecker Str. 80, Mon - Sun: 12 am - 2 pm / 6 - 9.30 pm, tel.: 7 71 79. Traditional café in the restaurant of the Hotel Steinburg with one of the most beautiful terraces in the whole of Münster situated next to the Aasee and providing a wonderful view of the lake. Ideal place for a stop if you're on a bicycle tour around the Aasee.

Wine Bars / Wine-cellars

L'Antica. Mauritzstrasse 22, Mon - Sat: 6 pm - 1 am, tel.: 4 55 45. Several thousand bottles of wine smile enticingly from their rustic shelves at the connoisseurs of fine wine. Delicious Italian snacks are served with the wine.

La Cantina. Tibusstr. 7-11, Mon - Sun: 6 pm - 1 am, tel.: 5 89 63. One of the most beautiful Italian restaurants in Münster. Very elegantly furnished interior. Probably the longest antipasti counter in the whole of the Münsterland.

Pane e vino. Neubrückenstr. 35-37, Mon - Thur, Sun: 5.30 pm - 1 am, Fri: 5 pm - 3 am, Sat: 12.30 pm - 3 am, tel.: 5 46 45. Absolutely crowded at the week-ends. You can even venture to speak to a complete stranger without the risk of getting strange looks.

Schoppenstecher. Hörsterstrasse 18, Tue - Sun: 6 pm - 1 am, tel.: 47114. One of the oldest wine bars in the city - the comfortable interior tempts you to stay for a long chat.

Wein- und Austernkeller in the **Butterhandlung "Holstein".** Bogenstr. 9, Tue, Wed: 10 am - 7 pm / Thur, Fri: 10 am - 7.30 pm / Sat: 9 am - 3/4/6 pm, tel.: 4 49 44. One of the 14 best delicatessens in Germany - with a wine and oyster cellar to match their excellent reputation.

Beer Gardens

Johann Conrad. Sonnenstr. 82, Mon - Sat: 10 - 1 am, Sun: 1 pm - 1 am, tel.: 4 35 14. Pub with a nice little beer garden; situated right next to the Promenade.

Kristall. Kanalstr. 133, Mon - Sat: 6 pm - 1 am / Sun: 2.30 pm - 1 am, tel.: 29 66 37. Attractive beer garden. During the winter months, the conservatory furnished with carefully chosen antiques is a fitting substitute.

Krusebaimken. Am Stadtgraben 52, Mon - Sun: 4 pm - 1 am, tel.: 4 63 87. The large beer garden has become a general meeting-place for the students of Münster.

Maikotten. Maikottenweg 208, in winter: Wed - Fri: 5 - 12 pm, Sat: 3 - 12 pm, Sun: 11 am - 11 pm, in summer: Mon, Tue: 6 - 12 pm, Wed - Sat: 3 - 12 pm, Sun: 11 am - 11 pm, tel.: 3 10 95. Popular destination of Sunday excursions.

Wienburg. Kanalstr. 237, Tue - Sun: 10 am - 12 pm (closed Mon), tel.: 29 33 54 / 27 32 34. Large beer garden as an ideal destination after a walk through the Wienburgpark.

Zum alten Pulverturm. Breul 9, Mon - Sun: 5 - 12 pm (winter), Mon - Fri: 4 - 12 pm, Sat, Sun: 12 am - 12 pm (summer), if it's "beer garden weather": Mon - Sun: 12 am - 12 pm, tel.: 4 58 30. Very popular beer garden right next to the Promenade.

Tourist Cafés & Restaurants

Böttcher Keller. Markt 4, 48291 Telgte, Mon - Sun: 5 - 12 pm, Sun + pub. hols also from 11.30 am to 2 pm, tel.: 0 25 04 / 30 59. Beautiful historic wine cellars (since 1776!), they alone are worth a trip to Telgte - ideal for a romantic tête-à-tête.

Burg Hülshoff. Café-restaurant. 48329 Havixbeck. Mon - Sun: 9.30 am - 6 pm (mid-March - December), tel.: 02534-6 57 21/ 10 52. After a tour of the museum and following in "Droste's" footsteps for a while, this is the ideal place to end a visit to the Burg Hülshoff.

Café Longinus. In the "Longinusturm". Baumberg 45, 48301 Nottuln. Mon - Fri: from 11 am, Sat, Sun + pub. hols from 10 am, tel.: 0 25 02/79 11. Before you go and try the delicious cakes, we strongly recommend that you climb up the tower first: a) to enjoy a marvellous view of the Münsterland and b) to compensate for the high-calorie cakes.

Haus Klute. Art-Antiques-Café. Poppenbeck 28, (Havixbeck). Wed - Sun: 2 - 7 pm, tel.: 0 25 07/29 58 or 29 55. A highly popular destination: home-made cakes and high-quality tea served in tasteful surroundings. And next door: **Historisches Brauhaus Klute.** Mon - Sun: 11 am - 12 pm, tel.: 0 25 07 / 9 83 90. Here the real ale brewed on the premises in their historic brewery is served; all the ingredients are produced in an environmentally friendly way.

Holtene Sluse. Am Max-Clemens-Kanal 303, Tue - Sat: 6 - 11 pm, tel.: 21 64 40. For long cosy evenings in front of the fireplace. The landlord, Mr Renfert, always has a fitting comment - better not try to outdo him as he is too quick at repartee.

Pleister-Mühle. Pleistermühlenweg 196, Thur - Tue: 11 am - 12 pm, tel.: 31 10 72. After a stroll along the River Werse you can relax in this beer garden.

Steverburg. 48301 Nottuln, café: Fri - Wed: 2.30 - 5 pm, tel.: 0 25 02/9 43-0. Have a nice cup of coffee at the foot of the Baumberge and enjoy the view of the Coesfelder Land.

Wilbers Kotten. Appelhülsener Strasse 15, 48301 Nottuln, Mon - Thur: 8 am - 7 pm, Fri - Sun: 8 am - 10 pm, tel.: 0 25 02/70 44 / 45. Rustic interior, typical of the Münsterland. Hearty meals are served on wooden plates.

Discotheques

Am Hawerkamp. Am Hawerkamp 31, **Sput-nikhalle** (Oldie and Heavy-Metal section) Fri, Sat: 10 pm - 5 am, tel.: 66 20 62/ **Triptychon** (different parties), Fri, Sat: 9 pm - 5 am, tel.: 66 18 88/ **Fusion-Club** (Techno-House section) Fri: 11 pm - 12 am, tel.: 6 34 50. Three discos on the premises of a former factory. Dance to your favourite tunes - until the morning comes.

Café del Arte. Königsstr. 45, Mon - Sat: from 9 am (Disco: Wed, Fri, Sat: 10 pm - 5 am) Sun: 10 pm - 1 am, tel.: 51 10 29. Hit the dancefloor of the disco downstairs or get your breath back in the café upstairs.

Casablanca. Dance hall. Hammer Str. 343, Fri: 9 pm - 4 am, Sat and before pub. hols: 9 pm - 5 am, tel.: 78 63 59. Very tastefully furnished and commodious dance hall with various bars that make it easy to have a nice chat.

Cascade in the **Café Fundus.** Berliner Platz 23 (central station), Fri, Sat: 10 pm - 4 am, tel.: 4 63 59. From Reggae and Soul to Pop: popular nightspot.

Depot. An der Kleimannbrücke 5/ Schiffahrter Damm, Mon : 10 pm - 4 am / Wed: 9 pm - 4 am, Fri, Sat, Sun: 10 pm - 5 am/ After-hour: Sat: 7 am - 7 pm / Sun: 7 am - 5 pm, tel.: 32 95 56. Music that gets under your skin. From Oldies to House, from Funk to "Schlagernacht" (German pop songs) and single party.

Der Elephant. Roggenmarkt 15/16, Fri, Sat and before pub. hols.: 9 pm - 5 am, tel.: 4 32 00. Here, Mum and Dad can shake a leg without risking burst eardrums from the Techno beat.

Dockland. Hafenweg 17, Wed: 10 pm - 4 am, Fri, Sat: 10.30 pm - 5 am, tel.: 6 03 01. For kids who like House, HipHop, Funk etc.

GoGo. Servatiiplatz / Friedrichstr. 9, Wed - Sun: 10 pm - 5 am, tel.: 4 57 26. Meet some nice people and hit the dance floor (Rock, Indie, House, Charts, HipHop).

Grand Café. Hörsterstr. 51, disco: Fri, Sat: 11pm - 3 am (pub: Tue - Thur: 5 pm - 1 am, Fri, Sat: 5 pm - 3 am, Sun: 6 pm - 1 am), tel.: 5 75 17. Despite air-conditioning, a hot crowd dancing to the top tunes from the charts.

Jovel Music Hall. Grevener Str. 91/ former Germania brewery, Wed/ Fri/ Sat: 9 pm - 5 am, tel.: 20 10 70. A real dance palace - Münster's largest discotheque.

Le Club. Cocktailbar/discotheque. Roggenmarkt 11-12, Wed - Thur: 10 pm - 3 am/ Fri, Sat: 10 pm - 6 am, tel.: 51 16 15. Guest are carefully hand-picked by the doorman. Bar and dance floor in the stylish vaults. Wed: reduced prices for students.

Le Différent. Hörster Str. 10, Fri, Sat: 10 pm - 5 am, tel.: 51 12 39. Nomen est omen.

Nachtcafé. Bahnhofstr. 44, Mon, Tue, Thur: 7 pm - 3 am, Wed, Sat: 7 pm - 5 am, tel.: 4 24 90. Pub and disco - not only for House and HipHop fans.

Odeon. Frauenstr. 51-52, Thur, Fri, Sat: 9 pm - 3 am, tel.: 4 34 47. What?? - Yeah, right... You might not be able to hear your own words, but the music here is great.

Shopping

Naturally, there are numerous shops in Münster that sell everything from basic necessities to luxury items. As a means of quick orientation, we have prepared a small list of shops for you. These shops offer high-quality, very useful or exceptionally original goods.

Most of the shops stick to the usual opening-hours. Only if there are considerable deviations have we added the individual opening-hours separately.

Presents / Souvenirs

Art-Shop. In the "Otmar". Ludgeristr. 100. Art goes public: Hundertwasser, Warhol, St Phalle and others for every occasion.

Crazy. Rothenburg 52, tel.: 4 43 44. Funny and eccentric presents.

Flaschengeist. Harsewinkelgasse 1-4, tel.: 4 20 36. Theme shops are in: wine, spirits, various brands of oil and vinegar can be bottled in the shop - a choice of decorative bottles and accessories is available, too.

Grün & Form. Rosenstr. 4, tel.: 4 76 22. Carefully chosen ceramics and an assortment of individual accessories for the house.

Hopla Hop Geschenkeshop. Salzstr. 25, tel.: 5 65 50. Wide choice of gifts.

Kadó. Spiekerhof 5, tel. 51 90 46. Looking for a choice present? - Try this shop.

Magnolia's English Shop. Annette-Von-Droste-Hülshoff-Str. 6, tel.: 0 25 34-23 13. English Goods, that you cannot find anywhere else in Münster.

Otmar. Ludgeristr. 100. From sushi-bar to art-shop: modern theme shops and superior fast food stalls under one roof.

Papier-Palast. Königspassage. tel.: 51 17 16. Pleasing packaging for personal presents.

Schinkenstübchen. Alter Steinweg 36, tel.: 4 30 88. More than 150 suggestions for typical Westphalian presents await the tourist.

Teehandelskontor Bremen. Salzstr. 26/Salzhof, tel.: 51 99 15. A special souvenir: a choice selection of teas and all sorts of accessories.

Terrakotta. Sprakeler Str. 216, tel.: 26 41 41. Not directly in the city centre, but well worth a detour: wide choice of terracotta items in all shapes and sizes.

Die Wohnkugel. Bergstr. 68, tel.: 5 12 12. High-quality gifts.

Fashion and Accessories:

Benetton. Rothenburg 40/ Salzstr. 61/Bogenstr. 15, tel.: 51 18 28/4 55 15/5 65 96. A lot of dispute over their adverts - no dispute over their clothes.

Bergmann. Ludgeristr. 116, tel.: 4 29 42. High-quality fashion for men and women.

Bernd Rasehorn. Aegidiimarkt 7, tel.: 4 48 89. Fine ladies' wear.

Boecker. Prinzipalmarkt 1-4, tel.: 4886-0. Clothes for the whole family.

Brambrink. Rothenburg 49, tel.: 5 84 62. Exquisite fashion for elegant women.

Country Classics. Prinzipalmarkt 33, tel.: 4 71 11. Finest quality clothing.

Creole. Salzstr. 61, tel.: 4 53 03. Ear-rings etc. to match your outfit.

Feminin. Ludgeristr. 5, tel.: 4 22 18. Sportswear for boys and girls.

H & M. Ludgeristr. 28, tel.: 4 28 30. Here, fashion changes quicker than the seasons.

Harenberg. Prinzipalmarkt 27 and 37-38-39, tel.: 4 20 05. Anything you can wish for in leather: international leather fashion.

Hasardeur. Königsstr. 43, tel.: 4 75 20. Fashionable and elegant clothes for men and women.

Ipuri. Prinzipalmarkt 32, tel.: 5 60 10. The name says it all: high-quality purist fashion presented in matching surroundings.

Jil Sander. Bogenstr. 15-16, tel.: 48458-0. Legitimate understatement.

Joop! Bogenstr. 1, tel.: 5 86 75. Well, even the top designers have realized that one shouldn't forget affluent Münster...

Kemmerich. Spiekerhof 13-14, tel.: 4 60 43. High-quality men's outfitter.

Kookai. In the Deilmannhof. Rothenburg 14/16, tel.: 5 10 53 46 Styling from top to toe.

Linea Italiana. Königspassage, tel. 51514. Boutique selling high-quality Italian men's wear.

Madeleine. Roggenmarkt-Drubbel 13, tel.: 5 55 80. Haute-couture for the lady.

Mannefeld. Roggenmarkt 7, tel. 43314. Men and women's outfitter with a long tradition.

Marc Cain Exclusiv. Bergstr. 75, tel.: 5 12 79. Credit cards: AX-DC-EC-MC-V.

Marc O'Polo. Lambertikirchplatz 1, tel.: 5 44 17. Sports fashion for young people.

Max DKNY. In the Deilmannhof. Rothenburg 14/16, tel.: 5 10 53 61. Fashion for business women as well as city girls.

Panther, Tiger & Tucano. Salzstr. 14, tel.: 4 29 51. Synthetic furs that can hardly be distinguished from genuine ones. Jewellery and fashion with a Latin-American touch.

171

Polo's für you. Rothenburg 48, tel.: 4 77 88. International proprietary sportswear for boys and girls.

Romana. Rothenburg 37, tel.: 4 47 72. Fine Italian shoes and accessories.

Sandy Blue. Ludgeristr. 86-87, tel.: 4 84 90-0. Boutique offering quality clothing for women.

Sandy's Bijoux. Königspassage, tel.: 4 84 90-0. Jewellery to match the latest fashion: costume jewellery.

Sandy Two. Hötteweg 8, tel. 4 84 90-0. Fashion for the sporty woman.

Schnitzler. Prinzipalmarkt 40 and 43, tel.: 4 14 90-0. Old-established clothes shop selling fashion for men, women and children. **Differente**: attached shop for young people.

Sinn-Leffers. Salzstr. 3-4, tel.: 5 10 24-0. Fashion to suit your personal style.

Spiegelburg. Königsstr. 42, tel.: 5 75 04. This shop in the Oer'sche Hof is definitely worth a visit: fine unique items (also tailor-made)

Tepe. Prinzipalmarkt 19, tel.: 4 84 50-0. International women's fashion.

That's me. Rothenburg 36 and Salzhof, tel.: 5 59 29/ 5 56 71. Young fashion for him and her.

Velvet. Ludgeristr. 54 / Aegidiistr. 61/62, tel.: 51 85 88/ 40851. Fine clothes for young women.

Wehmeyer. Ludgeristr. 75, tel.: 41 42 50. Big fashion store in the pedestrian precinct.

Weitkamp. Prinzipalmarkt 6/7, tel.: 5 47 22. Renowned men's outfitter. High-quality classic clothing.

Wolford. In the Deilmannhof. Rothenburg 14/16, tel.: 5 10 53 87. Specialist for hosiery.

Antiques

Antike Uhren - Alter Schmuck Dötsch. Ludgeristr. 85/ Hötteweg, tel.: 4 73 28

Antiquitäten & Kunsthaus Eibel. Mecklenbecker Str. 387, tel.: 71 24 40

Antiquitätenhaus Pleistermühle. Pleistermühlenweg 194, tel.: 31 67 18

Belle Epoque. Rosenplatz 10, tel.: 51 13 07. Art Nouveau and Art Déco.

Frye & Sohn. Hörsterstr. 47/48, tel.: 4 66 62

Münstersches Kunst- & Auktionshaus. Buddenstr. 27, tel.: 5 13 56

Saphir Antiquitäten. Bogenstr. 4, tel.: 44560

Schlummer's Laden. Ringoldsgasse 1/ Salzstr., tel.: 4 72 31

Music

CD-Forum. Alter Steinweg 4, tel.: 5 88 89. CD-shop in the city centre.

Das Ohr. Aegidiistr. 27, tel.: 4 14 58-0. Vast choice of CDs. Advance booking for concerts.

Discoteca. Windhorststr. 48, tel.: 5 67 54. *The* specialist for classical music (CDs). Advance booking for concerts.

Elpi. Windthorststr. 20, tel.: 5 70 30. Records, CDs. Advance booking for concerts.

JPC. Alter Fischmarkt 2, tel.: 4 14 53-33. CD-specialist. Advance booking for concerts.

Galeria Kaufhof. Ludgeristr. 1, tel.: 50 02-2 36. Top CDs and MCs on the 3rd floor.

Karstadt. Salzstr. 47-50, tel.: 5 02-0. Wide choice of CDs and MCs.

Delicatessen

Butterhandlung "Holstein". Bogenstr. 9, tel.: 4 49 44. Once rated in the Gault Millau among the 14 best delicatessens in Germany. Excellent wine and oyster cellar downstairs.

Delikatessa. Ludgeristr. 1, tel.: 50 02-0. A meeting-place for gourmets in the basement of the "Galeria Kaufhof".

Gastronomia Italiana. Warendorfer Str. 44, tel.: 3 38 07. Italian specialties: from Amaretto to zucchini. And an astonishing choice of 600 different Italian wines and 500 brands of Grappa.

Grünewald. In the fashion store Wehmeyer. Ludgeristr. 75-78, tel.: 4 71 65. Nice little café overlooking St Ludgerii; includes a delicatessen.

Wine dealers

Maison de France. Friesenring 49, tel.: 92 52 50. Mon - Fri: 11am - 6.30 pm, Sa: 10 am - 2 pm. Home offine French wine.

Nientiedt. Steinfurterstr. 57, tel.: 27 91 54. Mon - Fri: 9 am -1 pm / 2 - 7 pm, Sat: 8.30 am - 2 pm. You can choose from 800(!) wines.

Richter. Weinkeller. Melchersstr. 3, tel.: 27 92 91. Mon - Fri: 10 am - 1 pm / 3 - 8 pm, Sat: 10 am - 2 pm. Top quality wines from Germany, France, Italy and Spain.

Vino Classico. Königsstr. 42, tel.: 4 67 12. Mon - Tue: 3 - 6.30 pm, Wed - Fri: 11am - 8 pm, Sat: 10 am - 4 pm. Estate-bottled wines from all vine-growing regions.

Weinquelle. Steinfurter Str. 99a, tel.: 29 86 87. Mon: 3 - 6.30 pm, Tue - Fri: 11am - 6.30 pm, Sat: 10 am - 1 pm. Specialist for eco-wines.

Galleries

Artconsult Galerie Steinrötter
Rothenburg 16, tel.: 4 44 00

Clasing, Galerie Etage
Prinzipalmarkt 37, tel.: 4 41 65

Frye & Sohn
Hörsterstr. 47/48, tel.: 4 66 62

Hachmeister
Klosterstr. 12, tel.: 5 12 10

Galerie L'Hippopotame.
Ludgeristr. 55, tel.: 4 60 02

Laurin
Aegidiistr. 64, tel.: 5 58 19

Nettels
Spiegelturm 3, tel.: 4 62 93

Noran
Roggenmarkt 5, tel.: 4 05 12

Ostendorff Nachf.
Prinzipalmarkt 11, tel.: 5 74 04

Pohlkötter
Rothenburg 38, tel.: 4 45 11

Stefan Rasche
Sternstr. 17, tel.: 66 15 39

Galerie S der Stadtsparkasse
Ludgeristr., tel.: 5 98-14 56

Schnake
Beelertstiege 5, tel.: 5 82 19

Torhaus
Hindenburgplatz 78, tel.: 51 86 44

Tuckesburg Galerie Steinrötter.
Hüfferstr. 18a, tel.: 5 77 99

Wienhausen
Rosenplatz 10, tel.: 4 24 33

General Tourist Information for Germany

(for Münster in particular see *Münster from A - Z*, p. 179ff)

Important emergency phone numbers:

police: 110, *fire brigade*: 112 (also for urgent medical help)
Ärztenotdienst (doctors on call) (usually this number): 1 92 92
further important local telephone numbers (like <u>Lost Property</u>, <u>Breakdown Service</u> etc.) see p. 179ff)

Embassies:

US: 0228/339-1 / GB: 0228/9167-0 / CA: 0228/968-0 / AU: 0228/8103-0 / JA: 0228/8191-0 / see also <u>consulates</u> in Münster in *Münster from A - Z*

Quick reference:

A lot of Germans speak English. Especially in Münster, with more than 50,000 students, it should not be too difficult to find someone who can understand English. But to help you along, here are a few useful phrases:

Hello (Good day)	Guten Tag.
Do you speak English?	Sprechen Sie Englisch?
Do you understand?	Verstehen Sie mich?
Sorry?	Bitte?
I (don't) understand.	Ich verstehe (nicht).
Could you help me please?	Könnten Sie mir bitte helfen?
Could you translate that for me, please?	Können Sie mir das bitte übersetzen?
How do you say ... in German?	Was heißt ... auf Deutsch?
Could you please write that down?	Können Sie das bitte aufschreiben?
I'm looking for...?	Ich suche...
Where is...?	Wo ist ...?
How do I get to...?	Wie komme ich nach...
by bus/ train/	mit dem Bus/ Zug/
car/ bicycle/ on foot ?	Auto/ Fahrrad/ zu Fuß?
station/ bus stop/	Bahnhof/ Bushalte-
taxi rank/	stelle/ Taxistand/
airport / petrol station	Flughafen/ Tankstelle
right / left	rechts / links
straight ahead	geradeaus
Can you show me (on the map)?	Können Sie es mir (auf der Karte) zeigen?
What's up?	Was ist los?
What's your name?	Wie heißen Sie?
My name is (John Doe).	Ich heiße (Hans Müller).
Mrs/ Miss/ Mr/	Frau/ Frau/ Herr/

Ladies and Gentlemen	Meine Damen und Herren
Are you Mr ...?	Sind Sie Herr ...
I'm pleased to meet you.	Sehr erfreut.
Where are you from?	Woher kommen Sie (polite)/ kommst Du?
How are you?	Wie geht es Ihnen (polite) / Dir?
Well, thanks.	Danke, gut.
Yes. / No.	Ja. / Nein.
Perhaps.	Vielleicht.
Please.	Bitte.
You're welcome.	Bitteschön.
Thank you.	Danke.
Help! A Thief! Fire!	Hilfe! Ein Dieb! Feuer!
Call the police / a doctor/ the ambulance.	Rufen Sie die Polizei/ einen Arzt/ den Krankenwagen
Where is the nearest telephone?	Wo ist das nächste Telefon?
Is it serious/ harmless?	Ist es ernst / harmlos?
Excuse me./ I'm sorry.	Entschuldigen Sie./ Es tut mir leid.
Goodbye.	Auf Wiedersehen.
When is...?	Wann ist ...?
Sure.	Klar!
What time is it?	Wie spät ist es?
How much is it?	Wieviel kostet dies?
I'd like a receipt.	Ich hätte gerne eine Quittung.
What's up?	Was ist los?
I want to exchange some money.	Ich möchte Geld umtauschen.
What is the exchange rate?	Wie ist der Wechselkurs?
I'd like to book a room please.	Ich möchte ein Zimmer reservieren.
I'd like a single room	Ich hätte gerne ein Einzelzimmer.
I'd like a double room	Ich hätte gerne ein Doppelzimmer.
I'd like a one-way/ return-ticket	Ich hätte gerne eine Einzel-/Rückfahrkarte.

Cardinal numbers:

0	null	8	acht
1	eins	9	neun
2	zwei	10	zehn
3	drei	20	zwanzig
4	vier	50	fünfzig
5	fünf	100	hundert
6	sechs	500	fünfhundert
7	sieben	1000	tausend

Ordinal numbers:

Add "-te" (female, neuter) or "-ter" (male) resp. to the cardinal numbers after indefinite article (irregular: first = erste(r), 3rd = dritte(r), 7th = siebte(r)).

Days:

Monday	Montag
Tuesday	Dienstag
Wednesday	Mittwoch
Thursday	Donnerstag
Friday	Freitag
Saturday	Sonnabend
Sunday	Sonntag

Months:

January	Januar
February	Februar
March	März
April	April
May	Mai
June	Juni
July	Juli
August	August
September	September
October	Oktober
November	November
December	Dezember

Measures:

Linear Measures

1 m (Meter) = 3.281 ft/1.094 yd
1 km (Kilometer) = 1000 m = 1094 yd/0.621 mi.

Square Measures

1 qm (Quadratmeter) = 1.196 sq.yd
1 qkm (Quadratkilometer) = 1,196 sq.yd

Measures of Capacity

1 l (Liter) = 0.264 U.S.gal./0.22 imp.gal.
1 hl (Hektoliter) = 26.42 U.S.gal./22 imp.gal.

Weights

1 g (Gramm) = 15.43 grain
1 kg (Kilogramm) = 2.2 lb.
1 t (Tonne) = 0.984 tons

Air distances from the local international airport FMO in kilometer / miles (only some flights are direct): (1mi = 1.60934 km)
For a rough calculation of flying time in hours, divide kilometers by 750.

Amsterdam 200/124	Madrid 1666/1035
Athens 2050/1274	Mex. City 9794/6086
Berlin 391/243	Montreal 6101/3791
Bombay 6812/4233	Moscow 2277/1415
Brussels 296/184	Munich 512/318
Buenos Aires 11732/7290	New York 6441/4002
Cairo 3164/1966	Paris 518/322

Cologne 171/106	Rio d. Jan. 9815/6099
Frankfurt 243/151	Rome 1191/740
Hamburg 270/168	Seoul 8887/5522
Hong Kong 9413/5849	Stockholm 1083/673
Jakarta 11365/7062	Sydney 16740/10402
Johannesburg 8933/5551	Tel Aviv 3190/1982
London 542/337	Tokyo 9783/6079
Los Angeles 9554/5937	Zurich 525/326

Public holidays: N = not in all Lands of the Federal Rep. of Germ.; M = movable feasts (dates given refer to **1998**)

1.1.	Neujahr / New Year's Day
6.1.	Heilige Drei Könige / Epiphany (N)
10.4.	Karfreitag / Good Friday (M)
12.4.	Ostersonntag / Easter Sunday (M)
13.4.	Ostermontag / Easter Monday (M)
1.5.	Tag der Arbeit / May Day Holiday
21.5.	Christi Himmelfahrt/Ascension Day (M)
31.5.	Pfingsten / Whitsuntide (M)
1.6.	Pfingstmontag / Whitmonday (M)
11.6.	Fronleichnam / Corpus Christi (N) (M)
15.8.	Mariä Himmelfahrt / Assumption (N)
3.10.	Tag der Deutschen Einheit/ Reunification of Germany
31.10.	Reformationstag / Reformation Day (N)
1.11.	Allerheiligen / All Saints' Day (N)
18.11.	Buß- und Bettag / Day of Prayer and Repentance(N)(M)
25.12.	1. Weihnachtstag / Christmas Day
26.12.	2. Weihnachtstag / Boxing Day

(Banks and shops are closed, restaurants and pubs etc. are usually open)

The Germans: The weather is not always nice - it really cannot be compared with the Mediterranean climate. For this reason, you should not expect an overwhelmingly hearty welcome as, for example, in the Mediterranean area. Normally, when you meet someone, you shake hands. Kisses on the cheek (also between members of the same sex) have become quite common and do not necessarily indicate a close personal relationship. Women are addressed as 'Frau' (Mrs/Miss), men as 'Herr' (Mr). NB: When you're asked 'How do you do?' (Wie geht es Ihnen?), a more or less honest answer is expected - Germans don't always feel 'fine' or 'great'. And, if they are excited, they normally won't express it as ebulliently as a typical Californian on the sunny beach. But there is a sphere where Germans do express themselves: on the "Autobahn" (motorway) according to the motto: "Unrestricted driving for free citizens!" or at the national obsession of soccer (Fußball).

And this may please you: you can drink alcohol anywhere and as much as you want to! Smoking is actually only forbidden in special zones in some restaurants. There is a prejudice that in Germany children should be seen but not heard, and that sometimes people treat their neighbour's dog better than their children. But find that out for yourself. Furthermore: times are changing - even on the *old* continent, so: in the above-mentioned situations, the exception proves the rule!

Warnings: Don't park in prohibited zones. You'll have to pay up to 320 DM if your car is towed away. Don't buy drugs - if you feel like trying marihuana, go to the Netherlands: there it is allowed. Don't insult a police- officer - it's costly! You had better buy your condoms at the chemist's rather than in a pub, for quality reasons. Buying contraceptives is a completely normal thing to do and - after all - it's better to be safe than sorry.

Police (Polizei): 'your friend and helper': they are normally correct and polite and are eager to help. Compared with the situation in other European countries, they are usually less aggressive and - presumably because of the recent dark phase in German history - more aware of the democratic rights of the citizens (but beware if you demonstrate against nuclear power plants, even though you are perfectly entitled to do so...).

Travel documents: EU citizens require only an ID card to enter the country. Citizens of the following countries, among others, require only a valid passport: Argentina, Australia, Brazil, Canada, Columbia, Hong Kong, Israel, Japan, Mexico, Monaco, Slovakia, Slovenia, South Korea, Hungary, USA. Citizens of other countries require a visa, for example those of S. Africa, India or Russia.

Best time to visit (Münsterland): all year round, but especially May to Oct (if snow falls, then only a little between Dec and Feb)

Climate (Münsterland): mild winters and relatively cool summers (average over the last 135 years: 9.2 °C); ø 195 days of rain per year, but on the other hand ø 1,600 hrs of sunshine per year. To convert °C into °F multiply the °C figure by nine, then divide by 5 and add 32. Thus:
$$((°C \times 9) : 5) + 32 = °F$$
Examples: 25°C = 77 °F; 15 °C = 59 ° F; 10 °C = 50 °F; -5°C = 23 °F

Clothing: If you take the following items along, you won't go far wrong: all year round long trousers and an umbrella, in the summer a light jacket, in the winter a warm jumper and jacket and a scarf; all year round comfortable walking shoes and in the winter perhaps warm boots.

Time: (GMT): Greenwich Mean Time + 1 hr, Summer time (last weekend in March to last weekend in October) GMT + 2 hrs

Money / Currency:

coins: 1, 2, 5, 10, 50 Pfennig, 1, 2, 5, (10) (Deutsche) Mark
bank notes: (5), 10, 20, 50, 100, 200, 500, 1000 (Deutsche) Mark
Attention: In German, decimal points are written with a comma (i.e. 12.50 $ = 22,50 DM) numbers above a thousand with a point (i.e. 3,000 $ = 5.400 DM) (But in this book all numbers and German prices are written in the form you are used to.)
Exchange: at banks and post offices; credit cards and Eurocheques very widespread; traveller's cheques accepted only in banks, post offices & hotels

The climate in Münster: (average figures)

	temp. °C / °F (day)	temp. °C / °F (night)	hrs of sunshine/day	rainy days
January	3.7 / 38.7	-0.8 / 30.6	1.4	12
February	4.9 / 40.8	-0.8 / 30.6	2.4	10
March	8.5 / 47.3	1.4 / 34.5	3.7	11
April	12.8 / 55.0	3.9 / 39.0	5.5	10
May	17.4 / 63.3	7.7 / 45.9	6.7	10
June	20.6 / 69.1	10.8 / 51.4	6.9	11
July	21.7 / 71.1	12.5 / 54.5	6.0	12
August	21.7 / 71.1	12.4 / 54.3	6.0	11
September	18.8 / 65.8	9.9 / 49.8	5.0	9
October	14.1 / 57.4	6.6 / 43.9	3.5	10
November	8.2 / 46.8	3.0 / 37.4	1.8	13
December	5.0 / 41.0	0.6 / 33.1	1.3	13

What you get for German Marks:

(average prices; students and disabled people often get certain reductions)

Museums: admission free, otherwise: 5 - 10 DM
Bus journey inside town: 1.70 - 2.80 DM
Taxi journey 5 km: 13.30 - 14.60 DM
Trip round town: 1 1/2 hrs: around 70.00 DM
Hotels: Single room from 40 DM, double rooms from 30 DM (per person)
Cinema: 8 - 13 DM
Theatre: 15 - 50 DM
Sandwich: 2 - 6 DM
Cake: take-away: 1 - 4.50; in cafés: 3 - 5.50 DM
Hamburger: 1.85 DM
Cup of *coffee* (in pavement cafés usually only small pots of coffee): 1.50 - 4.50 DM
Beer 0.2 l: 2.60 - 3.50 DM (in beer gardens usually only a large beer, 0.4 or 0.5 l): 4.50 - 6 DM
Decanted *wine*: glass or 1/4 l: 5 - 9 DM
Evening meal (main menu): from 10 DM (cheapest) or 30 DM (average) to 70 DM (more expensive)

Accommodation: cheap: youth hostels (International Youth Hostel Card required) or camping on camping-sites; reasonable prices in the country in pensions and inns, in towns, hotels are sometimes categorized (1 to 5 stars) to indicate different levels of comfort. But the classification is a voluntary one, so that even hotels without a category may have a similar level of comfort!

*	= tourist, simple appointments
**	= standard
***	= comfort, medium quality of appointments
****	= first-class, high quality of appointments
*****	= luxury, very high quality of appointments

Electricity: AC 220 V./ 16 A., two-pin safety plugs, don't forget to bring an appropriate transformer, an adapter or a two-pin Euro plug if you want to bring any electr. appliances along.

Medical Services: All hospitals have an emergency ward. **In case of emergency, call 112**. You should inquire in your home country about the agreement with Germany, since the arrangements for claiming back costs differ from country to country. EU citizens have to exchange the form E 111 in Germany at a medical insurance institution (gesetzliche Krankenkasse; see telephone directory or inquiries) for a form known as the "Anspruchsbescheinigung", which then has to be presented to the doctor.

At the **chemist's** you receive any necessary medicine. For some you need a prescription, for others not. For any medication you require regularly, make sure that you bring a prescription with you from your own doctor at home, since medicine (even some type that you can get without a prescription at home) may be available only with a prescription in Germany.

Security: Normally, Germany is known for its relatively secure cities compared with other countries. You can walk almost anywhere, even in the middle of the night, without any great risk to your person, except perhaps, around the railway stations in Frankfurt or Berlin. Keep your eyes open, and women shouldn't walk unaccompanied after 10 pm or in dark areas of the city.

Media: CNN and other world-wide TV and radio programmes can be received; one can usually get the international press at kiosks at railway stations.

Restaurants: service and VAT always included, tips welcome (amount of your own choice, average of 10%); usually closed on Mondays (if at all); no difference between drink prices at the bar or at the table; closing time usually 1 am, sometimes 3 or 6 am; vegetarian meals common.

Tip: In Germany, people working in the service sector have fixed wages, but will naturally be happy about a tip. But, as you may have heard, the service in Germany isn't always quite as good and professional as you might be used to in your own country. But times are changing. And the best thing is to give people like taxi-drivers, chamber maids or waiters and waitresses a good tip if they have really deserved it. So you could effectively help to change what is sometimes called in an inflated manner the "service desert" of Germany.

Public conveniences: In Germany, your are allowed to use the toilets in hotels and restaurants without being guest there. Sometimes people may be rather indignant, but don't worry about it.

Shopping: VAT is included in the prices. As a tourist from outside the European Union (EU), **you can save up to 10 % Value Added Tax. 1.** Buy from stores with the **Tax Free** sign (almost every shop participates in this system). **2.** Ask in the store for a Tax Free Cheque. **3.** Have the Cheque stamped by German customs when leaving Germany. If you leave Germany for another EU country, before returning home, you should ask for a customs stamp at the point where you finally quit the EU internal market. **4.** Hand the Cheque in and collect cash at more than 3,000 payment points in Europe.

Haggling over prices is not usual; however, in a case of more expensive purchase, don't hesitate to try to get a reduction. 3% is legal, but, unofficially, you might get more. **Opening hours:** bigger shops from 9 or 9.30 am to 8 pm (smaller shops sometimes only until 6 pm and with a lunch hour from 1 to 3 pm in small towns and villages and the suburbs), Saturdays only until 4 pm, on Sundays shops generally closed (except at railway stations and many petrol stations);

Sizes:

Ladies' wear:

D	36	38	40	42	44	46	48	50	52
GB	34	36	38	40	42	44	46	48	50
US	10	12	14	16	18	20	22	24	26

Gents' wear:(suits, coats)

D	44	46	48	50	52	54	56	58	60
GB/US	34	36	38	40	42	44	46	48	50

Gents' wear:(shirts)

D 36 - 37 - 38 - 39 - 40 - 41 - 42 - 43
GB/US 14 - 14,5 - 15 - 15,5 - 16 - 16,5 - 17 - 17,5

Shoes: D 36 - 36,5 - 37 - 37,5 - 38 - 38,5 - 39 - 40
GB/US 03 - 03,5 - 04 - 04,5 - 05 - 05,5 - 06 - 6,5
 41 - 41,5 - 42 - 42,5 - 43 - 43,5 - 44 -   45 - 46
07 - 07,5 - 08 - 08,5 - 09 - 09,5 - 10 - 10,5 - 11

Traffic: drive on the right; cars coming from the right have the right of way if there are no traffic signs; streets can be used without toll-charge; **speed limit** for cars in built-up areas (unless otherwise stated): 50 km/h, country roads: 100 km/h, motorways (Autobahn): no speed limit; **max. alcohol level in the blood**: 0.5 (0.8) ‰. Exceeding the speed limit can be very costly. On motorcycles, you have to wear a helmet. In cars, you have to fasten your seat belts.

Parking: Parking in inner cities is becoming more difficult; better go by bus or hire a bicycle; when you park in inner cities, you usually have to pay in advance. You put coins in the metre to cover the amount of time you are likely to park there (usually a max. of 2 hrs permitted) and receive a ticket, leave that clearly visible in your car. Sometimes you also find parking metres for each space (max. 1 hr). Parking in prohibited zones or overrunning the time costs you around 20 - 50 DM, depending on the amount of time; if you park in the wrong place or obstruct others, your car will be towed away, and you could end up paying up to 320 DM.

Car hire: as in other countries (credit card necessary), see also *Sought & Found: Münster ...*

Petrol stations: normally self-service, often with a little supermarket with longer opening hours than normal shops, also open on Sundays.
Taxis: mostly in cream with a "Taxi" sign (black on yellow ground) on the roof; you can go to a taxi rank, sometimes stop one as it goes past, or call it by telephone (Münster: tel.: 6 00 11)

Communication:

Internat. Phone Codes. From Germany to ... add:

Australia	0061	Korea, Republic	0082
Austria	0043	Luxembourg	00352
Belgium	0032	Mexico	0052
Canada	001	Netherlands	0031
Czech Republic	0042	Newsealand	0064
France/Monaco	0033	Norway	0047
Great Britain	0044	Poland	0048
North Ireland	0044	South Africa	0027
Greece	0030	Spain	0034
Honkong	00852	Sweden	0046
Ireland	00353	Switzerland	0041
Italy	0039	Russia	007
Japan	0081	USA	001

Telephoning: Telephone unit 0.12 DM, only some coin-operated (unit 0.20 DM), others with phone cards (available in post offices, Telekom shops and kiosks; cheapest 12.00 DM for 100 units; calls from post offices 2.00 DM plus units. **International inquiries**: 11834 (8 units + for every 3.8 sec. 1 unit). **Domestic inquiries**: 11833 (8 units + for every additional 3.8 sec. 1 unit) or 11880(5 units), for additional info like German addresses etc. call 01189 (8 units + for every 3.8 sec. 1 unit). If your stay is extended, inquire about telephone companies with cheaper rates. In 1998, the liberalization of the telephone market has been completed, and there are several private companies with lower rates. Thus, you can make all your calls with these companies, or only a few (call-by-call system). At **post offices** (yellow signs), you can use the full service for telegrams, faxes, money orders, stamps, letters and parcels and so on. Often a bank ("Postbank") is integrated. By the way, letter boxes are yellow and are identifiable by a black post-bugle with two arrows on a yellow background.

Customs regulations: One can bring goods

into the country to the value of 350 DM without paying customs duty, but there is a max. of 200 cigarettes and 1 l of alcohol. One can take currency and goods **out of the country** without any limitation (but you should remember the regulation of your own country). See also Shopping (**VAT refunding via Tax-Free Cheque**)

SOUGHT & FOUND: MÜNSTER FROM A - Z
Dialling code for Münster: 02 51

Agencies for arranging lifts:
Extratour. Überwasserstr. 19,   40 40-0
Asta-Laden. Mensa II,   833-22 22

Airports:
Münster/Osnabrück (FMO) 48252 Greven
Info: 0 25 71 / 94-33 60
Administration: 0 25 71 / 94-0
Lost luggage: 0 25 71 / 94-33 51
Transfer from Münster: busses S 50, D 50 and RT 51, departure from bus platform A2 at the central station, several stops in the city.
Transfer from Osnabrück: e.g. from the central station: FAST-Flughafen-Anruf-Sammeltaxi (taxi for small groups): 0 25 71 / 45 25
Private transfer services:
G&D-Flughafentransfer: 0 25 71 / 94-45 00
Haus-zu-Haus-Service: 0 25 71 / 5 55 67
Parking: short-term parking 2 DM/hr; long-term parking 6 DM/day (max.: 60,- DM); multi-storey car park 12 DM/day (max. 120 DM)
Regular flights: Berlin, Dresden, Frankfurt, Leipzig, Munich, Stuttgart, Eindhoven, Geneva, London, Paris, Venice, Zurich
Reservations: (dialling code 0 25 71)
94-34 36 (Base Airlines), 94-34 35 (Crossair), 94-44 11 (Eurowings), 9 10 32 (Deutsche Lufthansa), 94-42 40 (LTU)
Holiday flights: info & reservations at the indiv. travel agencies at the airport FMO: 0 25 71 / 94-33 69
Club airfield in Telgte 0 25 04 / 33 66

Bicycle-hire:
Deutsche Bahn, central station Münster
(luggage counter):   6 91 33 20
ADFC Fahrradverleih, "Westfalen" petrol station, Sentruper Strasse 169:   8 11 12
Fahrrad Hof, Siverdesstr. 8:   27 93 89
Hansen KG, Hörsterstr. 7:   4 49 98
Rad & Tat Pues, Kanalstr. 47:   20 19 54
Weigang, Grevener Str. 434:   21 23 45

Breakdown Service: (town breakdown service of the *ADAC*) 24 hrs: 0 13 08 / 1 92 11 or 0 18 02 / 22 22 22 (if you use a handy 22 22 22 without dialling code)

Car-hire:
Avis: Georgskommende 10,   4 31 43
Bismarck: Weseler Str. 316,   7 70 06

Europcar. Hammer Str. 139,   7 77 73-0
Henkenjohann & Liebers:
   Am Mittelhafen 51,   66 31 62
Hertz: Hammer Str. 186,   7 73 78
Sixt Budget: Rudolf-Diesel-Str. 5,   32 53 10

Cinemas: films showing: 01 15 11

Consulates:
French Consulate,
Bismarckallee 1,   5 20 30
Dutch Consulate,
Prinzipalmarkt 13,   69 01 06
Turkish Consulate General,
Lotharingerstr. 25,   4 70 07

Emergencies:
Police: 1 10
Fire brigade/ ambulance: 1 12
Doctors on call: 1 92 92
Poisoning: 02 28 / 2 87 32 11
Emergency dental treatment: 8 34-70 01

Events: see Information; *Münster aktuell* (brochure with list of events, available from *Stadtwerbung und Touristik* and *Bürgerberatungsstelle* (see Tourist Information))

Exhibitions: calendar of events in *Münster aktuell* available from the *Stadtwerbung und Touristik* and *Bürgerberatung* (see Tourist information).

Flea markets:
Promenade / Hindenburgplatz:
   Flea markets in the summer from May to Sept. on the 3rd Sat of the month
Halle Münsterland, for events call: 66 00-0

Guided tours of the town :
Information: 02 51 / 4 92-27 10
                          or 4 92-27 21 / 22 / 23
All the guided tours listed below (apart from the last two) start from the historical City Hall on the Prinzipalmarkt.
Guided tours of the old part of the town:
Mon - Sat: 11 am - 12.30 pm,
Sun: 10 - 11.30 am, tickets: 6 DM

Evening stroll through the old part of town: Tue: 7 - 8.30 pm (Apr. 8th to Dec. 19th), tickets: 6 DM

Guided city tour in English language: Each Saturday: 11 am - 12.30 pm from May to Oct. Special arrangements at other times are possible (tel.: 02 51 / 4 92-27 21). Price per person: 6 DM. Starting point: City Hall on the Prinzipalmarkt (Information Counter / Bürgerhalle)

Extended city tours on foot or by bus; preceded by a tour of the old part of the town: Sat and Sun: 10.30 am - 1 pm, Wed: 2.30 - 5 pm (all year round), tickets: 14 DM

Guided tours of the City Hall: Sun: 11.30 am - 12.30 pm (except on days when events take place), tickets: 6 DM

Guided city tours on foot or by bike to the less well-known parts of town offered by
StattReisen Münster   52 16 00

Tours of the town by taxi daily
24 hrs, headquarters: 6 00 11

Hotels: see Hotels on p. 184f

Information:

Doctors on call: 1 92 92
Citizens' Advice Bureau, Heinrich-Brüning-Str. 9, Mon-Fri: 9.30am-6pm, Sat: 9.30am-1pm: 492-1313
Info on bus timetables
Mon - Fri: 7 am - 7 pm, Sat: 7 am - 2 pm: 6 94 16 80
Airport: 0 25 71 / 94-33 60
Lost Property: (see Lost Property) 492-3216/17/18
Hotel reservations: (see p. 184f)   4 92-27 12
Cinemas: 01 15 11
Emergency nos: police: 110, fire brigade: 112
Municipal Theatre & concerts: 59 09-1 00
Road conditiont   0 11 69
Theatre / concerts: 01 15 17
Tourist information: 4 92 - 27 10/11/13
www.muenster.de/publikom/touristik
(see also Tourist information, Guided tours ...)
Events:

The *Stadtwerbung und Touristik* of Münster publishes a monthly programme: *Münster aktuell* can be bought for 1 DM at the *Stadtwerbung und Touristik* (see Tourist information) as well as in many pubs, restaurants and hotels. Apart from that, you will find information on what is going on in town in the local daily newspapers (*Münstersche Zeitung, Westfälische Nachrichten*) and in several weekly and monthly magazines that appear free of charge (*Na dann, Ultimo, Gig*). They can also be found in many shops, restaurants and cultural institutions.
Weather forecast: 0 11 64

Emergency dental treatment: 834-70 01
Accommodation service: see Rooms in ...
Rail information: timetable and tickets: 1 94 19
Mon - Fri: 7 am - 9 pm, Sat/ Sun: 8 am - 9 pm
long-distance trains to the north: 01 15 33
long-distance trains to the south: 01 15 34

Keys: 39 27 37 / 61 55 33 / 6 40 66 / 27 78 78
If you lose your car keys, you can get help at the numbers above-mentioned if you can show them your car documents.

Leisure-time activities:

Some tips for leisure-time activities in and around Münster and the Münsterland: some telephone numbers of people who can advise you and provide further information; you can also turn to *Stadtwerbung und Touristik*:   4 92-27 10 and
Sportamt (Bureau of Sport):   4 92-52 14
Münsterland Touristik: 0 25 51 / 93 92-91
Angling: 32 65 25 / 21 78 15
Swimming: see Swimming pools
Ballooning: 6 04 48
Boule / Boccia: 4 92-52 14
Camping: 32 93 12 u. 31 19 82
Germania Therme: 9 25 35-0
Sky-diving: 21 13 14
Soccer: 78 81 74 (SC Preußen 06)
Golf: 38 12 57 (public course), 21 12 01
Go-kart: (indoors)   7 63 68 66
Jogging: (where there's a will there's a way)
Canoeing: 6 42 63
Climbing (indoors):   02536-341168
Minigolf: 31 10 72 / 3
Museums: see p.145f
Lazing around: (carpe diem)
Observation of nature: 16 17 60
Paddling: 8 03 03
Bicycle tours/"Pättkestour": 0 25 51 / 93 92-91
Picnicking: (a taste of nature)
Covered wagon tours: 4 92-27 21
Riding: 29 31 61, 61 43 14, 31 51 81, 71 98 55
Rowing: 6 42 63 / 8 03 03
Sightseeing flights:
helicopter: 0 25 71 / 94-44 30
Sport. aircraft, Greven: 0 25 71 / 94-33 60
0 25 71 / 13 00
Sport. aircraft, Telgte: 0 25 04 / 13-3 27
0 25 04 / 7 20 01
Epicurism: see pp. 156ff
Ice-skating: 9 68 97
Gliding: 0 25 04 / 7 20 01 + 3366 + 13-327
Sailing: 8 03 03, 79 82 60
Skating: 4 92-52 14 / 7 63 68 66

Burg Hülshoff

48329 Havixbeck · Tel. (0 25 34) 10 52 + 6 57 21

Welcome to the Castle!
(from middle of march to december)

• castle with café-restaurant
• park-grounds
• preserve
• Droste-museum

park, museum & café-restaurant
daily from 9.30 a.m. to 6 p.m.

Sculpture exhibitions:	cf. p. 149
"Speckbrett":	4 92-52 14
Squash:	9 79 13 33, 2 55 95
Surfing:	8 03 03
Tennis:	78 51 91, 9 32 01-0
Pedal boating:	8 03 03
Keep-fit trails:	595-231
Farmhouse holidays:	5 99-3 05 / 5 99-3 27
Hiking:	("In the early morning dew...")
Moated-Castles tour:	492-2721,02551/9392-91
Yachting:	23 58 80

Local public transport:
cf. bus routes on p. 186f

Tickets can be bought from the driver or at the following offices: *Info-Pavillon* at the centr. station (Mon - Fri: 7 am - 7 pm, Sat: 7 am - 2 pm) or at the *Stadtwerke-Verkaufsbüro*, Syndikatgasse 9, behind the "Stadthaus I", Mon - Fri: 8.30 am - 6.30 pm, Sat: 9 am - 2 pm.

Tourists are recommended to buy multi-tickets or tickets valid for all buses for a whole day (Mini-, Maxi-, Mega-tickets for families or small groups).
bus timetable:
Mon - Fri: 7 am - 7 pm, Sat: 7 am - 2 pm: 6 94-16 80

Lost Property:
Ordnungsamt. Berliner Platz 8: 4 92-32 16/17/18
Mon-Wed: 8am-3.30pm, Thur: 8am-6pm, Fri: 8-12am
Stadtwerke Münster. Syndikatgasse 9: 6 94-28 35
Deutsche Bahn. Central station: 691-33 94
or 02 01 / 1 82-43 64

Money Matters:
Post offices: (Postal bank, Eurocheques & traveller's cheques) *Postamt 1* - Berliner Platz (Centr. station): Mon-Fri: 8 am-7 pm, Sat: 8 am-1 pm. *Hauptpost* on the Domplatz: Mon-Fri: 9 am-7 pm, Sat: 8 am - 2 pm.
Cash Dispenser in the city centre: Domplatz (*Post*), outside the "Karstadt" store (*Commerzbank*), Ludgeristr. (*Sparkasse*), Rothenburg (*Sparkasse/ Sparda-Bank*), Königsstr. (*Dresdner Bank/ Commerzbank*), Alter Fischmarkt (*Dt. Bank*), near and in the central station (*Sparda-Bank*), Berliner Platz at the centr. station (in *the post office* at the opening hrs indicated above), Neubrücken-str./opposite the Munic. Theatre (*Volksbank*)
Exchange: at banks or post offices: Mon - Fri from 9 am - 4/6 pm, depending on individual opening hrs; Mon - Sat: at the usual opening hrs at the *Commerzbank* in the "Karstadt" store.

Municipal Library: see pp. 43, 144

Parking: see also <u>city map</u> bet. pp. 144 & 145

Look out for the electr. signs indicating parking facilities as you enter town.

multi-storey car parks: *Aegidimarkt*, Mon - Sat: 7 - 2 am. *Bahnhofstr.*, daily: 6 am - 12 pm. *Bremer Platz*, daily: 5.30 am - 12 pm in the parking garage. 24 hrs at the parking metres on the ground floor. *Klemensstr./Karstadt*, Mon - Fri: 7.45 am - 8.30 pm, Sat: 7.45 am - 4.30 pm. *Theater* (can be reached via Tibusstr.), Mon - Sat: 7 - 2 am. *Kaufhof*, Mon - Fri: 7 am - 9 pm, Sat: 7 am - 5 pm. **Parking lots:** *Georgskommende* and *Hindenburgplatz:* Mon - Fri: 7 am - 9 pm, Sat - 7 am - 5 pm. *Hörsterplatz:* Mon - Fri: 6.30 am - 9 pm, Sat: 6.30 am - 5 pm. *Stubengasse:* Mon - Sat: 7 am - 12 pm, Sun: 9 am - 7 pm.

Press / Media:

daily: *Münstersche Zeitung* (MZ), also via the Internet: www.westline.de/MZ; *Westfälische Nachrichten* (WN), also via the Internet: www.muenster.net

weekly: *Kaufen + Sparen, MS am Sonntag* (delivered free of charge to all households), *Der heisse Draht* (small ads newspaper at every kiosk), *na dann* (most important source of information on the student scene, available free of charge everywhere)

bi-weekly: *Ultimo* (cinema and culture, available free of charge everywhere)

monthly: *MUZ - Münsters Universitäts-Zeitung* (official university publication), *Gig-Magazin* (mag. with info on musical events), *Münsterland Anzeiger* (regional monthly paper), *Moritz* (mag. on various themes and events for people with children) are available free of charge; *"draußen!"* (socially committed, Münster's only street mag., sold on the streets)

local computer networks (via Internet): Advantages of local communication by Internet: info on town, culture etc., communication within Münster via: **Stadtnetz** *publikom:* **www.münster.de**
or: www.buergernetz.muenster.de
or: www.muenster.org
Network of the **local daily** WN: www.muenster.net
Local radio: *Radio AM* on 95,4 FM

Reading tips:

City Guides in English:

Bergenthal, Josef: **Münster Curiosities and Treasures.** 6th ed. Münster 1995 (ISBN 3-7923-0441-4) 18.50 DM

Neumann, Wolfgang/ Schaepe, Ralf (Translated by Rund um Buch & Skript): **Münster. A City Guide.** 1st ed., Münster: NW-Verlag, 1998. [Quo Vadis? Stadt- und Reiseführer. Vol. 3] (ISBN 3-932927-10-9) 19.80 DM

Illustrated volumes on Münster (English)

Krewerth, Rainer A /Rensing, Dieter: **Münster - Schöne Hauptstadt in Westfalen.** Münster 3rd ed., impr. and enl., 1995. 168p, 118 colour photographs. (ISBN 3-402-06040-X) 49.80 DM

Küster, Dagmar: **Münster international.** Im Spaziergang durch die Hauptstadt Westfalens. Münster 1992 (ISBN 3-923606-09-5) 19.80 DM

Otto, Werner/ Klein, Günther: **Münster. Das Herz Westfalen.** Hameln (ISBN 3-928261-06-1) 26.80 DM

Schilgen, Jost: **So schön ist Münster.** Grafberg 1996 (ISBN 3-921957-15-X) 16.80 DM

Illustrated volumes on the Münsterland:

Babovic, Toma (Ill.) Hörig, Monika: **Münster und das Münsterland.** Bildreise. 1996. (ISBN 3-89234-626-7) 19.80 DM

Claes, Holger/ Fischer, Bernd: **Münsterland.** Hameln n.d. (ISBN 3-928261-19-3) 36.80 DM

Rooms in private flats or houses:

Asta-Laden. Mensa II,   83-3 22 22
Mitwohn-Zentrale. Weseler Str. 35,   1 94 45

Semi-weekly market: on the Domplatz:

Wed + Sat: Apr 1st - Oct 31st: 7 am - 1.30 pm, Nov 1st - Mar 31st: 8 am - 1.30 pm, (one day earlier if Wed or Sat are pub. hols). *Ecological market* with produce direct from the farmer: Domplatz: Fri: 1 - 6 pm.

Swimming pools:

For opening times and prices, see free brochure available in the swimming pools.

Swimming pools (indoor):
Handorf: Heriburgstr.17,   32 40 39
Hiltrup: Westfalen Str. 201,   0 25 01 / 34 88
Kinderhaus: Idenbrock Platz 8,   21 30 30
Mitte: Bade Strasse 8,   51 83 60
Ost: Mauritz-Lindenweg 101,   37 54 93
Roxel: Tilbecker Strasse 36,   0 25 34 / 81 91
Süd: Inselbogen 36,   79 82 79
Die Therme: Grevener Str. 89-91
daily:10 am - 11 pm   9 25 35-0
Swimming pools (outdoor):
Wellenfreibad Handorf:
Heriburgstr.17,   32 40 39
Hiltrup: Zum Hiltruper See 171,   02501/1 69 22

- Palace Nordkirchen, the **"Westphalian Versailles"** and it's historical park
- Art and music at the Palace
- Biking and walking in the Muensterland
  250 km of marked bike-paths - bike-rentals
- Hay-Hotel, Golf, Tennis, Squash
- Life on a farm - see it live

**Verkehrsverein Nordkirchen e.V. , Bohlenstraße 2,
59394 Nordkirchen, Tel.: 0 25 96-917 137, Fax.: 0 25 96-917 139**

Stapelskotten: Laerer Werseufer,   31 18 20
Sudmühle: Dyckburgstrasse,   32 55 55
Koburg: Grevener Strasse 125,   9 2203-0

Taxi: 6 00 11
(for taxi ranks see city map bet. pp. 144 and 145)
Rickshaw-Taxi: 6 00 02

Theatre: see <u>Information</u>
Boulevard Münster
Königspassage/Königsstr. 12-14,   5 45 64
Charivari Puppentheater
Körner Str. 3,   52 15 00
Kleiner Bühnenboden
Schillerstr. 48a,   66 17 59 or 27 19 57
Pumpenhaus
Gartenstr. 123,   23 34 43
Rebeltanz-Theater
Berliner Platz 23,   4 78 49
Städtische Bühnen
Neubrückenstr, 63,   59 09-1 00
Studio-Bühne der Universität
Domplatz 23,   832-44 29
Wolfgang-Borchert-Theater
Berliner Platz 23,   4 00 19

Bühne der Theaterpädagogik
Scharnhorststr. 100, 83-393 29/ 83-393 13

Tourist Guides: Call: 4 92-27 10/11
Guides for city tours on foot or by coach or for special tours are provided by the town.

Tourist Information:
Internet www.muenster.de/publikom/touristik
(among other things: on-line hotel reservation)
Info-Shop Klemensstr. 9: 4 92 27 10/ 1 94 33
Mon - Fri: 9 am - 6 pm, Sat: 9 am - 1 pm.
Advance booking for the theatre, cinema concerts and other events in the Info-Shop: 4 92 27 13
Stadtwerbung und Touristik
Stadthaus I, Klemensstr. 10,   4 92 27 10
Information counter Bürgerhalle des
Rathauses, Prinzipalmarkt: 4 92 27 24
Mon - Fri: 9am - 5pm, Sat: 9am - 4pm, Sun: 10am - 1pm

Tours: see <u>Guided tours of the town</u>

University: (WWU)   83-1

Youth Hostel: Bismarckallee 31, 53 24 70

HOTEL-INDEX

So that you can relax - perhaps after a long flight and do not have to search for ages, we have prepared a list of hotels for you. You can reserve your hotel room easily by phoning up the numbers listed below. There, you can also obtain further advice. A lot of hotels are located in the city centre, so that it will be easy for you to get to know Münster on foot or by bicycle (supplied by the hotel). And they can also probably lend you an umbrella ... (Ha, ha). On the other hand, the hotels further out towards the edge of town in beautiful surroundings will make it easy for you to stroll out into the natural surroundings of the Münsterland.

Categories of accommodation: cheap: youth hostel, call 532470/7 (International Youth Hostel Card required) or camping on camping-sites near town call 311982 (Stapelskotten) or 329312 (Wersewinkel) for example with a hired caravanette.

In the following, some hotels are categorized (1 to 5 stars) for different levels of comfort. But the classification is a voluntary one (TIN standard), so that uncategorized hotels might also have a comparable level of comfort!

*	= tourist, simple appointments
**	= standard
***	= comfort, medium quality of appointm.
****	= first-class, high quality of appointm.
*****	= luxury, very high quality of appointm.

HOTEL RESERVATIONS:

Münster:
tel.: 02 51 / 4 92 27 12
fax: 02 51 / 4 92 77 43

Münsterland:
tel.: 0 25 51 / 93 92 91
free of charge: 0 130 / 83 42 29
fax: 0 25 51 / 93 92 93

On-line hotel reservations:
www.muenster.de/publikom/touristik

hotel		address	sg	db	phone
Town centre/on the outskirts of the city centre: (dialling code: 02 51)					
----	Am Ring	Steinfurter Strasse 68	95,-	67,50	2 05 55
* * *	Am Schlosspark	Schmale Strasse 2-4	145,-	97,50	2 05 41-4
*	An'n Schlagbaum	Weseler Strasse 269	60,-	55,-	79 21 80
----	Bockhorn	Bremer Strasse 24	55,-	55,-	6 55 10
* *	Busche am Dom	Bogenstrasse 10	65,-	60,-	4 64 44
* * *	Central	Aegidiistrasse 1	150,-	92,50	51 01 50
* * *	City-Hotel	Friedrich-Ebert-Strasse 55-57	125,-	82,50	9 72 80
* * *	Coerdehof	Raesfeldstrasse 2	116,-	79,-	92 20 20
----	Coerheide	Königsberger Strasse 159	70,-	55,-	24 97 80
----	Conti	Berliner Platz 2a	69,-	54,50	4 04 44
* * * *	Dorint Hotel	Engelstrasse 39	225,-	142,-	4 17 10
* * * *	Europa	Kaiser-Wilhelm-Ring 26	159,-	99,-	3 70 62
----	Feldmann	Klemensstrasse 14	90,-	65,-	41 44 90
* * *	Fränd	Warendorfer Strasse 58	105,-	75,-	3 02 41
* * *	Hansa Haus	Albersloher Weg 1	70,-	55,-	6 09 25-0
* *	Haus Niemann	Horstmarer Landweg 126	90,-	65,-	8 28 28
*	Haus v. Guten Hirten	Lindenweg 61	55,-	47,-	37 87-0
*	Horstmann	Windhorststrasse 12	90,-	82,50	41 70 40
* * *	International	Neubrückenstrasse 12-14	99,-	79,50	48 48 40
* * *	Jellentrup	Hüfferstrasse 52	98,-	80,-	98 10 50
* * *	Kaiserhof	Bahnhofstrasse 14-16	120,-	85,-	4 17 80
* * *	Kolping Tagungshotel	Aegidiistr. 21	128,-	75,-	48 12-0
*	Krone	Hammer Strasse 67	65,-	55,-	7 38 68
* *	Landhaus Kahl	Untietheide 2	110,-	70,-	97 10 30
----	Lohmann	Mecklenbecker Strasse 345	78,-	62,50	7 15 25
* *	Martinihof	Hörster Strasse 25	71,-	57,-	41 86 20
* * * *	Mauritzhof (Design-H.)	Eisenbahnstrasse 15-17	185,-	117,50	4 17 20
* * * *	Mövenpick	Kardinal-von-Galen-Ring 65	220,-	130,0	8 90 20
* * *	Münnich	Heeremannsweg 13	95,-	70,-	6 18 70
* * *	Pleistermühle	Pleistermühlenweg 196	80,-	70,-	31 10 72/3
* * * *	Schloss Wilkinghege	Steinfurter Strasse 374	170,-	137,50	21 30 45
----	Steinburg am Aasee	Mecklenbecker Strasse 80	100,-	77,50	7 98 07-0
* * *	Tannenhof (Design-H.)	Prozessionsweg 402	110,-	70,-	3 13 73
* * *	Überwasserhof	Überwasserstrasse 3	150,-	100,-	4 17 70
----	Wienburg	Kanalstrasse 237	98,-	80,-	29 33 54
* * *	Windsor	Warendorfer Strasse 177	128,-	84,-	13 13 30
* * *	Windthorst	Windhorststrasse 19	150,-	97,50	48 45 90
----	Zum Schwan	Schillerstrasse 27	90,-	75,-	66 11 66
Albachten (dialling code: 0 25 36)					
*	Sontheimer	Dülmener Strasse 9	40,-	40,-	10 94
* *	Zum Ausspann	Dülmener Strasse 20	88,-	58,-	2 32 + 86 69
Amelsbüren (dialling code: 0 25 01)					
* * *	Zur Davert	Davertstr. 40	99,-	74,50	6 91 10
----	Landhaus Kessler	Raringheide 226	88,-	58,-	64 40
Handorf (dialling code for Münster: 02 51)					
* * *	Deutscher Vater	Petronillaplatz 9	75,-	65,-	93 20 90
----	Dorbaum	Dorbaumstrasse 145	65,-	47,50	32 62 55
* * *	Handorfer Hof	Handorfer Strasse 22	80,-	60,-	93 20 50
* * *	Haus Eggert	Zur Haskenau 81	125,-	103,-	32 80 40
* * *	Haus Vennemann	Vennemannstrasse 6	95,-	72,50	32 90 71
* * * *	Hof zur Linde	Handorfer Werseufer 1	150,-	105,-	3 27 50
Hiltrup (dialling code: 0 25 01)					
* * *	Hotel Ambiente	Marktallee 44	120,-	80,-	27 76-0
* *	Gästehaus Landgraf	Thierstrasse 26	100,-	70,-	12 36
* * *	Hiltruper Hof	Westfalenstrasse 148	85,-	62,50	40 25
* * * *	Waldhotel Krautkrämer	Am Hiltruper See 173	180,-	135,-	80 50
* * *	Zur Prinzenbrücke	Osttor 16	139,-	89,50	4 49 70
*	Zum Ollen Duorp	Westfalenstrasse 156	50,-	45,-	20 18
Nienberge (dialling code: 0 25 33)					
* * *	Hüerländer	Twerenfeldweg 4	85,-	68,-	5 61
* *	Pilgrim's Hotel	Nienberger Kirchplatz 4	50,-	45,-	13 30
*	Zur Post	Altenberger Strasse 8	49,-	49,-	12 92
Roxel (dialling code: 0 25 34)					
* *	Brintrup	Roxeler Strasse 579	65,-	71,50	70 39
* * * *	Parkhotel Schloss	Hohenfeld/Dingbänger Weg 400	150,-	107,50	80 80
Wolbeck (dialling code: 0 25 06)					
----	Klostermann	Münsterstrasse 25	60,-	55,-	22 34
----	Tanneneck	Alter Postweg 26	45,-	42,-	73 19
* * *	Thier-Hülsmann	Münsterstrasse 33	134,-	72,50	83 10-0

185

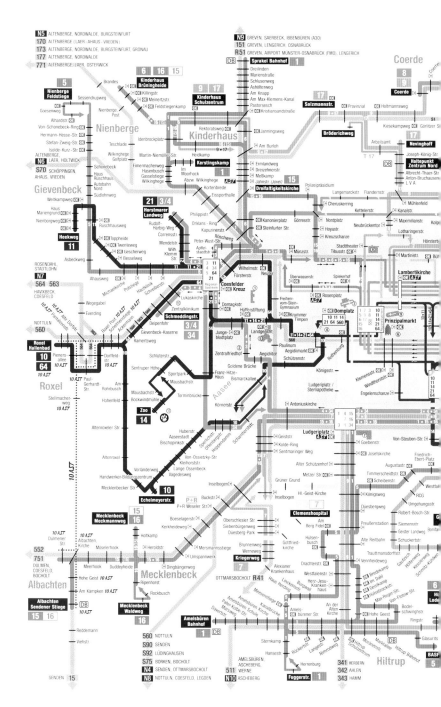

Bus Stop Area »Ludgeriplatz«

Bus Stop Area »Hauptbahnhof« (Main Station)

Bus Stop Area »Prinzipalmarkt«

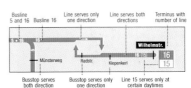

Information-Timetable: 0251 - 694 16 80

CITY TAKT: busstops having this symbol are served every 10 minutes.

CITY EXPRESS: (fast coach) only stops at busstops marked with the CE symbol.

T 7 TAXI BUS: only pre-booked journeys by taxi possible. (Tel. 0251 - 66 66 05 or ask the bus driver)

Call-Collect-Taxi: only pre-booked journeys by Call-Collect-Taxi possible. (Tel. 0251 - 66 66 05)

Night-AST: Tel. 66 66 05   During the following nights:
Sunday – Thursday: 23:45 – 01:15
Friday: 23:45 – 03:15
Saturday: 00:45 – 03:15

S70 SchnellBus: (fast coach) no service in town.

N1 Night Bus: Saturday/Sunday – does not stop at all busstops. N5 also on Friday/Saturday.

① Castle	⑧ Theatre
② Main Cemetery	⑨ St. Lamberti
③ Cathedral	⑩ University Medical Center
④ Westf. Museum	⑪ Zoo, Planetarium, Museum for Natural History
⑤ County Court	
⑥ Municipality I	
⑦ Municipality II	

Designed by Arne Kämpgen

BUS MAP
STADT MÜNSTER
28.9.1997

STADTWERKE
MÜNSTER GMBH

187

Index

I. Illustrations: (© photographers and institutions)

Allwetter Zoo/Westfälischer Zoologischer Garten Münster, photographic archives: pp. 35, 133

Hans Eick, Emsdetten/Hamburg: pp. 66 / 67

Michel Grunwald, Münster: pp. 18, 58 bottom

Helmut Hillebrand, Münster: p. 152 top left

Michael Hörnschemeyer, Münster: photo on the cover, p.22 top right, p. 24 bottom right

Mühlenhof Freilichtmuseum, Münster: p. 141

Franz-Josef Nasch, Münster: 152 bottom right, 152 top right, 152 centre right, 153

Wolfgang Neumann, Münster: pp. 9, 11, 13, 15, 17, 19, 22 top left, 27 both bottom, 30, 31, 33 bottom, 39 top, 42, 47, 49, 50, 52, 53, 55, 56, 61, 62, 64, 65, 70 bottom, 86, 87, 89, 96, 102, 107, 108, 109, 113, 117 top, 121 bottom, 122 bottom, 143, 147, 152 centre left

Christian Richters, Münster: pp. 44 / 45 (3x)

Jürgen Röttger, Münster: p. 110

Stadtarchiv, Fotosammlung Werbe- und Verkehrsamt: pp. 25(V.a./10), 28 (IV. c./60), 29 (IV.b./135), 77 (XXVII. a./1), 83 (XXXIX./42), 84 (XXXIX/226), 224 (XIX/10)

Stadtmuseum Münster/ Foto: *T. Samek*: 74, 75, 82, 90, 138, and p. 92 (*Rainer M. Kresing*)

Stadtwerbung und Touristik: pp. 2-3, 16, 22 bottom, 24 top, 24 bottom left, 33 top, 39 bottom, 58 top, 69, 70 top, 71, 72, 73, 76, 114, 117 bottom, 118, 119, 122 top, 124, 128, 135, 151, 152 bottom left

Städtische Bühnen: p. 98 (*Michael Hörnschemeyer*)

H. Tscharn (driver: Chet Thomas): p. 126

Verkehrsverein Nordkirchen e.V.: p. 121 top

Vollmer, Manfred: p. 106

Westfälisches Landesmuseum für Kunst und Kulturgeschichte Münster / R. Wakonigg: pp. 20 (permanent loan; priv. prop.), 27 top, 78, 94 (permanent loan from *Westfälischer Kunstverein*), 95, 127

II. Maps:

© by *Ravenstein Verlag GmbH*, Bad Soden a. Ts., 6203 Nordrhein-Westfalen: Münsterlandkarte (Lizenz-Nr. 7/130) between pp. 144 and 145

© by *Stadtwerbung und Touristik*: folded city map between pp. 144 and 145

© by *Stadtwerke Münster GmbH*: bus routes pp. 216 and 217

III. Sources:

Joke on p. 14 taken from: *Kleine Bettlektüre für herzhafte Münsteraner*. Chosen by Lütge, Jürgen. 1980 Scherz-Verlag, p. 70

Commandments on p. 14 taken from: *Münster und die Münsteraner in Darstellungen aus der Zeit von 1800 bis zur Gegenwart*. Ed. by Bruno Haas-Tenckhoff. Münster 1924, p. 69ff

Translation on p. 76 taken with kind permission from: Bergenthal, Josef: *Münster. Curiosities and Treasures*. Münster: Regensberg 6th ed. 1995, p. 23

various data from the *Amt für Stadtentwicklung und Statistik*

✑ For kindly providing photos, maps and information, we would like to thank the photographers and institutions.

Special thanks to all those who have also contributed to the preparation of this book.